The

Torch of K̶̶ ̶̶ ̶̶owledge

Darren

2004.

2

Painter

2009.

The
Torch of Knowledge

A story about the twentieth century, and the changes which
will take place as the result of increased knowledge.

BY

ARTHUR FINDLAY

" Ignorance is the curse of God. Knowledge is the wing
wherewith we fly to Heaven."—*Shakespeare*.

SNU PUBLICATIONS

Other titles by Arthur Findlay
On the Edge of the Etheric
The Rock of Truth
The Unfolding Universe
Where Two World's Meet
The Way of Life
The Physic Stream
The Curse of Ignorance

© SNU Publications

First published by Psychic Press.
This edition published in 1996 by
SNU Publications
Redwoods
Stansted Hall
Stansted Mountfitchet
Essex CM24 8UD

ISBN 0902 036 09 2

Reprinted in England by Booksprint, Bristol

THIS BOOK
IS A REPLY TO
THE ATTACKS ON SPIRITUALISM

made by

THE BISHOP OF LONDON
in his Diocesan letter of July 1935,

and by

THE BISHOP OF WINCHESTER
in his Diocesan letter of July 1935.

IT IS ALSO A REPLY
TO THE ATTACKS
MADE ON SPIRITUALISM BY
MANY THOUSANDS OF PRIESTS AND PARSONS
ON NUMEROUS OCCASIONS
OVER THE PAST EIGHTY YEARS.

CONTENTS.

FOREWORD TO THE FIRST EDITION

James Arthur Findlay, who was born in Glasgow in 1883, comes of a line of ancestors who have been prominently connected with the commercial and financial life of Glasgow and the West of Scotland for the past 170 years.

After leaving his preparatory school he went to Fettes College and then to Geneva University. At the age of 25 he was called on to take his father's place as Head of the Stockbroking side of one of the leading Stockbroking and Chartered Accountant firms of that city.

He retired from business at the age of 40 and bought the Estate of Stansted Hall in Essex where he now resides. As a Magistrate for Essex and Ayrshire and Chairman of Administrative Councils in these counties he has given much of his time to county work. He is also a Freeman of the City of Glasgow.

Ayrshire is his home county and there his ancestors in the reign of James II played a prominent part in their opposition to being forced to attend the Episcopal Church, one being hung in the Grass Market of Edinburgh while another was imprisoned, awaiting the same fate, when William of Orange landed and he was pardoned.

During the Great War Mr. Findlay was awarded the Order of the British Empire for his organisation work in connection with the Red Cross.

Agriculture is one of his interests and the improvements he has effected in methods of production are generally well known. As a director of several companies he still retains his interest in finance, on which he has written many articles.

Arthur Findlay, however, is best known to the public through his books and addresses on Spiritualism, Philosophy and Religion. He has spoken in the largest halls of most of our great cities, and his books have been read in practically every country throughout the world.

He has been Chairman of the International Institute for Psychical Research since its inception. He founded the Glasgow Society for Psychical Research and is its Vice-President. He is a Past-President of the London Spiritualist

Alliance, the originator of the Quest Club, and is an Honorary Vice-President of the Spiritualists' National Union.

Always a student and a great reader he had read many of the standard books on Comparative Religion and Mythology before he was 21 years of age, and for the past 30 years has made a special study of this branch of science. Readers of his Trilogy will realise how intimately this subject is connected with Spiritualism. How thoroughly he has covered the entire field by his three books will be best realised by turning over the pages of the Index to the Trilogy, which has just been published. Here we find nearly sixteen thousand references to the contents of these three books, which in itself emphasises the amount of labour and research involved in their compilation.

Having thus completed his great work, the author's mind then turned to the best way of popularising the subject and of introducing the public to a new and wiser way of thinking. He decided that a story would be the best medium for conveying the message he has to deliver. For this reason *The Torch of Knowledge* came to be written. It is written in a style which makes the reading easy, and yet the reader all the time is probably learning much which is new and of vital interest.

To those who are enquiring into Spiritualism for the first time and have accepted without deep thought the religious teachings, considered from childhood as sacred and true, this book may prove disconcerting. Nothing can be too sacred to be investigated and discussed. Discussion leads to the truth and an increase in our knowledge, which in turn leads to the greater comfort and happiness of the race.

D.M.M.

AUTHOR'S PREFACE.

Sallust of old, once said that if you present Religion to the-people in mystical veil they will accept it. This remark by a wise old man set me thinking that if I told the public about Spiritualism in the form of a story they would read, mark, learn and inwardly digest the facts of the greatest and most vital subject on earth, and at the same time enjoy their lesson.

So I present *The Torch of Knowledge* to the public in the full anticipation that the story I have to tell will be found interesting, instructive and in places thrilling.

One thing I would like to emphasise, which is that all the characters in this story are fictitious and are not portrayed to resemble anyone. Having said this I wish also to emphasise the fact that all the psychic phenomena, which run through this story, have actually happened. What I have done has been to change their setting and the details.

On 3rd February 1936 my mother passed on. Within a fortnight of her passing she had communicated to me, through two separate mediums, one in Glasgow and one in London, who had never known her or seen her, and who knew nothing about our private family affairs, one hundred and forty-six facts of an intimate private nature which were only known to the members of my family. Some of the information she gave me was new to me but on enquiry I found it to be true. Nothing said was wrong.

Besides this she told me where some old letters, which she had hidden away before her death, had been put, and how entrance could be effected to the secret place of concealment.   By following the instructions given I found the letters, of whose existence I was quite unaware.   What I have experienced others have experienced.

With regard to the various psychic happenings related in this story, I and many others have had similar experiences and similar conversations with those called dead.   I, therefore, emphasise the fact that I have experienced all the psychic phenomena referred to in this book, that what I relate are facts and not the product of my imagination.   When this is remembered the reader's interest in the book will be much increased.

All that I have written with regard to the Christian and other world religions is likewise true and can be verified by reference to the standard books on the subject.   Those who wish further details on the subject are recommended to read *The Rock of Truth* and *The Unfolding Universe* if they have not already done so, as in these two books the leading authorities and their books are referred to.

In a story such as this it is impossible to give all these references, but, as I have been very careful to be accurate in what I make the characters of this story, say, the reader can feel that he may accept their remarks as true and reliable, and as having been written by me with the same care and accuracy as I employed when writing my Trilogy.

The Trial of the Bishop of Alfortruth, as given in this story, is based on what took place at the Convocation of York on 7th June 1934 when the Bishop of Liverpool was arraigned before his brother bishops because he allowed one who was not an orthodox

Christian to speak in Liverpool Cathedral on the subject of our life after death. The opinions I make the orthodox bishops of this story express, correspond to the opinions· expressed by the bishops at this Convocation of York when the Bishop of Liverpool was censured for his action.

Priests and parsons have forever shown their deep antipathy to Spiritualism, which in itself should show the average intelligent man and woman that it is a subject well worth consideration. Spiritualists, by the priesthood, have been associated with the Devil and termed his servants and followers. They have been cursed, maligned, sneered at and jeered at, and every conceivable lie has been told about them. Their miserable condition was not confined to this world, but they have been consigned by these men of God to Hell for all eternity. This book will put this question in its true setting, but it is well to remember that these curses and warnings continue at the present time. Not only have the rank and file of Christian priests and parsons been guilty of these despicable utterances but they have also come from Popes, Cardinals and Bishops, who have used their position and their ingenuity to frighten the people from investigating Spiritualism.

Dr. Winnington-Ingram, the present Bishop of London, is always making opportunities to warn the people against the dangers of Spiritualism. He devotes his entire Diocesan letter of July **1935** to the subject, because, to quote his words, of " the revival of Spiritualism, which has again raised its head in the diocese." Then he goes on to tell his people that "it is all wrong, it is very dangerous, it is dishonouring to the dead, it is a waste of time for the living and has been condemned in the Bible. Because God has spoken to man through the Church and through the Bible, I do most earnestly exhort those whom I personally know and love to give up this unauthorised attempt to communicate with the other world," and so on. Dr. Garbett, the Bishop of Winchester, in his Diocesan letter of July 1935, concludes with the words " I have written strongly because I am convinced that real harm is done by Spiritualism," and goes on to advise the Christian mourner to find comfort in the doctrine of the Communion of Saints.

The only difference between these utterances and those of most others in the profession, of the past and present, is that on this occasion these two priests have not associated Spiritualists with the Devil or consigned them to Hell. Perhaps this is an indication, for the future, of more refined manners on the part of the clergy.

Spiritualism and Christianity have no connection whatever. They are as far apart as the poles. Spiritualism is a philosophy of life and claims that life after death has been proved, that those who die live on in a world much the same as this, with the same characters as they had on earth, and that given suitable conditions they can communicate with us on earth. Christianity, on the other hand, is a sacrificial religion and the Christian Church is an organisation, to keep alive a belief in a sacrifice for sins, and for the performance of the rites and ceremonials connected with this belief. For this reason Spiritualism and Christianity will never join, and no Spiritualist who thinks deeply desires such a fusion.

The Eucharist, or Holy Communion, of the present day is directly descended from the primitive savage, who sacrificed man or animal on his altar. Primitive man sacrificed man on his altar for the purpose of placating the gods. The Christian, instead of a slain man on his altar, has him represented in the form of bread and wine, as symbolical of his body and blood. Likewise the priests of our primitive ancestors performed before their altar of stone in much the same way as Christian priests perform before the Christian altar.

Likewise the idea of a Christ or Saviour springs from the same primitive source, and in Mythology we find the same ideas and beliefs as are expressed in the creeds of Christianity. Though the names have been changed the beliefs and ceremonials are still the same. Primitive man, for want of an efficient vocabulary, and because of his ignorance, produced a religion which was crude and cruel. Christianity is this religion's direct descendant and is likewise both crude and cruel.

It will probably take the better part of a century before people generally come to look on Christianity in its true light. The whole issue has been befogged because of the rascality of the early Church fathers in associating the man Jesus with ancient pagan beliefs. Jesus had nothing whatever to do with Christianity, which is just another name for Paganism. He was made use of by the early Christian priests to bring the people back to the belief in the old Pagan Mythology, from which they were drifting. The belief was then fading from men's minds that the gods had come to earth. Consequently there was nothing to

link the old Mythology to earth.   The Pagan priests,
who called themselves Christians, made use of Jesus
as the link between earth and heaven, and round this
unknown man were wound all the miraculous stories,
associated with the other pagan gods who had come
to earth.   Thus a man became associated with one
of the three gods of the Pagan Trinity.   Thus the
priests brought a god back to earth !

We do not believe in the stories about these
ancient gods coming to earth and living as men.
These stories are all part of the Mythology of the
ancients.   Some day the entire Christian story will
be looked on just as we now look on the story of
Osiris and other similar gods of the past.

What is important is this.   From our study of
Mythology we realise that the ancients had feelings
and desires akin to our own.   Being more ignorant
they were more fearful, but through all the Mythology
of the past the thread can be discerned of a belief that
earth-life is but a preparation for another world to
which we pass at death.   They imagined Saviours to
help them into this unknown abode and they invented
beliefs, ceremonials, incantations and prayers to comfort the living and help the dead.   The instinct of the
after-life produced what we now call Mythology,
which was the religion of the ancients, just as it is the
cause of what we call Religion to-day.   Where
Christians have gone wrong is in considering all these
creedal drapings, and the ceremonials attached to
them, as religion.   Naturally the Church, which is
the custodian of the creeds and ceremonials, fosters
this idea and discourages everything which helps to
place religion in its proper setting.

I draw attention to these facts in this preface because I wish the reader to differentiate clearly between Christianity and Spiritualism and to realise that Christian beliefs prevent the general acceptance of the truths of Spiritualism. Christianity and other religions of the past and present draw their strength from man's inherent belief in an after-life, and to support this they have wound round it draping after draping of primitive beliefs and ceremonials which are considered essential to religion. Spiritualism, on the other hand, proves that these primitive instincts are based on a great reality, but it utterly discards all the drapings which have been wrapped round this vital truth. Its philosophy is based on this cardinal fact which needs no church, no creeds, no dogmas and no ceremonials to support it.

Towards the end of the story I have tried to envisage the change which better education and greater wisdom will bring about within the next fifty years. This development is what everyone should strive for as it is our character, our knowledge and our wisdom which we carry with us to the next stage of our existence, and will forever remain part of ourselves.

Having now made all the explanations necessary and not wishing to keep the reader from judging the story for himself, I shall conclude by saying that if he does not, on this occasion, accept as true all I have to tell, it is probable that he will some day if he studies the subject without prejudice and with the necessary care and thoroughness.

ARTHUR FINDLAY.

Stansted Hall,
Essex, August 1936.

CHARACTERS

in the order they come before the reader.

JOHN MATTERSON,	-	- A Scientist and Materialist.
FAITH CHURCH, -	-	- A devout Christian.
ANGELA BRIDGE,	-	- A Medium.
GRACE LOVEALL,	-	- A Humanist.
ANTHONY GOODENOUGH,		- A keen Hunting man.
FRANK WISEMAN,	-	- A Medical Student & Rationalist.
GEORGE TRUEMAN,	-	- A Chartered Accountant and Spiritualist.
MRS. TRUEMAN,	-	- A highly-developed Medium.
HOPE TRUEMAN,	-	- Their daughter.
RALPH LEADER,	-	- A Politician.
BOLES, - -	-	- Butler at Sureway Court.
DR. CUREALL, -	-	- A village Doctor.
MRS. CUREALL, -	-	- His wife.
MISS NOTEALL, -	-	- Secretary to Mrs. Trueman.
MR. FARMER, -	-	- A Sussex Farmer.
DR. EDWARD LEADER,		- Bishop of Alfortruth.
MRS. LEADER, -	-	- His wife.
ERNEST KEEN, -	-	- A London Stockbroker.
LORD KILFORFUN,	-	- A Master of the Hounds.
LADY KILFORFUN,	-	- His wife.
GLEN, - -	-	- Butler at Huntingham.
DIANA HUNTER, -	-	- A Hunting woman.
AGNES, - -	-	- A Housemaid.
THE DEAN OF ALFORTRUTH,		A liberal-minded Parson.
COLONEL WISEMAN,	-	- Father of Frank Wiseman.
MRS. WISEMAN, -	-	- Mother of Frank Wiseman.
RUTH, - -	-	- A Housemaid
HENRY LAW, -	-	- A Lawyer.

THE ARCHBISHOP OF CHURCHISALL, ⎫
THE BISHOP OF DIEHARDHAM,
THE BISHOP OF CREEDALBURY,
THE BISHOP OF DOGMAHAM, ⎬ Christian Priests.
THE BISHOP OF LATITUDEHAM,
THE BISHOP OF FAITHFORD, ⎭

HORACE STOREY,	-	- A Professor of History.
MRS. CLARA HEARING,		- A Clairaudient Medium.

CHAPTER I.
AT TURNBERRY.

"What a simply glorious view! See how those peaks of Arran stand out against the sky."

"Yes, isn't it glorious? I am so glad I decided to come here instead of going to Frinton, with its monotonous sea. I feel as if I could gaze on those changing colours for hours."

The two speakers were John Matterson and Faith Church, who with other friends were staying at this popular golfing resort, consisting of only a large modern hotel and a golf course.

A number of friends had gathered together for golf and tennis; all were young, and just beginning life on their own. Everything pointed to a happy future for each and none gave much thought to the cares and troubles of life.

They were all typically young people of the year 1936, with its wider outlook and greater freedom of expression. How changed were the times from the Victorian and Edwardian days with their circumscribed outlook on life! The Great War had acted as a tremendous stimulus to thought, to freedom of thought and action. Liberty was the order of the day.

John Matterson and Faith Church were cousins, and they had arrived by car the previous day with two of Faith's old school friends, Angela Bridge and Grace Loveall. This was the first morning they had experienced the Firth of Clyde with all its charms and

graces.   Scotland, when the weather is good, depicts
nature in its most perfect setting.

" Have you seen any of the others yet, or are
they still slumbering and blissfully ignorant of all that
they are missing ? "

" No," answered John, " they don't seem to be
down yet.   Have you ever thought how silly people
are to come down to breakfast at nine, after two or
three hours of a fine summer morning have passed ?
We sit up till eleven, using artificial light, and then
sleep during the best part of a summer day.   What
slaves of fashion we are ! "

" I quite agree," replied Faith, " but are we
not in everything slaves of custom ?   I know I am.
I just accept and slip through life.   You, John, are
different and always have been.   You are a thinker
and never have accepted just what you have been
told.   All the same, I have the feeling that those who
think as deeply as you do don't get so much happiness
out of life as people like myself."

" Well, Faith, we are all built differently and we
are as our heredity and environment have made us,
but let us keep off deep subjects before breakfast.
I'm feeling hungry.   Let us feed the inner man first.
If this weather continues we shall have plenty of
stimulus for thought in these surroundings."

At the breakfast table they were joined by
Angela and Grace.

" Why have you both been so lazy ? " asked
Faith.   " John and I could not tear ourselves away
from the view from the terrace.   Arran is looking a
perfect picture.   And the plum pudding looks just a
mile away."

" I suppose you mean Ailsa Craig," said Grace. " It does look like a plum pudding. We must sail over to it some day, if we can find time. It is a veritable hive of bird life. Did you see Ireland, John? I heard a man saying yesterday that you can see the coast of Ireland on a fine day."

" I did not look specially," replied John, " but to the south of Arran there is land which I take to be the Mull of Kintyre."

" I am told," Angela remarked, " that the further up the Firth you go the more beautiful it becomes, islands and mountains. I won't go south till I have been across to Arran and up the Clyde. I want to explore those numerous sea lochs. Daddy says that they are unique in their beauty and setting. Keen as I am on tennis and golf, I feel much more inclined to go exploring than to play games."

" Well, we may be able to work in both," Grace replied. " I feel as you do, Angela, that there is so much to see and so little time to see everything. Let us hope that the weather keeps fine."

" Here come Tony and Frank. No, we have not finished everything, but you must be quick, the day is getting on."

Anthony Goodenough and Frank Wiseman sat down and gave their orders to an attentive waiter. They were both tall athletic youths, keen golfers, and had been guests at the hotel for the past week. Anthony lived in Essex, not far from Faith's home, and it was on his recommendation that Faith and her two school friends had decided to come to Turnberry. John, when he heard of the holiday being planned, had offered to take the three girls in his car.

"Well," said Anthony, "here we are again. I hope you have all slept well. You girls look as fresh as rosebuds. What a topping day for golf! Frank and I are having a round after breakfast. If we don't hurry we shall have to queue up ; people will be coming from all over the place a day like this."

"Are you going round, Faith, or is it tennis?" asked Frank.

"I think I shall play tennis this morning, if Angela and Grace agree. I know someone who will make a fourth."

Angela just then rose, remarking, "I must go to see if there are any letters."

"Only one for me," she replied on her return.

On opening her letter she hurriedly read it through, and then exclaimed, "We shall have no difficulty now in getting a fourth for tennis. I have a letter here from a friend of mine saying that she and her father and mother hope to arrive to-morrow for a few days on their way south."

"What is her name?" asked Faith.

"Hope Trueman," replied Angela. "She lives in Sussex, about twenty miles from my home. They have been touring the Highlands. Rob Roy, she says, would not have had the ghost of a chance to get away these days. The roads are marvellous. They slipped through Glencoe before they had time to wonder where the massacre took place."

"Trust modern science," said John. "I pin my faith to science and all it means to us to raise humanity out of the slough of despond in which it wallowed during the ages of superstition. Railways, good roads and the motor car have opened up to us a paradise of beauty and civilised a lot of savages, who lived in the mountains and raided these fair lowland plains. But I must be off. I want to have a look at *The Times.*"

" How very profound and learned," remarked Faith, with a smile. " The poor fellow can't help it, so we must not be too hard on him."

Frank and Tony arrived at the first tee at ten o'clock and had to wait ten minutes before their turn came.

" Just time for an easy round before lunch. You drive off, Tony."

Tony took up his stance and with an easy swing sent the ball well over two hundred yards straight down the fairway. It was a beautiful shot and earned from Frank the well deserved remark. " Good shot, Tony."

Frank did equally well and they both holed out in four. It was a ding dong game and at the finish Tony was two up.

After leaving the clubhouse Tony said, " We have just time for a stroll to the shore before lunch."

They crossed the golf course and went between the sand hills. The sea was placid. All nature seemed at peace. A small boat was slowly gliding out of *The Maidens* harbour wafted by the soft breeze.

" That little hamlet over there has a queer name," said Frank. " I wonder how it came to be called *The Maidens*. It must have been a lonely spot before the railway and the motor came on the scene. Have you ever read *The Grey Man?* You should ; it makes this coast to live again. What a history it has—Robert Bruce, Smugglers, Raids, the feudal lords in their castles and the people living in caves, like savages. Then at the end of the seventeenth century all round here religious persecution reached its height and was probably nowhere more intense throughout the length and breadth of the land."

"I seldom read," said Tony. "Books don't interest me. I enjoy Wodehouse, especially his golf stories. Anything about sport interests me. I prefer exercising my muscles and not my brain. Your mind and mine run on different lines. You must always be reading, thinking and wondering. I don't think it makes you any happier."

"Yes, I love books," said Frank, "but let us be strolling back ; it is nearly one. If I did not love reading and studying, I never could become a doctor. You are in the fortunate or unfortunate position of having been born with a silver spoon in your mouth. I wasn't, and in a way I am glad. You will doubtless slip through life enjoying yourself. I must work, and I think my life will be the happier one."

"Perhaps you are right," said Tony, "but when the old man gives me an allowance of five hundred, to be increased when I marry, I don't feel inclined to exert myself unduly, especially when I know that there is much more to come after his day. That is the advantage of being an only child."

"I look on life differently," replied Frank. "I don't think we are here just to enjoy ourselves. Something in me urges me on to greater and greater effort.   I have the love of healing.   I never see anyone sick or ill but I want to cure him.   I shall not rest satisfied till I have a house in Harley Street and my daily round consists of making sick people well."

Talking thus, they crossed the golf course and the road running from Ayr to Girvan and entered the grounds of the hotel.   There they met Angela and Grace, and together they started to climb to the terrace of the hotel by the long flight of steps.

The hotel stands high above the road and is approached by a winding drive, but the quickest way up is by the steps.   This is the way always taken by pedestrians, the drive being used only by cars.

The situation of the hotel, perched high on the hill, gives it a commanding view over the golf course to the sandhills beyond and thence to the sea.   In the distance, in a northerly direction, lies the beautiful island of Arran, with its towering peaks stretching northwards for twenty miles.   Further south behind the island can be seen the Mull of Kintyre, near the south end of which can be seen Campbeltown Bay. At its southernmost point lies the island of Sanda, and between it and the mainland Ailsa Craig, a mountain of rock rising sheer up out of the sea.

On a fine day, south of the Craig, can be seen the Antrim Coast of Ireland, which blends with the Ayrshire Coast as it winds in and out, throwing headland after headland into the sea, a truly grand and inspiring sight which makes the hotel terrace a popular resort throughout a fine summer day.

Here it was after lunch that the party of young people gathered to discuss their morning games.

" What happened to you, John? " asked Tony.

" Oh, I found that the girls had finished their game and as they had nothing special to do I took out the car and we all went along the shore road till we came to Dunure Castle.   I never knew a place where one could find more old ruined castles than here in Ayrshire.   I would like to read up their history. The very stones seem to speak of battle, murder and sudden death."

" I know something about Dunure and the other historical places round about here," said Frank.   " I have been here before, and I like to read up the history of a place at which I am staying.   Dunure has a terrible history.   Its dungeons during the dark ages were filled with prisoners and they suffered every conceivable form of torture.   Dunure belonged to a branch of the Kennedy family and these Kennedys were continually fighting each other.

At Dunure, the Kennedys once roasted alive the Abbot of Crossraguel, and some years later, when some more roasting was taking place, a scene occurred, the tale of which has been handed down from generation to generation.   A tall man sat on a grey horse observing the poor wretches being burned. He could scarcely be seen as he sat in the gloomy archway of the gate at the entrance to the courtyard. He was clad from head to foot in a cloak of grey, having his face shaded by a high-crowned, broad-brimmed hat.   Asking for a Bible, he swore an awful oath that he would roast out and utterly slay the entire Kennedy family.   Then he threw the book into the flames and rode away."

" And who was this mysterious individual ? " asked Angela.

" Just wait a minute," replied Frank, " and you will hear.

The people quite approved of the killing of their enemies because the Holy Book told them to do so, but the fact that this man in grey threw into the flames what is still called in our Churches *The Word of God* aroused the indignation of the onlooking crowd. It broke into a cry of horror at the sacrilege. ' This is Devil's work ! ' said one. ' The fires of Sodom and the brimstone of Gomorrah will light upon us all for this deed ! ' said another.

Their protestations were, however, cut short by their gaze being turned to a knoll on the left of the entrance, because there sat on his horse the one who was responsible for it all, silent and still. The dying flames gave him a weird and unnatural appearance. ' The Devil and none other ! ' they shouted, and fled in terror to their homes."

" We must make you our guide, philosopher and friend during our stay here," said Faith. " I was reading about the Abbey of Crossraguel in the Guide Book. It has been unearthed and is a grand sight in all its ruined glory. It is not very far from here."

" I am only too glad to tell you what I know," said Frank. " That old castle on the left as you pass *The Maidens*—you must have noticed it on your way to Dunure—is old Culzean Castle. The new one is the handsome pile built on the rocks, which you see when coming home as you turn the corner to come round Culzean Bay. The old castle has been a ruin now for many years. It is another old home of the Kennedys, which family in the old days owned most of the land and castles round here. In those days they were called the Wild Kennedys, and their mad escapades are known to everyone in Ayrshire."

" I do love the past," said Faith ; " it interests me more than the present. I was sure that there was something romantic about this coast. A wild, rugged coast stirs the imagination, and these old castles dotted along it help one to picture those old days when knights were bold."

" Bold and bad," said Frank. " To me there is little romance about it all. I can picture too vividly the sufferings of the people. Don't you agree, Grace? Your thoughts always turn to the down-trodden and the suffering."

" Yes," she replied, " I always think like that when I see the old castles and their dungeons. I always think of the suffering, of the cruelty these so vividly call to mind. I remember seeing a hole in Dunvegan Castle in Skye where prisoners were let down by a rope. To-day they let down an electric light to enable you to see to the bottom. It made me shudder, and I had to get away as fast as possible."

" Our ancestors were little better than beasts, and cruel beasts at that," said John. " I always ask myself what good has Christianity ever done. It has given comfort but never educated nor raised the people socially. It was only as people came to rely more and more on themselves that we have become more civilised."

" Quite true," said Frank, " but you won't find Faith agreeing with you. To her, all that we are is due to the faith that she professes."

" Of course," Faith replied, " I cannot understand why so many people now-a-days are becoming indifferent to Christianity. I could not live without it."

"Tell me, Faith," enquired John, "what is Christianity, and what does it mean to be a Christian? Until we know that we are at cross purposes."

"Christianity," she replied, "is the religion of Jesus Christ, the second person of the Trinity, who came down from Heaven, became man, and died for our salvation ; and all who believe this will be saved from their sins, while those who do not will not be. A Christian is one who believes this, one who does not is not a Christian."

"Right you are, first time, Faith !" remarked John. "A clear and correct definition. All have the right to their own religious opinion. I can only state facts and wait till the mental level rises so that they can become accepted, but I do object to the word Christian being so misused as it is to-day. To be a Christian has nothing to do with conduct. It only applies to one holding the belief you have just mentioned. To talk about Christian conduct, or Christian ideals, or Christian this or Christian that, is entirely wrong. Christian ideals are no higher than mine. I am not a Christian. A Christian is one who believes that his sins have been atoned for by Christ. There it begins and ends."

"You are quite right, John," remarked Frank. "Some people say it is unchristian to go to war, others say it is not. Some say it is unchristian to have slums, not to educate the people, and so on ; all of which is rubbish. It is only unchristian not to believe the creeds of Christianity. Why ! during the age of Christendom more wars have been fought than in any other period of the world's history, and most of them were the direct result of this religion. The people have lived in hovels and they only began to be educated at the end of last century, because by then their intelligence had increased sufficiently to overthrow the power of the Church, which had kept them ignorant for its own purposes."

"I saw it reported the other day," remarked Angela, "that a parson said it was unchristian to wear black at a funeral. If it is unchristian, why have Christians always worn black at funerals?"

"There is no end to the misuse of the word," replied John. "Nowadays it is used for everything that we call good, but a hundred years ago it was used for everything that we now call bad. It was quite Christian then to have slaves, for the people to live in slums, to work eighteen hours a day, and to send little boys up chimneys to clean them, and for prisons to be dens of iniquity. To-day it is quite Christian to participate in blood sports and hunt foxes, otters and stags. It is quite Christian to trap and vivisect animals, and hang people for murder. When the mental level rises, I suppose it will become unchristian to do this.

In the eighteenth century, a schoolmaster named Peter Annet criticised some of the blood-thirsty passages in the Psalms. He said it was not right to sing or read about dashing babies against the wall, hating our enemies, and the righteous washing their feet in the blood of the wicked. The people in his days considered it was quite Christian to do so, just as they do to-day, because in every Parish Church in the land the people still lustily sing these Psalms.

Some day, I suppose, it will be called unchristian to do so, but the mental level of present-day Christians will have to rise before it is stopped. Peter Annet, however, had to suffer in his attempt to make Christians humane. He was brought before the King's Bench and sentenced to one month's imprisonment in Newgate, to stand twice in the pillory with a label round his neck, on which was printed ' For Blasphemy.' Then he was given a year's hard labour and made to find sureties for his good behaviour during the rest of his life.''

" To go further back," said Frank, " it was quite Christian to burn, torture and imprison all unbelievers and witches, and to break your faith with a non-Christian. This was done over and over again from the time of the Crusaders to the Christian invasion of America. To-day we are witnessing the most Christian nation in the world carrying on a war of aggression against Abyssinia, in a way which barbarous savages would be ashamed of, bombing defenceless towns, women and children, with never a word of rebuke or criticism from the Pope, the chief representative of Christ on earth and the head of the Christian Church. The Pope was right when he said, a few days ago, that Christianity has nothing to do with social problems and that the priest's only function is to act as an intermediary between God and man.''

" And to enforce this claim on the people," said John, " every fiendish device that could be imagined was employed by the Church. The crucifix and the instruments of torture always went together. After the trail of poison gas and bombs which have blinded and maimed thousands of men, women and children in Abyssinia we need not therefore be surprised that the Christian Church is now going to erect a large statue of Jesus in Addis Ababa.   Christian priests, throughout the Christian era, have always blessed and supported the barbarities of Christian fiends, and in blessing the Italian soldiers they have lived up to their past reputation.   Before every bull-fight the toreadors receive Holy Communion and the blessing of the priest.   No wonder that those who know the history of the Christian religion despise the name and resent being in any way associated with it.''

"Well, John," said Faith, who seemed anxious to change the conversation, "you live like a Christian, and you are more of a Christian than many who profess Christianity.''

"My dear Faith," said John, "doubtless you think you are paying me a compliment and will be surprised when I tell you that I consider it quite the reverse.   I have no wish whatever to be compared with either good or bad Christians.   The way Christian people to-day favourably compare the lives of materialists, agnostics and atheists with what they are themselves is doubtless done to give the impression of broadmindedness.   If they only knew how those of us who are not Christians despise their patronage, they would be surprised.   I have never observed that Christians, either individually or collectively, as they appear now or in history, have managed to exhibit so lofty a character that it excites my admiration.   True, many bearing the name have been outstanding in their goodness, but they are dwarfed by the much greater number, who likewise bore that name, and were recognised as such by their fellows, who were the greatest scoundrels and blackguards it has been the misfortune of the world ever to breed."

" I am sorry, John, if I have said the wrong thing," said Faith, " but you see, that to call a person a Christian is the nicest thing I could think of, though I should have remembered that you started off this conversation by insisting that it was belief which made a Christian and not deeds. It is unfortunate that the word is used in such a loose way as evidently it means to you something quite different from what it means to many. Christianity has been a great comfort to me, and I hope that some day it will be an equal comfort to you also."

" If it satisfies you, Faith," said Frank, " stick to it, but there are millions it does not satisfy. To-day, the tendency is to give up belief in the old, and this generally ends in agnosticism, the philosophy of those anxious for a satisfactory explanation of existence but who have to admit that it is beyond human understanding. The majority of thinking people at the present time are agnostics though they will not admit it."

" What we need to-day," said Angela, " is a new religion, one that will satisfy our inmost longings and assure us of our destiny."

" I quite agree," said Frank, " but let us get away from controversial subjects. I think it is long enough after lunch now to have a dip in the Swimming Bath. After that, what do you say to a round of golf, John? You need some exercise."

The company broke up and after tea John and

Frank started out for their game while the others paired off and followed them round the links.

After the game was finished the two men strolled down to the shore and walked towards the lighthouse, so prominently situated that it can be seen for miles around.

" I did not like to pursue the subject further on the terrace, John," said Frank, " but very few people realise how much the fear of offending God has kept back the human race, so far as Europe is concerned.   Only here and there you come across someone who has studied the subject apart from popular history books.   The more you study the question the clearer it becomes how this fear has obstructed all progress and education.   Without education there is no civilisation."

" I was taught, " replied John, " that the fear of God is the beginning of wisdom.   History teaches the very reverse.   I have given up all belief in religion.   I am not ashamed to say that I am an atheist and a materialist.   It is the only sensible attitude of mind for any intelligent man.   No one who thinks of all the cruelty and suffering in the world can believe in a God directing the universe.

I look forward to the day when all organised religion will be abolished, and good deeds and kind thoughts will be the only religion practised by humanity.   Nature to me is God and this earth life is the only life we have.   Let us keep our attention centred on it and make the best of it.   One world at a time is my motto. This worrying about another world has brought in its train nothing but cruelty and misery. Humanity will become freed from the shackles of religion only when it realises that the only time to be happy is now. All these religious speculations about a future life, and what we have to believe in order to be happy in a fantastic heaven, are humbug and not worthy of intelligent men and women. I can find no place for God in the Universe, as we to-day understand it, certainly not for a Being who expects our worship."

"You live up to your name," replied Frank; "I look at things somewhat differently. I admit that you are perfectly logical looking at things from a human standpoint. You will believe only what you see, feel and hear, but my point is this, do we humans see, feel and hear everything there is in the Universe? Is the Universe, in other words, made up only of electrons and protons? I instinctively cannot believe it. I have no proof that it is not so but something tells me not to be too sure. I admit that what goes under the name of religion to-day is enough to disgust any thinking individual ; but I ask you this : why did the first religion come into being, and why did it give seed to every other religion the world has ever known?"

"Ignorance of the facts of nature. As science has revealed the reason for everything, there is no place for religion," replied John.

"When science explains everything and reveals the reason for everything," Frank replied, "I admit that there may be no place for religion, but I do not admit that science has yet done so. Modern science is but four hundred years old, and up till last century it had to fight for its very existence.   There seems no end to the limit of our knowledge.   He would be a bold man who said that our present-day scientific text books contained all that there is to know and all that ever shall be known.''

   '' Science is my religion.   I believe that it and it only is the saviour of mankind,'' said John. '' Only since men began to think, to examine, to wonder and to doubt all the Church has told them has humanity risen.   When the Church ruled, Europe was in misery and poverty, cruelty reigned everywhere, the Church lorded it over kings and princes, and tyrannised over everybody.   Ignorance was elevated, knowledge was denounced and every-one who expressed an honest thought was either burned, tortured or imprisoned.   The wonder is that we are what we are to-day when such an institution of reaction held Europe, until quite recently, beneath its iron grip.   Dean Swift once remarked that ' We have just enough religion to make us hate, but not enough to make us love one another.'   I would prefer to say that, as people become less religious, they become kinder and more tolerant and charitable to others.''

   '' All true,'' replied Frank, '' but you have not got me.   You must not confuse religion with Chris-tianity or some other cult.   Every intelligent person knows that all you say is true and much more, but why, I ask you, is there such a word as religion in the dictionary?   There is a reason for everything, and if our ancestors lived in hovels and spent their labour and earnings in building Cathedrals and

Churches, and in the East in building Temples, Mosques or Pagodas, they must have done so for a purpose. Now, what was that purpose?"

"Because they were ignorant of the facts of nature, thinking that they were pleasing the gods or god, and that they or he would not punish them after death if they honoured them or him in life," answered John.

"Exactly," said Frank. "You have given me the only possible answer, and that is why I am not a materialist. I am a rationalist, which is quite different. I use my reason in religion just as in my daily life. Nothing is higher than reason ; it is our only guide. I am proud to call myself a rationalist, and I live up to my name of Frank Wiseman, just as you live up to yours. When you sleep you do so to satisfy a natural desire. You need sleep as you need food. Humanity needs religion, and up till now legends and fables, holy books and holy places have satisfied its desire. These will go as education increases, but it does not follow that the desire will also go. Religion will remain, though what it means in the years to come will be very different from what it has meant in the past, and means to most people to-day."

" ' The world is my country, and to do good is my religion,' " quoted John. " Tom Paine summed it all up in these few words, and that is enough for me."

"Well, you won't go far wrong if you follow that," replied Frank, "but why have we this urge to do good instead of evil, to be unselfish instead of selfish? To think noble thoughts is something apart

from the material universe, something in us that is
related to a higher order.   In fact, thinking is super
material, something quite apart from the physical
universe.   To me, this urge for an ideal means
that there is something in us, or, to be more
correct, we are something more than mere flesh and
bones.   If that is so, then that mysterious something
has been the cause of religion, is to-day the cause,
and will remain the cause till it is satisfied."

"I can't follow you, Frank.   Brain and brawn
are all that I am made up of, so far as I can tell."

The two men had by now reached the lighthouse
and had turned to come home.   The sea was glistening and every wavelet was a mirror to the bright,
blue sky overhead.   There was a soft gentle breeze
and the gulls were circling and swooping gracefully
to and fro.

"Out yonder, John, you see Arran through the
misty haze.   You see the soft and ever-changing
colours of both sea and mountain.   Now tell me how
do you see all that?   What is it about you that sees?
Flesh and bones cannot see any more than they can
feel, any more than that stone can see and feel, and yet
you see the beauties all around you, you feel the sand
you tread on, and you enjoy the sensation of harmony
and peace.   Why, I ask you, do you do all that if
you are only made up of brain, flesh and bones?"

"My brain," he replied, "is stimulated through
the nerves running from my eyes, just as it is stimulated by my nerves running from my feet.   That is
surely a good enough answer.   Let us, however,
step out as it is getting late.   I know of no answer
but the brain.   Its cells are stimulated and give me

the impression of all that I hear, see and feel."

" I know no more about the how and the why than you do, but as a rational thinker," said Frank, " I cannot accept that as an explanation. You have still to explain who ' me ' is. Your brain, you tell me, is made up of matter, just as much matter as that stone. If you won't admit that, then you must admit that the brain is a different order of matter from any other matter, and you have no proof that it is. If your skull were opened your brain would be like a sheep's brain, which you eat. Savages eat human brains just as they eat human flesh. You can't deny that it is just as material as any other part of your body."

" I don't deny it," said John, " but I have given you the only explanation I can think of."

" Well, I can't give you the correct reason, but I am sure of this, that your explanation is not the right one," replied Frank. " I am, however, going to try to find out the reason as I have never yet read of one which satisfies me."

Talking thus, they reached the steps leading to the hotel, and climbed slowly to the top just in time to change for dinner.

CHAPTER II.
FRANK STARTS HIS QUEST.

After dinner the three men and the three girls were sitting on the terrace discussing the day's doings.

"By the way," said John to Tony, "how long have you been here?"

"Just a week," he replied. "Frank and I left the place we were staying at near Cambridge after breakfast and arrived here just after dinner."

"You must have travelled fast to do the trip in a day. Which way did you take?" asked John.

"We came by the Great North Road," Tony answered, "joining it just past Huntingdon. What a topping stretch of road that is between Cambridge and Huntingdon! I think it must be one of the straightest roads in this country. You can keep up sixty for miles. After that, it is just slogging on through Stamford, Grantham and Doncaster till you reach Scotch Corner. There we turned over the Westmoreland Hills, through Brough, and joined the West Coast Road at Penrith. Then we came by Carlisle, Newton Stewart and Girvan. We stopped at Doncaster for lunch and at Penrith for tea. We reached Carlisle by 6-30."

"Just the way we came," said John. "Fine country after you leave Scotch Corner, coming over to Penrith, and after Carlisle through Galloway, which was once a kingdom all of its own. If you had taken the coast road after Dumfries you would have passed the scenes of many incidents referred to in Scott's *Guy Mannering*—Dirk Hatteraick's cave, for instance.   All this coast from here right down to the Solway Firth was a hot-bed of smugglers a hundred and fifty years ago.   Just forty-five miles south from this hotel is the point of land nearest to Ireland, if you except Kintyre, over there, where, in the old days, ships from abroad dumped their contraband goods, which were run across in a few hours to Scotland, when the coast was clear.   The channel is only twenty miles across.''

" That would have taken us miles out of our way," said Tony, " but we can easily go back from here and have a picnic and explore the place.   I am sure you girls would not say ' no ' to that."

The next day it was decided that the morning would be spent in playing golf and tennis and that in the afternoon the two cars would take the party to Dirk Hatteraick's cave, where they would have tea, explore the place, and then return in time for dinner.

" Well, Frank is our guide," said John.   " You had better get hold of that copy of *Guy Mannering*, Frank, I was looking at yesterday, and be able to answer all our questions.   You will find it in the bookcase in the writing room."

" I have read the book more than once," said Frank, " but I shall take it with me and read you all the exciting bits at tea."

After lunch, the two cars were brought from the garage and the party set off.

It had been decided to take the coast road as far as Stranraer, cut across Wigtonshire to Newton

Stewart, then make for Creetown, at the top of Wigtown Bay, where they would then ask where they would find the cave.   Frank said it was only a few miles further on but was not sure of the exact spot.

Without much difficulty the cave was discovered, and after it was explored, when the party was at tea, Frank was called upon to tell its history.

" This was a centre of villainy in the eighteenth century," he commenced.   " Just listen to Sir Walter Scott's description of the laird's son being kidnapped from this spot—

> ' After the bloody deed was done we retreated into a cave close beside, the secret of which was known but to one man in the country ; we were debating what to do with the child, and we thought of giving it up to the gipsies, when we heard the cries of the pursuers hallooing to each other.   One man alone came straight to our cave, and it was that man who knew the secret, but we made him our friend at the expense of half the value of the goods saved.   By his advice we carried off the child to Holland in our consort, which came the following night. to take us from the coast.   That man was———' "

" Who ? " all shouted in chorus.

" Who ?   Why, none other than that villain over there, drinking his tea with his mouth full," and all faces were turned on John Matterson, who nearly choked in his attempt to suppress a laugh.

" I can't be serious any longer," explained Frank.   " In any case it is not fair to put this load on my shoulders. Read the story for yourselves and it will be all the more interesting now that you have seen the place."

So laughing, talking and scrambling about the rocks, the afternoon passed and they were on their way home again by six, arriving back at the hotel in time for dinner.

When Angela came down to dinner she saw Hope Trueman at a table at the further end of the room and made straight for her.

" Delighted to see you, Hope, and you also, Mr. and Mrs. Trueman. I hope you have had a good holiday. I must hear all you have to tell me."

" Sit here beside us," said Hope, " the table holds four. The waiter can tell your friends where you are."

Angela sat down and was soon hearing all the news.

" We have been up to the north of Scotland," said Mrs. Trueman. " We went over the Grampians by Blair Atholl to Inverness and then through Lairg right up to Durness, the furthest north we could go. On our way home we came by the new road from Inverness by Loch Ness, through Glencoe and down the side of Loch Lomond. The roads were perfect."

" Nothing to the scenery," said Hope. " North of Lairg it was just one loch after another and mountain after mountain rising behind the other."

" No one knows the beauties of Scotland till they get north of Lairg," said Mr. Trueman. " The beauty and grandeur of the scenery are beyond description. Now that the roads are so good a new country is opened up to motorists and more and more people will find pleasure in their own country. We need not go abroad for beautiful scenery."

"What a wonderful road that is between Inverness and Glasgow," said Hope. "No, we did not see the Loch Ness monster, Angela, though we looked for it all the time we were passing down the loch."

"Our party here," said Angela, "has just come back from a picnic at Dirk Hatteraick's cave. You may not have heard of this bold, brave kidnapping smuggler, but the rocky coast and caves gave him and his crew every chance to evade the law."

"Yes, I have read about him in one of Scott's books, *Guy Mannering* is it not?" said Mr. Trueman. "There is romance and history wherever you go in Scotland. I hope to-morrow to run over to Ayr and see Burns' Cottage. His love of nature always appealed to me. Will you come with me?" he enquired, turning to Angela.

"With pleasure; and I am sure some of the others will come also. There are six of us, all about the same age, and Hope makes the seventh. We find that there is so much to see and so much to do that the days just fly past."

After dinner, the Truemans were introduced to the others, and when the coffee had been drunk most of them found their way into the ball-room.

When the dancing finished and the ladies had gone to bed, the four men were left seated in the lounge.

"Well! another wonderful day over," said Tony. "I am tired and will turn in."

"Goodnight, Tony," replied the others, "don't dream of smugglers or golf."

" You played topping golf to-day, I hear," said John, "and went round in just two over bogey. We must have a game to-morrow."

" If you can fit it in with your golf," said Mr. Trueman, " I would suggest that, as a matter of education, you should see Burns' Cottage when you are here. He has been an inspiration to millions."

" I am afraid Burns never appealed to me," called out Tony, who had risen to leave.   " But John and Frank are the thinkers.   I am afraid I am just a drifter.   Goodnight."

" I would like to go with you, Mr. Trueman," said Frank.   " I always admired the humanity of Burns, his love of the people and his democratic outlook.   Did anyone write anything finer than *A Man's a Man for a' that*? "

" I admire the way he slanged the Kirk Session of Ayr," said John.   " If he had lived fifty years earlier he would have been put in prison for writing *Holy Willie's Prayer*."

" Sir Walter Scott described it as the most exquisite piece of satire ever written," said Trueman. " Nothing ever written in that age showed up better the hypocrisy and bigotry of the Presbyterians of his time.   Did you ever read that wonderful poem composed by Ingersoll, that great American advocate of free thought, when he visited the Cottage during his visit to this country towards the end of last century? I can't remember it, but we may get a copy of it at the Cottage."

Mr. George Trueman was a man of outstanding ability, a graduate of Cambridge, about fifty years of age, above the average in height, handsome, and

still young-looking. He had made his mark as a
chartered accountant in London and was a worthy
representative of a long line of ancestors who, for the
last two hundred years, had occupied a prominent
place in the business community of the city of London,
his great grandfather having been Lord Mayor. He
was head of the well-known firm of Trueman, Solid
& Swift, one of the leading accountancy firms in the
city, and had carried through the amalgamation of
some of the largest companies, being frequently called
in by the Treasury and the Board of Trade when
difficult and intricate work had to be done. His grasp
of figures was remarkable, and the thorough way he
carried through his work made him trusted implicitly
by his clients.

Besides this, he was chairman of several large
companies, and his judgment, caution and courage,
all blended to perfection, made his decisions always
respected by his colleagues.

His home life was a happy one. He lived in
Sussex in a beautiful house, placed in a large well-
timbered park, and he and his wife were always
generous in their support of all local activities. He
had a well-stocked library and was a great reader.
Only in one way was he considered peculiar, but his
other qualities made his friends forget it. He was a
Spiritualist, and always expressed the gratitude he
felt towards his wife, whose mediumistic gifts had
brought him round from materialism to the wider
outlook he now had.

From Mrs. Trueman's appearance no one could
realise that she was in any way different from other
women. She was a handsome, middle-aged woman,

well preserved, of medium height, and from her face
shone kindness and good nature.   She was a devoted
wife and mother and was beloved by all who knew her.

Few of Trueman's friends in the city were
interested in Spiritualism, so he rarely mentioned it ;
but at home, if his guests were anxious to hear about
his experiences, he was always glad of the opportunity
to make known his beliefs.   He was a good public
speaker and his lectures were always appreciated by
his audiences.

Sitting at the present time in the lounge at Turnberry Hotel he was discussing with John and Frank
the revolutionary character of some of the works of
the great Scottish poet, Robert Burns.   After this,
the talk became general, but before separating for
the night Frank asked if he could join the party going
to the Cottage to-morrow, to which request he
received a cordial affirmative from Mr. Trueman.

After lunch the next day the car set off for Ayr,
about fourteen miles distant, with George Trueman,
Grace, Frank and Hope.

Taking the shore road they were able to see the
beauties of the Firth right up to where it begins to
narrow between Garroch Head in Bute and Farland
Head on the mainland.   A slight haze hung over the
distant peaks of Arran and the sea was calm and still.
In the distance could be seen ocean liners on their
way to Glasgow from some distant ports and others
on their mission abroad.   Dotted here and there
moved the various Clyde passenger steamers, which
link up the islands with the mainland.

" Do you see that point of land away in the distance?" said Trueman. " Round that you come on an island called the Great Cumbrae, and on it is a little town called Millport. The parson there, some time last century, distinguished himself every Sunday by praying ' for the adjacent islands of Great Britain and Ireland.' "

" I can tell you a good story, too," said Frank. " My mother told me about the parson at Brodick, over there in Arran, who in his sermon once said that his congregation need not expect to hang on to his coat-tails on the day of judgment, as he would wear a jacket that day. On another occasion, when preaching on the same subject, he told how some of his congregation on the last day would cry ' Oh Lord we didna' ken, we didna' ken,' and on that great day the Lord will look down on you and in solemn tones will say, ' Ah weel, ah weel, ye ken noo.' "

" I suppose that is Scotch humour," said Grace.

" Yes, and it is very rich at times," said Frank. " I shall give you an example which my mother, who came from Ayrshire, told me was true—and I am sure it is—because she said she got it from the direct descendant of Jock Thomson, the hero of the tale."

The car was just passing over the *Heads of Ayr* and Frank pointed across the bay. " Over there, you see that town with the harbour jutting out to sea. Its name is Saltcoats. Now, not far from Ayr is a village called Tarbolton. On these two places hangs my tale.

Some time early last century a village lad called Jock Thomson disappeared from his native village of Tarbolton, and no one knew what had happened to him. Many years passed, and a Saltcoats man of the name of Elliot, who was the son of the local minister, was at Vera Cruz, in Mexico, as master of a sailing ship, and lying off shore was the Spanish Navy in all its glory.

Much to his surprise he received an invitation from the Admiral of the Spanish Fleet to dine with him that night. He arrived and found him in company with his officers, all of whom were in full naval dress. Rather shyly he took his place on the right of the Admiral and was treated as an honoured guest, wondering all the time why all this attention should be paid to him.

When the dinner came to an end, he was much astonished to receive a similar invitation for the following night, which he accepted. On returning at the hour appointed, he was more than ever surprised to find that he and the Admiral were dining alone. His surprise increased when the Admiral plied him with questions about Ayrshire and its people.

'Why all this interest in Ayrshire?' asked the Saltcoats skipper. 'You seem to know it well. Have you ever been there?'

'Losh man, Elliot, I'm Jock Tamson frae Tarbouton. Do ye no ken I'm Scotch, as Scotch as yersel. I was the laddie who ran away frae hame and was thocht to be deed.'"

"What an extraordinary story," said Hope. "Trust a Scotchman to get to the top. It rather reminds me of the story of Joseph and his brethren. I suppose Tarbouton is the local pronunciation of Tarbolton."

Further comments were impossible as the car now drew up at the cottage in which Burns, Scotland's national poet, saw the light, one stormy January morning, in the year 1759.

George Trueman gave the others the impression that they were entering a shrine, and his first question of the caretaker was for a copy of Ingersoll's poem on Burns.

"We hae no copey for sale, but ye'll get it hinging up yonner," was the reply. Trueman went over to the wall, to the place the man pointed.

"Yes, here it is ; just listen to this. How Burns still stirs the imagination in all parts of the world !

' Though Scotland boasts a thousand names,
   Of patriot, King and peer,
The noblest, grandest of them all,
   Was loved and cradled here.

Here lived, the gentle peasant prince—
   The loving cottar king;
Compared with whom the greatest lord
   Is but a titled thing.

'Tis but a cot roofed in with straw;
   A hovel made of clay;
One door shuts out the snow and storm,
   One window greets the day.

And yet I stand within this room,
   And hold all thrones in scorn;
For, here, beneath this lowly thatch,
   Love's sweetest bard was born.

Within this hallow'd hut, I feel
   Like one who clasps a shrine,
When the glad lips at last have touched
   The something deemed divine.

And here, the world, through all the years
   As long as day returns,
The tribute of its love and tears,
   Will pay to Robert Burns.'

Isn't that fine, written by one of the world's greatest
orators and champions of liberty about one whose
very simplicity made him great?"

After spending half-an-hour inspecting the relics
the party returned home. The Cottage and all its
associations had stirred George Trueman to the
depths of his impressionable nature and he waxed
eloquent, so much so, that the others found little
opportunity to do more than listen.

"Robert Burns," he commenced, "born in
poverty, was the greatest man of his day, the Shakespeare of Scotland. He was great because he
thought great thoughts and expressed them fearlessly
and honestly. As Burns put it :

> ' The honest man, tho' e'er so poor,
>   Is king of men for a' that.'

He expressed the ideals of the best that is in the
Scottish race. He made the common life beautiful
and elevated honest labour above that of titled idle-
ness and orthodox ignorance. In all he said and
did he showed his independence, his generosity.

> ' You see yon birkie (pert fellow) ca'd a Lord
>   Wha' struts and stares and a' that,
> Though hundreds worship at his word
>   He's but a coof for a' that.'

These lines helped to inspire the masses to rise from
being down-trodden wretches to what they are to-day,
and they will still inspire them to something greater
still. Then Burns ends up this greatest of all his
poems by the well-known lines :

> ' Then let us pray that come it may,
>   As come it will for a' that,

That sense and worth o'er a' the earth
    May bear the gree and a' that!
For a' that, and a' that,
    Its coming yet for a' that,
That man to man, the world o'er,
    Shall brithers be for a' that! '

Seldom does he touch on history.   In his poems
he shows little learning.   To him the every-day life
is his book.   What he sees and feels he writes about,
and turns the common things of life into something
sublime.

He wrote against political and religious injustice,
against all artificial distinctions.   To him, the Presbyterian creed was cruel and preposterous, and he
lashed it and its advocates.   He was one of our great
freethinkers, one of our early Rationalists.   He was
a reformer in his time, both political and religious,
and cared nothing for creeds and dogmas.   To him,
good deeds counted for far more than religious beliefs.
He struck a blow at caste, at social distinction, at
religious hypocrisy, at the parsons and their churches,
and all who bowed their ignorant heads in meek submission.   He left with a generous hand a legacy to
mankind and to the glory of Scotland."

" Who was Holy Wullie? " asked Grace.

" Holy Wullie," Trueman replied, " was one
of those miserable creatures who think that they and
only those who think like them are going to Heaven.
The world has been full of them.   His real name was
William Fisher, an elder of the Parish Church of
Mauchline, not far from here.   When Burns published the poem about him called ' Holy Wullie's
Prayer ' the Scotch Church clergy were so alarmed
that they tried to invoke the Law of Blasphemy

against the poet, but without success. Holy Wullie
met a drunkard's end and was found one morning
dead in a ditch by the roadside.''

'' Can you repeat his prayer, Daddy?'' asked
Hope.

'' Only bits of it.—It starts thus :

' Oh, Thou, wha' in the heavens dost dwell,
Wha' as it pleases best thyself,
Sends ane to Heaven and ten to Hell,
  A' for thy glory
And no for any guid or ill
  They've done afore thee!

I bless and praise thy matchless might,
Whan thousands thou has left in night,
That I am here, afore thy sight,
  For gifts and grace,
A burning and a shining light,
  To a' this place.'

And so on, and then after Wullie has prayed for the
damnation of all those about him, whom he terms
sinners, he ends up :

' But, Lord, remember me and mine,
Wi' mercies temporal and divine,
That I for gear and grace may shine,
  Excelled by nane,
And a' the glory shall be thine,
  Amen! Amen! ' ''

'' What a hateful character,'' said Grace. '' I
am glad people like that don't go about nowadays.''

'' Perhaps they do, but we have not a Rabbie
Burns to expose them,'' answered Frank.

Here the conversation ended as the car drew up
at the hotel door. How much more George Trueman had to say we shall never know as his eloquence
was cut short by having to get out of his car.

'' Well, you have kept us enthralled,'' said
Grace. '' We have done fourteen miles and it seems

as if we had just left the Cottage five minutes ago.
I love the humanity of Burns ; that is what appeals
to me."

"Well, though I am English," replied Trueman, "Burns has always appealed to me. My
mother was a Douglas of Castle Douglas and she
taught me to appreciate his poetry."

After dinner, George Trueman and Frank were
strolling up and down in front of the hotel enjoying
the long twilight, for which Scotland is so famous in
summer.

"How light it is in these northern regions,"
remarked Frank. "The sun has just gone behind
that highest peak of Arran. Goat Fell it is called,
3,000 feet high."

"One reason for the longer evenings in Scotland," said Trueman, "is that Scotland is from
2° to 6° west of Greenwich, and every degree of
longtitude means four minutes difference in time.
The sun is just setting here but it has set in London
sixteen minutes ago. Besides that, owing to the
tilt of the earth, the further north you go in summer
the longer the sun keeps above the horizon and the
twilight is also longer."

"Well, they get shorter days in winter,"
replied Frank, "so it is not altogether an advantage.
But there is another subject, sir, I would like to speak
to you about. You are so well-known as a Spiritualist that I would not like to lose this opportunity
of hearing something about the subject from one who
is such a recognised authority. Do you mind telling

me how it is Spiritualists seem so sure that there is another life beyond this one?"

"That, Frank, is rather a common-place way of putting it. It is incorrect to say that there is another life beyond this. It is the same life, the only difference being that life changes its environment at death, that is all; there is nothing so very mysterious about it."

"You see," remarked Frank, "John Matterson and I were having a talk about things after a game of golf the other day, and he says that nothing exists beyond what we can see, feel and handle. I disagreed with him. He says that he is a materialist, a matter of fact, hard-headed, believer in only what he can sense by touch, smell and sight."

"He is a brave man to be so dogmatic," replied Trueman. "If he had seen and heard what I have seen in the séance room he would come to a very different conclusion. There we get into touch with other expressions of nature which prove that matter, as we sense it, is only one expression and by no means the highest, perhaps one of the lowest, in the Universe."

"You are speaking rather above my head, sir, but tell me, will you, have you ever spoken to people after they have died? To me it seems impossible; but I have an open mind. I am a rationalist, you see, and I suppose, to be rational, I should hear all sides before I make up my mind about anything."

"So much the better," said Trueman. "A rationalist has no preconceived opinions to shed, as have those professing some orthodox religion. Take a Christian, for instance. He, when first introduced to Spiritualism, must make it square with his beliefs, and if it doesn't then he says it is wicked or of the devil. It takes a Christian a long time to be driven off his orthodox pedestal, to discard what is unessential in religion and to keep only to what is essential. That is why orthodox Christianity, or any other orthodox religion, is the greatest stumbling-block to the spread of the new knowledge.

You probably know already, as every well-educated person does, that the Christian Church has opposed everything that is true, and Spiritualism is no exception. For nearly a century now, since modern Spiritualism came into being, as a result of the Hydesville discoveries in 1848, priests and parsons have preached against it and denounced it as of the devil, just as the priests in the time of Jesus warned the people against him because they said that he was a servant of the devil. Christian bishops and priests, up to the present day, have issued manifestos to their flocks warning them against Spiritualism as being of the devil, and affirming that all who accepted it were the servants of the devil. The devil has always been brought in to frighten the people against any new revelation. ' Keep the people ignorant ' has always been the motto, and so for years past there has been this united opposition of the Church to the truths of Spiritualism.

Prior to last century, what we now term mediums were called witches, whom the Church nearly exterminated, by burning, during the Christian era. This capacity for mediumship is a hereditary gift and it was thus nearly lost to humanity. Naturally, the Church did not want the people to make contact with the other world except through its own organisation.

At times, when it could make use of this gift mediums possess for its own ends, it made saints of psychic people, but only if they accepted the teachings of the Church.   When, however, these mediums made use of their powers outside of the direction of the Church, it called them witches, burning and torturing them.   If it had not been for this burning of witches we, to-day, would have been in close and regular touch with a higher order of existence, which functions in what I call Etheria, which is our destiny after death.

Mediumship, as I say, is a hereditary gift, and it was almost stamped out by the Church's opposition to that which nature intended was to be ; but nature will not be denied, and will come into its own some day when intelligence increases.

That is why, in my addresses I give throughout the country, I try to show that Christianity has no foundation for its assertions, in fact that it is just paganism under another name.   Break completely the power of the Church and Spiritualism will flood Christendom.''

'' I quite agree about Christianity being paganism under another name,'' said Frank. '' I have read a good deal along those lines and have come to that conclusion also, but what I always wondered was why our ancestors and the people of to-day gave, and do give, time and wealth to supporting any kind of religion.   There must have been a reason behind all the frauds and falsehoods, behind all the claims made by the Churches of all the world's Faiths.''

'' Of course there was a reason,'' replied Trueman, "and that reason was because man is—not has—an immortal soul or mind. At least we know that he survives death, and the soul or mind seems to be indestructible and thus immortal. In the years gone by the people could not understand the deeper meaning of life, and they had fewer facts to go on than we have to-day to prove that life continues after death. They had only a vague instinct, and so the priests evolved legends and myths, which symbolised the central truth and so satisfied the people's longings. To-day, they still worship these drapings, and many forget, and many don't realise, that they are only symbols of the truth behind. It is not the drapings which are of any importance. When the people know the truth and have the knowledge which Spiritualism gives they are easily discarded. Unfortunately, these wrappings, which go under the name of creeds and dogmas, hide the truth, as the priests and people worship these and think that they and they only are of importance and that to believe in them leads to salvation."

"Yes, I see what you are driving at, but you are convinced that you have proof of survival, whereas I am not. I have never had any evidence that when we are dead we are not dead."

"That is easy to give you," said Trueman, "but first of all you see what I mean when I say that a rationalist can grasp the truth much more easily and quickly than a believer in any of the world's religions."

"Oh yes, I quite see what you mean. Creeds and dogmas don't bother me, I never could accept them ; but what I want is proof, and you say that is

easy to get. To me it seems the most difficult thing
on earth."

"Well, we shall try and get a chance to discuss
the subject further before I leave, but I promise you
this, that I shall see that you get proof. You may
be surprised to know that my wife is one of the best
mediums in this country, and through her you will
get the proof."

"Well, I never expected to hear you say that.
You seem very confident, if I may say so, with all
respect."

"You see, I know. My wife is one of the best
all-round mediums with whom I have ever sat, and
I have sat with many. You don't understand yet,
but you will. I promise that you will speak to those
you call dead, face to face, and hear their actual
voices, those they used when on earth. Don't think
I am talking rubbish. You must know that I always
keep to facts ; my life is one long dealing with facts,
and making each fit the other. Figures are facts.
I believe in nothing that I have not experienced.
Like you, I am a rationalist, and I bring rationalism
into my religious life just as I do in business and in
everything else. When I make a promise I keep it.
If you accept my offer I invite you now to my house in
Sussex. It is called Sureway Court, a good name,
you will admit, now that you know that I never
believe anything without being sure that it is true.
We shall fix up a date before we leave. I like your
caution. Don't accept anything without proof and
then, when you have it, stick to it as I have done
these last thirty years. Well, good-night, and don't
dream of ghosts."

The next day the weather broke, but in the fine intervals golf and tennis occupied the energies of our friends.   George Trueman and his wife went out in their car in the afternoon.   They motored inland to the uplands of Ayrshire, stopping to look at a number of martyrs' graves as they passed them.   In parts of the county these are placed not far from the roadside. When they came to Muirkirk, George remarked, " I am sorry it is too long a walk for you, my dear, to visit the memorial to John Brown of Priesthill, but it is up that valley and I see that there is no road.

He was a brave man and his wife equally brave.   He was shot at his cottage door before his wife and children.   Towards the end of the seventeenth century the Episcopal Church made a determined attempt to stamp out Calvinism in Scotland, and John Brown was only one of 28,000 who, between the years 1661 and 1689, were ruthlessly butchered, while many thousands were either shipped abroad as slaves or died from months of exposure in the Greyfriars Churchyard in Edinburgh, where they had no shelter from the wind and rain.

When William of Orange became King he brought to an end what is still known in Scotland as ' The Killing Time.'   This persecution came about because the Scottish people preferred their own form of worship to the Episcopalian brand.   It is just one of the many instances of Protestants murdering and torturing each other.   These men and women were bold enough to defy authority and worship as they thought right.   If it had not been for them, and for many others throughout our land, we should have no religious or political liberty to-day and should still be under the dictatorship of Church and State.   It is interesting to realise that many of the people in Ayrshire are the decendants of the Lollards, the followers of Wyclif, who took refuge in Ayrshire in the fifteenth century.   They were a tough lot of people, or otherwise they never could have endured what they suffered.''

''If you had lived then, George,'' said Mrs. Trueman, ''and I had been your wife, I would have been a widow for the same reason as Mrs. Brown became one.   These brave men, who were hunted like foxes all over these moorlands, and lived in caves so as to escape their pursuers, ushered in the era of religious liberty we now enjoy.   I suppose I should have been killed also for being a witch.''

''You would, indeed.   Five hundred thousand innocent women were burned by the Christian Church for no other reason than that they exercised a natural gift, because of the injunctions in Exodus that no witch must be allowed to live.   Pope Innocent VIII, in 1488, ascribed, in his famous Bull, all the troubles in life to mediums and ordered their extermination, which was duly carried out by Catholics and Protestants up till the eighteenth century.   Be thankful, dear, you live in the twentieth century and that the Church has lost its power.''

''When the people obtained freedom to think Europe became civilised,'' remarked Mrs. Trueman.

''Well, my dear, the Church was in full control up till the end of the eighteenth century and it made a most miserable mess of things.   The French Revolution was the beginning of its overthrow and ever since then it has been losing ground.   It is an interesting thought that six Scotsmen, who all lived at the same time early last century, did more to civilise and raise humanity than all the Christian priests and parsons put together since the beginning of the Christian era.   Telford and Rennie built the principal harbours, roads, bridges and canals of Britain.   Macadam, born in Ayr, which we have just passed through, discovered how to surface our roads.   Watt made the steam engine a practical proposition. Stevenson built our first locomotives and railways, and Symington the first steamship.   They made no preposterous claims, such as the priesthood make, of being God's representatives on earth, and yet they transformed mankind, mentally and morally, and raised us from what was little better than savagery to what we are to-day.   Before these men appeared our country consisted of scattered communities of poor, miserable and ignorant barbarians.   It took over two weeks in the eighteenth century to travel from London to Edinburgh, through quagmires. Murder and pillage prevailed everywhere.   News took months to travel.   Macaulay, the historian, tells us that the long Court mourning for the death of Queen Elizabeth was over before the people in Devon knew that she had died.''

"I think you are quite proud of your Scottish descent, George.''

"Indeed I am.   Every Scotsman should be proud of these six men who ushered in the era of modern civilisation.   Those of them who were offered titles showed their independence in refusing them. A man's name, without any addition to it, should be sufficient to enable his fellow men to place him in their estimation. If an omniscient being had the conferring of titles, justice would be done, but when we find to-day that such things are purchased, obtained by intrigue and descend to the progeny of the original recipients, who have no claim to be different from other people, titles become a farce and are despised by men of independent mind."

" I am not sorry now, George, that you refused that baronetcy you were offered. I would rather that you lived and were remembered as George Trueman, and all that stands for, than that anyone imagined that you paid for a title or intrigued to get it."

" When you come to think of it," he replied, " it is not titles that make men great, but their achievements. James Watt would have been no greater a man if all the titles and honours that this earth can bestow had been added to his name. We remember the great by their achievements, and no country has produced more great men than Scotland. Down the centuries this country has poured men of genius into England, and what they accomplished has been largely responsible for making England what it is to-day. Great scholars, physicians, statesmen, scientists, engineers, soldiers, sailors, men of business and financiers have moved in a procession southwards and spread throughout the British Empire. It is no exaggeration when I say that Scotland has produced more great men than any other country in the world, and nearly all were born in humble homes. This can be attributed to their strength of character and the fact that from the time of John Knox the poorest had the chance of some education, whereas elsewhere it was confined to the rich.

We must now turn back as it is getting late."

On returning home the sun broke through the clouds and silhouetted Arran amid a glistening sea. The setting made a perfect picture.

When nearing the hotel, Trueman pointed to a stretch of land jutting out to sea. "That is where Robert Bruce is supposed to have landed on his last attempt to liberate Scotland from English rule, which was so successful at Bannockburn. Have you ever thought of the great dis-service he really did to Scotland in his fierce fight for his country's liberty. Scotland became rich and prosperous only when it became united to England. This, Bruce and his followers, through their mistaken policy, kept from being realised at the time when a union was possible. For the four hundred years which followed there was nothing but strife and bloodshed between two countries which should have been one as they were of the same race and had the same ideals."

The car by now had stopped at the hotel door and there they found most of the others sitting in the lounge in earnest conference.

"We are all discussing plans for to-morrow," said Hope. "Come and join us and tell us what you advise."

"We are planning to go across to Arran to-morrow, if it is fine. A steamer sails every morning and we get back at night. We shall get out at Lamlash and walk over to Brodick, where we can have our lunch and then take a bus over to Loch Ranza. The guide-book says that it is the most beautiful drive in the island. First, along the coast, and then through a lovely glen to a bay right on the north of the island.

Do come with us.''

'' Of course I will, said her mother, ''and you will come also, won't you, George?''

'' Certainly,'' he replied. '' It is our last day here. Let us make the most of it. We must get south and make a start the day after to-morrow.''

The next day the three cars took the party to Ayr where they joined the L.M.S. paddle steamer '' Jupiter,'' one of the fleet of swift vessels which ply between the sea coast towns of Ayrshire and Renfrew-shire, the islands, and the mainland of Argyll. This county, boasting of the longest coast-line in the country, throws southwards long arms into the sea, the most southerly point being the Mull of Kintyre, nearly opposite to Turnberry but separated from it by twenty-five miles of sea.

Kintyre acts to the Firth as a natural breakwater, fifty miles long, against the fury of the Atlantic Ocean. The opening to the Firth of Clyde commences about twenty-five miles south of Turnberry and the Firth extends due north for seventy miles as far as Dunoon, that popular watering place, when the river narrows to about three miles in width. Here it turns south-east, gradually narrowing for a further twenty miles, where is situated the Port of Glasgow, which accommodates vessels of the largest tonnage. From Glasgow sail also pleasure steamers to all the coast towns on either side of the Firth.

Thus, for a distance of ninety miles, there is a water-way, so sheltered that at all times of the year these Clyde passenger steamers can ply with safety. Only occasionally, when a strong south wind blows during the winter, is the sea so rough as to make their journeys inadvisable.

As the traveller from the south enters the Firth he sees mainland on either side and islands in front of him. First comes the island of Sanda, to the west, then Ailsa Craig, and then, after passing the island of Arran, he passes the islands of the Big and Little Cumbraes and Bute. From here onwards stretch inland the sea lochs for which the Clyde is so famous. The Ayrshire coast is hilly, of a soft, deep verdure, but in the distance, northwards, the mountains of Argyll stand out in all their rugged glory. The further up the Firth one goes the closer in they come, but they are seen at their best at the Cumbraes—as distance lends enchantment to the view.

On this great stretch of water, known as the Firth of Clyde, ply twenty-four luxurious passenger steamers, owned by the L.M.S. and the L.N.E. railways, and their rapid journeys to and fro enhance the interest of this famous waterway. Sailing boats become more and more numerous as the Firth narrows and these, and the ocean-going vessels, make it necessary for the river steamer captains to keep a sharp look out.

The " Jupiter," the steamer our friends boarded,

made the journey across to Arran in about an hour, and the party kept to their plans. On reaching Loch Ranza in the afternoon they were all charmed with the beauty of the bay, with the old castle standing in its lonely majesty, where its waters reach furthest inland.

" I have just been talking to the oldest inhabitant," said John, on his way home. " You won't believe me when I tell you that you can't hire a small boat on Sunday, or Sabbath, as he called it. That, I suppose, is what is called ' Keeping the Sabbath.' "

" Well, it is no worse that the restrictions imposed by our London County Council," said Trueman, " which won't allow a Sunday entertainment in a London Theatre if the actors use paint or wear wigs. To wear these on Sunday is sinful, according to our city rulers. This is about the last folly we have to overcome before we have a sane Sunday in London, freed from all the taboos of the past."

" I remember reading," said Mrs. Trueman, " that the laws about Sunday, now nearly all abolished, fortunately, originated in Babylon ; in fact that they have been recovered, written on clay tablets. It seems one of the most remarkable things in history that we, to-day, four thousand years after they were enacted, are still tied to what the Babylonians thought should not be done on ' the Sabatu, ' as they called it. The Jews just copied them during their captivity and adopted their laws when they returned home."

" You remember me telling you some days ago, Faith, that we are just slaves of custom, and you seemed to glory in it," said John.

" I never knew that the laws about the Sabbath came from Babylon," replied Faith. " I was taught that God gave them to Moses. But you see, I have always accepted what I was told and what I have read in the Bible. I have never read anything about those subjects outside the Bible, so I am rather ignorant."

" It was Dean Inge who said, the other day, that the only way to remain orthodox was never to think," said Frank. " Many never read, except along their own line, and are blissfully ignorant of all the discoveries scholarship has made over the last hundred years. I hope you are not offended with me, Faith, for speaking like this. I hate saying anything to hurt. It came out without thinking. But, to change the subject, here we are back at Brodick and the steamer is waiting at the pier."

On the steamer, Mrs. Trueman touched her husband on the shoulder. " George, do you see those two over there?"

" Yes," said he, " what of it?"

" Well," replied his wife, " I have been watching them since we arrived at Turnberry and I am sure that they are in love with each other. When he comes to Sureway Court we might ask Angela also."

The two in question were none other than Frank and Angela.

CHAPTER III.
AT SUREWAY COURT.

To a chorus of good-byes, Mr. and Mrs. Trueman and Hope left Turnberry the next day on their way south. Before they left, however, George Trueman had a further talk with Frank, and it was decided that he would come to Sureway Court for the week-end a fortnight hence. He was to come by the two o'clock train from Charing Cross to Tunbridge Wells, where the car would meet him.

As Frank was strolling up the platform looking for a vacant corner seat he was much surprised to see comfortably seated, in a first-class smoking carriage, his old school and college friend Ralph Leader.

" Hello, Ralph," he said, " whoever expected to see you here !"

"Well, Frank, old man," he replied, "delighted to see you. I can say that I am equally surprised to see you. I am on my way to spend the week-end with some friends near Tunbridge Wells."

Frank stepped in and after he had seated himself opposite to Ralph the two men discovered that they were bound for the same destination and that Ralph, like Frank, was to be a guest over the week-end at Sureway Court.

Ralph and Frank had been at Eton together and afterwards had gone up to Cambridge, Frank going to King's and Ralph to Trinity. They had seen a good deal of each other there, but had not met since they had both come down a year ago.

Ralph had taken his degree in history and was

a keen politician, as his ancestors had been before
him.   His father, who had died, had left him well
off, so that he could give his entire time to what he
intended to make his life work.   His mother and he
lived together, spending part of the year in their
country home in Hertfordshire and the rest of the
time at their house in London.

He, like Frank, was tall, and no one needed to
look at him twice to realise that he was a young man
above the average in intelligence.   He had inherited
the family ability which had been responsible for his
ancestors making their mark not only in business but
in politics.

The journey to Tunbridge Wells took just over
an hour, and when the train drew into the station the
two young men alighted and soon found the car from
Sureway Court.

"Have you started on your career yet?"
enquired Ralph.

"Yes, I have started at Guy's, but it will be four
years before I am qualified.   I had a splendid holiday
in Scotland and I was keen to make a start at the
hospital as soon as possible.   So you see I am now
a budding doctor."

"You have my best wishes, Frank.   I am
waiting for a constituency to invite an ignoramus like
me to represent them in that august assembly at Westminster.   I hope I have not to wait till the next
election.   I intend to devote my life to promote peace
amongst nations.   If I don't get a seat soon I shall
go out to Geneva and get some experience there in
the work of the League of Nations."

Talking thus, the five mile journey was soon

completed and the car swung in between imposing gates, beside which was an ivy-clad lodge. The winding drive through the park, dotted with oaks and beeches, led up to the mansion perched on rising ground and commanding an extensive view over the surrounding country.

"What a beautiful place," said Frank. "These old Elizabethan houses are the pride of England. The mullioned windows are so attractive."

"They certainly knew how to build in those days," replied Ralph. "The pleasure grounds are evidently at the back, on the south front. It makes for privacy, having the front door facing north."

The car was approaching the house through an avenue of cedars and swung round the courtyard to draw up before a heavy timbered door.

The door was opened by the footman and they both entered the house, to be relieved of their coats and hats by Boles, the butler, who then piloted them to the library.

"Delighted to see you both," said Mrs. True-man, when she arrived a few minutes later. "Angela Bridge arrived last night. I am sure, Frank, you never expected to see her so soon. She and Hope are out in the garden. I don't know where my husband is—probably in his sanctum. Now I shall first show you your rooms and then you can go out and join the girls."

The afternoon up till tea time was spent on the lake, Ralph and Hope going in one boat and Frank and Angela in the other.

From the lake the beauties of the surroundings charmed the visitors. The sloping lawns led from the lake up to the rose garden, beyond which there was a terrace surrounded with climbing roses. A door from the house gave on to the terrace, and it was there that the family sat when out of doors. This aspect of the house faced south, and through avenues of stately trees distant vistas opened on the country beyond.

" You have a lovely home," said Ralph ; " you must love the place."

" To me, these beautiful summer days, the place is just a dream," replied Hope. " I cannot think of anything better one could wish for than to live in one of those beautiful old houses, given electric light and central heating."

" That is essential. Grandeur and cold don't appeal to me, Hope. I would rather live in a less stately house and have electric light than in a mansion with only lamps."

" In my grandfather's time," said Hope, " there were just lamps, but after he died and we came here, fifteen years ago, daddy fitted up the place with both electric light and central heating. Before that we had a lovely home near Epsom. There goes the tea bell ; we must pull for the shore."

At tea, conversation was general.

" I have just heard from Bill," said Mrs. True-man, addressing Hope. " He will be home on Wednesday, and Dicky on Friday."

" I suppose they are both at school," enquired Frank.

" Yes, I have two boys. William, called Bill, is at Winchester. He is sixteen, and Richard, called Dick, who is twelve, is at a preparatory school at

Sevenoaks. They are both counting the days till they are home for the holidays.''

''They keep us lively,'' said Mr. Trueman, ''the young scamps are up to every mischief. By the way, Frank, I promised to prove to you that we never die. Has he told you of our conversation, Ralph?''

''No, sir, but if you mean that you are going to have a séance, I hope you will let me be present. I recently read a very interesting article on Spiritualism. It made out a good case for its further consideration. I would like to read some solid book on the subject if you can tell me of one.''

''Much better than reading is to have practical experience,'' replied his host. ''I can prove to you in two hours that the dead have never died, whereas you might read for a week and never be sure.''

''You need not trouble to prove it to me, Mr. Trueman,'' said Angela, ''I know already.''

''You rather surprise me,'' he answered, and the two young men seemed rather amused.

''It is because people always treated anything I said on the subject as a joke that I have kept quiet and never spoken about it for years,'' replied Angela. ''Mummy and daddy told me not to be silly, my nurse told me not to tell what was not true, and I have come to think that I am different from every other person.''

''Most interesting,'' remarked Mrs. Trueman. ''You will never find anyone in this house laughing at you. I can quite understand what you must have suffered. I suffered as you did because I too was different from other girls. But please, dear, tell us

why you think you are different from other people.
Are you psychic?"

"I don't quite know what psychic means,"
replied Angela, "but if to see people you know are
dead, and hear them speak to you, is to be psychic,
then I am. I have been like that all my life."

"How very interesting," said Mr. Trueman,
"and it helps to confirm one of my pet arguments that
we are all potential mediums. Since the cessation of
witch burning, mediumship has steadily increased, and
now that mediums are safe it will go on increasing till
some day our descendants will all be mediums, and
will see and hear the finer vibrations of what I call
Etheria."

Ralph and Frank had sat silent and Mr. Trueman
turned to them. "I hope you young men will both
excuse this conversation, which is doubtless rather
strange to you. Frank asked for it and he must take
what he gets, but you, Ralph, did not, and if you
would like us to change the subject, we will. I can
talk to Frank alone, but we don't wish to inflict these
things on our guests if they are not interested in
them."

"Fire away," replied Ralph. "I am no bigot.
I know nothing about the subject, but I am intensely
interested."

"Now, there is no need for you to attend our
séance to-night," said Mrs. Trueman, "because if
you say you will not come, we can defer it till to-
morrow afternoon when you and Hope could go for
a walk. We would never leave a guest out in the
cold. If, however, you would like to experience
something quite new to you which will do you no

harm, and may do you good, then I propose that we ask Dr. and Mrs. Cureall to join us at dinner. They are good sitters, help the conditions, and are always glad to come. They are both charming people.''

'' Of course I shall attend,'' said Ralph ; '' I am looking forward to it more than I can say.''

'' Now I propose that we rise, as you have all finished,'' said Mrs. Trueman. '' I want to take Angela away with me and we shall have a quiet talk. I think I understand you, Angela, as few others can. You must be a medium, just as I am, and that is something you may well be proud of. Mediums have been given great gifts which it is their duty to use for the comfort and upliftment of humanity.''

The ladies left the lounge, where tea had been served, and George Trueman invited the two young men into the library.

'' I hope you are both as fond of books as I am,'' said he. '' A house without a library is like a man without a soul. Here you will find books of all kinds. The lighter literature, such as novels, we keep in another room. I have no room for them here. On this side are my psychic books. These occupy a considerable amount of space. Next are my books on science. Then comes philosophy, and you will see that I have a large number of works on comparative and early religions. Here we come to my books on history and next to those on travel. These volumes of the Encyclopedia Britannica I find invaluable. I often say that if the orthodox only knew what is contained within these pages they would be staggered. I don't suppose they often refer to it, except on general every-day affairs.''

Trueman selected three volumes and referred to the sections on Greek Mythology. " Read what Hesiod the Greek who lived in the ninth century B.C. has to tell us of the beliefs in his day.   Here we have the entire story of the fall of man, the flood, the Son of God coming to earth to take the punishment for men's sins, his death, resurrection and ascension, the convulsion of the earth and the dead coming out of their graves when he gave up the ghost.   All this was believed to have happened at least a thousand years before the date the Christian Christ is claimed to have come to earth."

" You do surprise me," said Ralph.   " My study of history was political and secular.   I have never heard of this in any sermon, and I have listened to many."

" Not likely," said Frank.   " The parsons who know keep their knowledge to themselves.   They call themselves the chosen of God, and to maintain this claim their energies are spent in preaching false doctrines.   No wonder they are despised by all honest thinking people."

" Remember their training," said Trueman. " From youth upwards and at the Theological College their minds have been trained to think in only one direction.   They have been made to think as the Church wants them to think, and after a few years they cease to be able to think differently.   In course of time, when they become the leaders, they teach those who come after them the same dishonest way of thinking.

What appears to be dishonesty to a layman whose mind has been trained to think clearly and logically, is not necessarily so with them. The critical faculty has become atrophied ; they have never been trained to think logically. They have been taught that faith is more than reason, so consequently they never reason things out, and the result is that parsons as a body are the most foolish lot of men on earth. Whenever you get them down to fundamentals they flounder and come out with the most irrational and nonsensical remarks it is possible to make.''

Trueman's gaze wandered round the bookshelves.

'' Ah, here is the book I am looking for. It is called *Pagan and Christian Creeds,* by Edward Carpenter. Sit down if you are interested, as I would like to read you a passage which sums up what I have just been telling you. Make yourselves comfortable while I find it. Yes, here it is on page 20 :—

' At the time of the life or recorded appearance of Jesus of Nazareth, and for some centuries before, the Mediterranean and neighbouring world had been the scene of a vast number of pagan creeds and rituals. There were temples without end dedicated to gods like Apollo or Dionysus among the Greeks, Hercules among the Romans, Mithra among the Persians, Adonis and Attis in Syria and Phrygia, Osiris, Horus and Isis in Egypt, Bell and Astarte among the Babylonians and Carthaginians. And an extraordinarily interesting fact, for us, is that notwithstanding great geographical distances and racial differences between the adherents of these various cults, as well as differences in the details of their services, the general outline of their creeds and services were, if not identical, so markedly similar as we find them.

I may roughly say that of all or nearly all the deities above-mentioned it was said or believed that :—

(1) They were born on or very near Christmas day.

(2) They were born of a Virgin-mother.

(3) And in a cave or underground chamber.

(4) They led a life of toil for mankind.

(5) And they were called by the names of Light Bringer, Healer, Mediator, Saviour, Deliverer.

(6) They were, however, vanquished by the Powers of Darkness.

(7) And descended into Hell or the Underworld.

(8) They rose again from the dead, and became the pioneers of mankind to the Heavenly World.

(9) They obtained Communion of Saints and Churches.

(10) And they were commemorated by Eucharistic meals.' ''

Trueman shut the book and continued : '' I would advise you to read the subject for yourselves, but you will get all that he says amplified in the pages which follow, and confirmed in other standard books dealing with Christian and Pagan mythology.

The ancients peopled the heavens with angels and demons. They had minds like those of children, and instead of giving a natural interpretation to psychic phenomena they wound round these natural events myths and legends, transforming etheric human beings into gods or devils, who were graded in the heavens just as people were graded on earth. The hierarchies of earth were likewise believed to exist in heaven and this grouping of the inhabitants of the Etheric World now goes under the name of Mythology. In this way the ancients found their comfort ; this, to them, was religion, and these heavenly beings they worshipped.

Spiritualism is mythology rationalised. We now have more developed minds. We do not allow our imagination to run riot. We keep to facts, and accept only what can be proved. When an etheric being speaks to us on earth, or is seen by a clairvoyant, he is likened unto ourselves, and we do not call him either a god or a devil. We have come to realise that Etheria is a real place, that its inhabitants are human beings, and that they are like ourselves because, though they function in a finer body, they still have the same minds as they had on earth. Just as we attribute physical phenomena to natural law, so likewise we attribute psychic phenomena to natural law. Just as physical phenomena have ceased to be looked on as the manifestation of a god or gods, so psychic phenomena can now be regarded as a natural event and not translated into the activities of angels and demons, gods and saviours. The study of mythology, moreover, impresses us with the fact that psychic phenomena, as they occur to-day, have occurred throughout the ages, the only difference being that we now interpret them differently owing to our more advanced minds.

Christianity borrowed all this mythology and turned it into history. What to the ancients was legend and myth the Christian Church preached as facts—as history. The poetic story of the two worlds which the ancients handed down to us became focussed on a certain place on the map, at a certain time in history, the Christian Church asserting that this, its own revelation, was a temporal intrusion into the ordinary laws of nature for the special benefit of all who termed themselves Christians. Christianity thus materialised those ancient stories, it brought etheric speculations down to the level of earth affairs, and because it did so it destroyed what was beautiful in mythology and falsified history.

The Church even went the length of changing the old Roman calendar to make it commence from the date it fixed for the birth of Christ. Every scholar knows that this date is false and that no Christ was born one thousand nine hundred and thirty-six years ago in Palestine. The entire structure of lies reared by the Church has thus no basis of fact, and the folly of our method of recording time from a mythological legend, having no historical foundation, will some day become apparent when education increases.

Christianity has burlesqued nature's revelation of the other world. It has materialised mythology and degraded history. It has condemned nature's method of revealing Etheria. But for Christianity, Spiritualism would now be recognised as the natural outcome of mythology, just as astronomy developed out of astrology. Spiritualism and Astronomy are the names given to our modern knowledge of the etheric and physical worlds which mean to us what mythology and astrology signified to the ancients. We have only changed words, because our knowledge has advanced and we have turned speculation into facts.

This mythology, when it became Christianity, made a mockery of nature's revelation. It has confused the issue and made it impossible for anyone who thinks to understand Christian history or Christian philosophy, because it has mutilated them both.

How few people in this country think along these lines, and yet that is how they should think. I know that I am one of a very small band who think like this. These thoughts have come to me slowly and surely, layer upon layer, as my study of Mythology, Spiritualism, and the origin of Christianity has advanced. I am, however, in a unique position to weigh up the whole question logically and correctly, because I can claim an intimate knowledge of all these three subjects ; there are others who know one or other of them ; but there are very few who have a knowledge of them all and can relate them correctly to each other.

What I am now telling you to-day must become known sooner or later, and when it is the Christian faith will cease to be believed. What will the people have to take its place? But for the knowledge which Spiritualism gives to a world now living in darkness materialism would become general, and our friend John Matterson would have the last say. Nothing would be believed to exist but what we see and feel, and our minds would never rise to the source whence comes all thought and inspiration.

Thus would end all philosophy, all religion, and we would bury our dead without any hope of ever seeing them again. Life would be truly an enigma.''

"Spiritualism you then believe will take the place of the dying creeds?" said Frank. "This gives you hope for both the living and the dead."

"Not hope, my friend," replied Trueman, "but certainty. The days of hope and faith are passing. We are entering the era of knowledge and that knowledge will increase our understanding of the Universe in a way that nothing else has. It will rank in the years to come as of greater consequence to humanity than the discoveries of Copernicus, great as those were."

"Is Spiritualism, then, your religion?" asked Ralph.

"I prefer the word philosophy to religion," replied Trueman. "Religion till now has been synonymous with a belief in a personal god who was worshipped by those who believed in him, with superstition, with creeds and dogmas, with holy books, holy churches, and holy men. It has been degraded in the minds of all thinking men and women because of its false claims, its cruelties, and its keeping the people ignorant, poor and miserable. All the same, there is nothing wrong with the word itself. Religion to me stands for a reaching out to the Source of Life and Thought, but the word Philosophy is the one I always use as it is more applicable and has not the disagreeable associations of the other word. Spiritualism, and it only, can help us to understand and direct aright this urge which is in most of us, though many are hardly aware of it. Without the knowledge it gives we cannot understand this vital part of man's make-up. We should be at sea without a compass, drifting hopelessly, not knowing why we are here or where we are making for.

Spiritualism, however, is just a name for this addition to our knowledge. The name means nothing in itself. What matters is what this name stands for. It is not associated with one particular medium who may be fraudulent or genuine but with the facts of survival and communication and all these imply. When this knowledge becomes general it will need no special label, though such is necessary to-day to distinguish the new knowledge from the old philosophies and theologies."

" If what you say is true about a life after death, I quite follow your meaning," said Frank. " As people become educated they slowly give up the superstitions and beliefs which satisfied their ignorant ancestors, but Spiritualism, you claim, has come along to take the place of the old beliefs, to give comfort to those in sorrow as well as an understanding of our right place in nature."

" Just so," replied Trueman. " Spiritualism will absorb Christianity and, in time, all the other world religions. Christianity will never adopt Spiritualism, as if it did so it would cease to be Christianity.

Spiritualism will take the place of the old beliefs quite naturally. These were just symbols of the truth we have now discovered. We have grown out of these old beliefs, or some of us have. All will do so in time and come to see that all those god-men who were supposed to have come to earth to suffer and die just symbolised man himself, who suffers on earth, dies and returns to the Etheric World. I shall make this much clearer to you on another occasion, but I want to use this time we are together in telling you something about what we may expect to-night at the séance and in giving you some scientific reasons why it is all possible.''

'' I wish you would,'' said Ralph, '' as the idea of the dead returning seems so fantastic that I cannot imagine myself ever believing it.''

Mr. Trueman lit his pipe, crossed his legs, leaned back in his chair, and in carefully chosen words commenced as follows :—

'' How many people at the time of Galileo realised that the world had entered a new era of thought? How many realised the change which the scientific method of thinking and recording of facts would bring about? For thousands of years man made little or no advance. In his mode of living, travel, warfare, clothing, little change took place over the centuries. The Chaldeans, two thousand years before the Christian era, had as great a command over their surroundings as we had in Europe up till the eighteenth century, and they probably knew just as much about natural phenomena as was known in Europe till the seventeenth century. The Egyptians and the Chinese were equally well-versed in knowledge as were our ancestors up to within the last two hundred years. China was in advance of us till an even later date. Its arts and crafts were then superior to those of Europe.

Up to within the last hundred and fifty years man knew how to build uncomfortable stone houses, how to clothe himself, how to make utensils and orna-

ments. Few could read or write and he lived in the
way our histories tell us that man lived prior to the
scientific age. The bringing of paper from China to
Europe and the invention of printing was the chief
cause of the mental development with which we are
all familiar.

Roger Bacon, in the thirteenth century, was the
first man to think in a scientific way. The scientific
method of investigation was adopted by Copernicus in
the sixteenth century. He was followed by Galileo,
and just as this method became recognised as the
right and only way to approach facts, so we have
advanced. The discovery of paper and printing made
it possible to pass on to others thoughts and discoveries and so gradually people began to think, to
study, to learn. As they did so the forces of nature
were gradually controlled and understood and utilised
for the comfort and happiness of the race. Paper
and printing have really made us what we are to-day.

Instead of humanity standing still and making no
progress for thousands of years the wheels of thought
quickened, and to-day we have comfortable homes
for the majority of the people, fast travel, good roads,
and all the discoveries which have prolonged life,
made us healthier and happier. Knowledge is
beginning to take the place of ignorance, and the
more it does so, so does life become easier and happier.
Pain and suffering are slowly but surely passing out
of our lives, but there is still much more to learn.
We are only at the beginning of things. What we
shall be, and how we shall live when we get still
greater control over nature, who can say? We have
been thinking rationally for only about one hundred

years. We have still, however, two great enemies
to destroy. One is war and the other is death.

War will end when we learn to limit the population to what each country can support. War is the
method adopted to-day by nations requiring to expand
their territories so as to support an increasing population. Those countries which are not over-populated
are not a menace to the peace of the world. In the
old days the nations of the world fought each other
just for the sake of plunder. Kings fought for
thrones, the Church for its creeds, and so on. That
is passing, and once you solve the problem of over-
population the last cause of war vanishes. That will
come slowly as the people become educated and
realise that it is possible. It will become easier just
as discovery along this line of research advances.

So much for the enemy, war. Now, as regards
the enemy, death. I said that this too will be destroyed, but that statement requires qualification. I
don't mean that we shall discover the elixir of life
and will live for ever on earth. That is not only
impossible but not desirable. This earth is but the
nursery of the race and it must leave the nursery and
find a larger, fuller life elsewhere. This enemy,
however, can be and is being destroyed in quite
another way.

I am now coming to my point. Am I interesting
you or are you bored?"

"Not in the least," they both replied together.
"Please go on," said Frank. "You are giving
me a new angle of thought. One I had an inkling
of but could never put into words."

"Well, to continue," said Trueman. "Death

will be vanquished when people understand it, just as disease has and is being vanquished by being understood. Think of the hopelessness of humanity in the past when, let us say, the plague swept over Europe. Think of the misery, sorrow and suffering it left in its train. This scourge was conquered by our coming to understand its cause and cure.

Now, when we come to understand Death the sorrow it causes will vanish. Moreover, our knowledge of the Universe and of our place in it will receive just as great an impetus as was imparted to Europe when the true relationship of the earth to the sun and planets was discovered by Copernicus. This discovery showed us man's place in the physical universe. Spiritualism is showing us man's place in the etheric and mental universe, because the Universe is made up of both physical and etheric and mental vibrations.

This being accepted, Spiritualism is slowly creating just as great a revolution in thought as did the scientific discoveries of the last four hundred years.

As to the effect of this revolution, just imagine, if you can, the difference it will make to us when it becomes possible for, say, a wife to converse with her ' dead ' husband, to see him again, and receive his love and embraces. This is happening to-day, but only to a limited extent because of our lack of mediums. With the increase of mediumship, the more general it will become. Think of the comfort this will bring, how mourning will cease and how the happiness of humanity will be advanced. The mother will not grieve for her ' dead ' child, the husband for his wife, nor the wife for her husband. Though the bodily presence will be missed the inconsolable grief will be banished by the realisation that in time those whom death separated will be together again. It is the uncertainty surrounding death, the longing to know that the ' dead ' still live, which causes so much sorrow and misery. The fear of death which is so strong in many will no longer be felt when knowledge of what death really is becomes general. If you could read the thousands of letters I have received from bereaved ones over the last twenty years you would realise how acute their sorrow is whenever their love and affection are broken by death. This knowledge opens a new world to us. As this happens, so our conception of how we should live on earth broadens to the lasting benefit and happiness of all mankind.

So much as an introduction to the subject. If you ask me how it is possible for us to live again, I must put it to you in a way that you can grasp or otherwise you will find it impossible to reconcile such a thing with your reason.''

'' Yes,'' said Frank, '' I want to know how it is possible we can live without a body, for you know as well as I do that we bury our body in the grave.''

'' That is where you make a great mistake,'' replied Trueman. '' We don't. Nature is a great illusionist. Till you know, you think that the sun goes round the earth. You think that the earth is flat. You think that that table is solid. You think that the sky is a dome, and so on. I could multiply nature's illusions indefinitely. You think you bury the body, but you don't.

How do we know that all these things I have enumerated are illusions? By thought, by correct thinking, by using the means nature has given us to prove that our senses mislead us. Nature deceives us but still she gives us the means of proving that she does so. Nature in effect says that if you will only think correctly you will find the truth for yourselves. We are looking at things upside down on earth, strange as it may seem, but it is a fact, and the more we come to realise that, the less difficulty shall we have in understanding nature.

" Now, first of all, what are we? Flesh, blood, and bones. No! that is just another of nature's illusions. We are something far different. We are Mind, and Mind only. What we think with is ourselves, and our body is only Mind's vehicle, the instrument it uses to express itself. Each one of us is an individual Mind. Where it came from, what it is I shall leave for discussion on another occasion, but let this be clearly understood, each of us is just an individual Mind, an individual thinker which makes images and these images it makes constitute our conscious existence."

" I never thought that way," remarked Ralph. " Rather deep, don't you think, Frank? "

" It is certainly deep, but it is not quite new to me," replied Frank. " My rationally-inclined way of thinking has made me realise that to sense our surroundings we require to bring in something besides just Brain and Brawn. I was having an argument with John Matterson at Turnberry on the subject. You remember him at Trinity, Ralph, a hard-headed materialist. He believes that matter, and matter only, exists.   I told him I had a vague idea that more than that was required to explain the Universe, but that I was going to try and find out if I possibly could do so.   Perhaps I am on the threshold of finding out what my instinct has told me is true.''

"You are, indeed," replied Trueman.   "Now, let me finish.   I must now turn your thoughts to physics.   You must be aware that the physical universe which we see is just a range of vibrations which reflect the light vibrations from the sun. These vibrations act upon our brain through our eyes and then create images in our mind.   Other vibrations also give us the sense of touch and smell.   If these vibrations did not exist our mind would have nothing to which to react.   It would be still, and if still then really dead.   The mind makes us conscious by re-acting to these physical vibrations, which, so far as sight is concerned, range between 34,000 to 64,000 waves to the inch.   By using instruments we can make it react to waves of faster and slower frequency. Its reaction consists of images which these vibrations, through our nerves, produce and what makes these images is our mind, our image maker, which is our-selves.

Am I making myself quite clear?" asked True-man.

"Quite ; but all this is quite new to me," said Ralph.

"Now, he would be a bold man who asserted that all the waves of vibration which we know on earth constitute all that exist," went on Trueman. "We Spiritualists know that others exist, and this is the pivotal point on which the whole subject turns.

Other vibrations, which we term etheric, constitute another vehicle for each individual mind in
which it functions after death, and the physical body
is only the earth covering of this etheric body. This
etheric body vibrates at a higher frequency than does
our earth body, but to the Mind in the Etheric World
it is just as solid as our physical body is to us on earth.
Keep that in mind and all else is easy to follow, and
when you hear Etherians at a séance talking about
being on another vibration, to what we are on, you
will understand that this is the common-place way of
expressing what I have put in more scientific
language.

Death is only the shedding of the physical
covering and nothing more. As the physical body is
not the mind's real home but just its temporary abode
on earth, the etheric body must be its true abode.

Now, this etheric body is just a duplicate of the
earth body. Each etheric body is composed of cells
which have attracted to them earth matter for its time
on earth, but this being only temporary, separation
takes place at death. When the etheric structure
leaves the physical body then the physical particles
fall away. This we call decomposition.

The etheric body, still guided by mind, operates
and functions, guided by the same mind, just as it did
on earth, but in an environment suited to its faster
vibrations. The mind is still in control. So, following
death, we are still ourselves, with the same memories,
affections and characteristics which we had on earth.

All that is changed is the environment in which
the finer body functions. Nature has provided this
environment to which I have given the name Etheria.

It is all about us though we sense it not.

When death takes place, we just enter this new environment and live in it as we used to do on earth. The ' dead ' can still sense the earth when they wish to, but they can do something more—they can read our minds and realise all we are thinking, because the mind makes images which constitute its thoughts. These images are pictures, so our minds can be read like a book.   When I think of a chair I image a chair, and those we call dead can stand behind me and see the picture of the chair in my mind.

You will realise that this is so after you have attended a few séances.   But I cannot bring this long talk to an end without telling you how those who live in Etheria can speak to us and thus prove that they are with us.

A medium supplies them with a substance which is part of herself or himself—this substance we term Ectoplasm.   A medium has a superfluity of this substance and Etherians borrow it during the séance. With it (after it has been treated by their chemists) they clothe their vocal organs and lungs and this enables them to vibrate our atmosphere and talk to us."

" What is this substance? asked Frank.   " As one who hopes to be a doctor some day, that interests me."

" We don't know much about it," answered Trueman.   " We do, however, know that it is part of the human body and that it has weight.   My wife will lose weight during to-night's séance.   We all shall do so, in fact, but she much more than others. I am inclined to guess that Ectoplasm is that part of the body which acts as the link between the physical body and the etheric body. Much research is needed to establish its actual composition, and perhaps, Frank, when you find out that what I have been telling you is true, you will make it part of your life work to discover the nature and origin of this substance.

We call it ectoplasm and our friends on the other side mix it with what they call psychoplasm, a composition of their own, and the finished product they call teleplasm. As teleplasm it can be seen and felt, and it is by means of this teleplasm that they manifest their presence to us earth people.

Now I have told you all you are fit to understand. It is a vast subject and I have only touched on its fringe. But I have given you food for thought —a good meal—and you have not yet digested it. I hope the séance, to-night, will act as a good digestive tonic, and you will begin to look on things differently after the experience you have after dinner.

Now I am sure the girls are longing for your company so we shall meet again in the drawing-room before dinner, at eight. The outside bell will ring at seven-thirty, when you will find your baths ready. I hope you will find your rooms comfortable and that you have everything you need."

The three men separated and met again at eight in the drawing-room where the ladies were assembled.

" Dr. and Mrs. Cureall should be here soon ; they are always punctual," said Mrs. Trueman, and just as she had spoken the butler threw open the door and announced them.

The company, after the introductions were made,

trooped into the dining-room and conversation became animated.

Dr. and Mrs. Cureall were, as usual, delightful
guests, and the conversation at dinner flowed like a
gurgling stream.

The doctor, who was sitting next to Angela, was
interesting her in some of the cures he had effected
by means of psychic healing.

" Most certainly it is successful," he remarked,
in answer to her enquiry.   " I know of some of the
most remarkable cures taking place after all other
means had been tried.   I have often remarked that
if people suffering from certain complaints went first
to a psychic healer how much easier it would be to
cure them.   As it is, they try every other means and
then as a last resort they visit the psychic healer."

" What, exactly, is psychic healing? " asked
Angela.

" Psychic healing is the healing of the body
through the etheric body.   We have an etheric duplicate, every cell in our body is duplicated, and bodily
disease is due to these cells being unhealthy and not
functioning properly.   Earth doctors try to cure the
physical body only.   Etheric doctors cure the physical
through the etheric by stimulating the etheric cells in
such a way that the physical cells become again
healthy."

" But how does the psychic healer know what is
wrong and what to do? " enquired Angela.

" He, himself, does not know anything because

he is in trance and the control of his body is taken over by an etheric doctor who diagnoses the illness, and then either cures it by passing healing rays through the medium to the patient by touch or passes, or he prescribes what the patient is to do or take."

" Tell me about a cure which you know has really taken place by this means," said Angela.

" Well, one of our greatest healing mediums, F. J. Jones, who unfortunately died a few years ago, could tell when in trance and under the control of his Etheric doctor the history of the past illnesses of the people who came to be cured, without, remember this, asking the patient a single question."

" How remarkable ; do tell me more," Angela remarked.

" Well, I shall tell you of a case I myself took to him. A woman patient of mine had recently undergone a serious operation, which had failed to cure her, and she awaited her turn in Jones' consulting room, quite unknown to anyone present, except myself.

Jones, in trance, when her turn came, lightly ran his fingers over her clothes. He asked no questions, but promptly informed her that she had had several operations. Then he traced over her clothes the exact course taken by the surgeon's knife. The symptoms, both before and after the operations, were correctly stated. ' No such operations were necessary,' the Etheric doctor said, through the mouth of Jones, 'but I can cure you' ; and prescribed a certain treatment which effected a complete cure. I could tell you of many other cases similar to this."

" How wonderful ! " exclaimed Angela. " The fact that he could tell her past medical history is re-

markable in itself.   Doctors should use mediumship
in diagnosing difficult cases.''

"They will, in time," answered the doctor.   "It
is all so new, and healing mediums are so few ; but
they are increasing.   More and more people are
finding that they have the power of healing by passes
and touch.   They can give out healing rays which
affect the etheric body and through it the physical
body.   It is, however, only when you are in the
presence of a powerful trance healing medium that you
realise that more than the medium's own healing force
is in play.   Then you feel the rays passing from the
medium to the patient.   I have had to draw my hand
away on occasions because they gave the sensation of
an electric shock.''

" I wish I could hear more another time, because
I think I could become a healing medium," answered
Angela.   " Mrs. Trueman tells me that I must be a
medium because I am both clairvoyant and clairaudient.''

" How interesting !   Well, we may find another
occasion to talk further on the subject ; but I have
spoken enough.   Let me hear about yourself.   Tell
me what you see and hear.''

So Angela told him about her own experiences,
but as conversation then became general it was impossible to do more than just tell him what she had
told the others at tea.

George Trueman then remarked, " Mrs. Cureall and I have been going over our holiday experiences.   I have been telling her of our time in
Scotland, and she, about the time they had in Corn-
wall.   I see that the doctor and Angela have been

equally engrossed, and so have you all with each other, but now that this lull has come in the conversation I would like to explain why the dinner is both simple and short. It is unwise just before a séance to eat a heavy meal. My wife, you will notice, has been on a very light diet. That is necessary because the medium must not demand too much from her digestive system. I just make this explanation for the benefit of our guests who are attending a séance to-night for the first time. After it is over, refreshments will be provided in the library."

Frank then spoke across the table to Angela. " You really have been absorbed. I only caught bits of your conversation, but I hope Dr. Cureall will also tell me something about psychic healing. I shall be most interested."

" I am sure you will, doctor," said Angela, turning to her partner. " Over there is a young man who intends to follow you in your noble profession. He, like me, wants to hear all about this new method of healing."

Dinner had ended, and Mrs. Trueman, with a glance at Mrs. Cureall, rose, and the ladies left the dining-room for the drawing-room, an old custom still kept up though no longer necessary, as it was in the old days when the men all became drunk and then slipped under the table.

Frank moved across and sat beside Dr. Cureall.

" Would it be possible for me to have a talk with you sometime about what you were telling Angela? We can't very well go into the subject now, but could you find time to-morrow? It is Sunday and you may not wish to be disturbed, as I am sure you try to make it as quiet a day as possible."

"I always go for an hour's walk," replied the
doctor. "I shall be only too delighted to tell you
what I can, and all the more so as you are becoming
one of us. My house is the second after entering the
village. Go down the drive and past the lodge, turn
right and you will come to it, standing back from the
road ; a garden is in front."

Frank had just time to thank him when Trueman
remarked, "Now, drink up your coffee and let us go
up to the séance room. I wish to tell our young
friends what all the gadgets mean."

Trueman and the doctor led the way out of the
room, and, looking into the drawing-room, asked
Angela to accompany them upstairs.

On reaching the upper landing they turned along
a corridor, at the end of which was a door leading into
a narrow passage, a few yards along which was
another door on the left, through which they entered.

Trueman switched on the electric light.
"Here," he said, "is where the two worlds meet."

CHAPTER IV.
WHERE TWO WORLDS MEET.

The room into which the guests were ushered had once been a bedroom but no trace of its original use remained owing to the alterations George Trueman had made.

Everything was so strange and unusual that it was some minutes before Trueman could command attention, and when he did so it was only after numerous questions had been asked and passed unanswered.

"I cannot answer everybody at once," he remarked, "so if you will allow me to explain things in my own way, it will be much simpler and better. I shall thus tell you all you want to know.

First of all this room is a room within a room. Let us just step outside the door and walk round the passage. I built this inner wall so as to enable access to be had to all the instruments without disturbing what is taking place at the séance."

On returning to the séance room Trueman went over to the wall and took down a plan of the room and handed it to Ralph.

"Now," said he, "you, Angela and Frank refer to this when I am speaking and everything will be quickly grasped.

I shall explain everything in its correct order, but let me just say this, that what you see in this room is more or less a copy of the séance room at the International Institute for Psychical Research in London.

PLAN OF SÉANCE ROOM AT SUREWAY COURT.

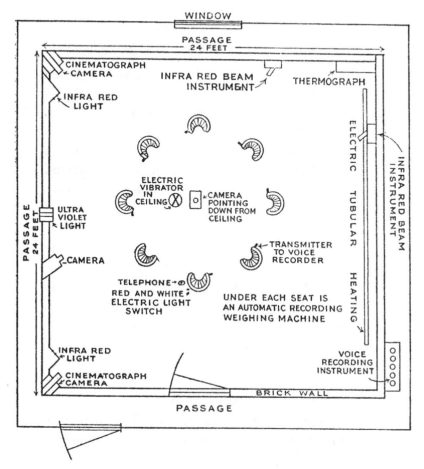

First of all the walls are brick, covered with plaster, coloured light blue. From roof to ceiling they are quite bare. The room is square, twenty four feet each way and twelve feet from floor to ceiling. It is better not to have the ceiling too high as the lower it is, and the smaller the room, the less chance there is of the teleplasm becoming dissipated.

As to the chairs, they look just like any ordinary

theatre seats except that they don't tip up. They are comfortable to sit in, which is important, but they are more than that. Under each is a weighing machine and on sitting down the sitter's weight is automatically registered. This continues in barograph fashion by clockwork till the sitter gets up. You will learn the reason for this in time, but it is important that we know the weight of each sitter every minute of the séance, and this is recorded as the clock is set at the minute anyone sits down. When you sit down the seats are raised so that your feet do not touch the ground. Otherwise you could alter your weight unconsciously by putting your weight on your feet, but as you lean back on these seats you feel no discomfort through not having your feet on the ground, because you can rest them on these foot rests which are attached to the seat.

Now, in the middle of the ceiling is an electric vibrator which keeps up a continuous vibration of the atmosphere, and this makes singing or the gramophone unnecessary. Next to it you will notice a camera aperture.

In these two corners of the room are also cameras. These three cameras are cinematograph cameras and when in operation take continuous photographs.

The two infra-red beams on either side operate these three cameras.

Let me explain what happens when the séance starts. The two infra-red beam instruments are switched on and each sends an invisible beam across the room so that they cross each other but do not touch because one is higher than the other. One is

four feet from the ground and the other is eight feet.
Now this is what happens. Two metal trumpets
each about three feet high stand in the middle of the
circle. The opening at the larger end of each trumpet is about five inches wide and at the smaller end
about two inches—something like a megaphone.
During the séance these float about the room, as you
will notice because they have luminous paint on them,
and whenever they come in contact with one or other
of these invisible beams the contact automatically
operates the flashlight connected with the beam. Thus
this camera here in this corner is operated when the
beam four feet from the ground is crossed, and the
other over there is operated when the beam eight feet
from the ground is crossed. The ceiling camera is
operated when either beam is crossed."

" How very ingenious," said Ralph. " I have
always heard Spiritualists spoken about in rather a
contemptuous way, as if they were just gullible fools,
who sit round in a circle in the dark, saying, ' Yes,
dear Aunt Marina, I am so glad to speak to you. I
hope you will come back again.' And Aunt Marina,
who is just the so-called medium, replies, ' Yes, it
will be so nice to speak to you again, my dear niece.' "

When the laughter had subsided Trueman remarked, " Well, wherever you got your information
from, Ralph, I don't know, but humbug such as that,
I am glad you realise, does not happen here. For
what may happen elsewhere I am not responsible,
but when you remember the low level of intelligence
and education prevailing amongst the great majority,
in every grade of society, small wonder that charla-
tans batten on and hoodwink many credulous fools

who dabble in what they call Spiritualism.

These foolish people are on a par with those other equally foolish people who, thinking themselves wise, deny the occurrence of all psychic phenomena. It is not the Spiritualists who are to blame, as they would like to see all fraud eliminated and every fraudulent so-called medium severely punished and disgraced. For many years Spiritualists have been trying to get a Bill through Parliament to enable them to register the genuine mediums, after they have been tested, but so far without success. As it is to-day, Spiritualism is not recognised in law, either as a religion or a science, but as representing only the activities of the devil. Legally, Spiritualism comes under the Witchcraft Laws, which were instituted when everything not understood was attributed to the devil and his angels. Until this is altered we Spiritualists can do nothing to stamp out the fraudulent so-called medium, and have to face misrepresentation and ridicule by the very people who will not allow us to clean up our own house.

Now, let me return to my explanation. On the wall, here, is another camera and next to it is an ultraviolet light. The plate in this camera is not affected by the infra-red beams, but by this light we can only take ordinary photographs, not cinematograph photographs. We use it for the purpose of photographing whatever the ultra-violet light will pick up, and we hope some day by this method, as we improve upon it, to get photographs of the Etherians present. Thus you see we are photographing throughout the séance whatever reflects the infra-red end of the spectrum, and we are also photographing anything that we can pick up which reflects the ultra-violet end of the spectrum. These cameras have a greater range of sight than have our human eyes.

By means of these cameras we can record the teleplasm building up. This teleplasm enables those on the other side to speak to us as it is by the Etherian entering into and becoming covered with this sub-stance, so far as his vocal organs and lungs are con-cerned, that he becomes sufficiently materialised to enable him to vibrate our atmosphere.

If you remind me I shall show you a photograph we got of the materialised vocal organs. After the photograph was taken they explained to me in detail how they produced the voice and the means they used, by materialising tubes and lungs, to obtain the air to vibrate the larynx.

Remember their organs are just like ours, only of a finer matter, which makes it impossible for them normally to vibrate our atmosphere and speak to us. If they could normally vibrate our atmosphere then there would be no need of a medium. Things being as they are, we require a medium, one who can supply Etherians with something to enable them to bring down their vibrations to the level of the earth vibra-tions.

Over there in the corner is the voice recording instrument which makes a record of all that is said during the séance, as on each chair is a transmitter with which it is connected. The transmitter picks up all that is said by both the sitter and the Etherian speaking. Thus we can go over everything after the séance and study how much or how little evidence has been accumulated of other personalities being present.

Similarly, we can at the same time record the movement of the trumpets on the screen, the convolutions of the teleplasm, the teleplasmic rods which move the trumpets, and the ectoplasm coming out of the medium's body and returning when the séance is over.

The thermograph over there records the temperature. Throughout the séance the temperature falls, whereas it should rise owing to the heat of our bodies. That electric tubular heating over there emits no light and keeps the temperature constant at sixty degrees during the time no phenomena take place, but when phenomena occur the temperature falls as much as twenty degrees Fahrenheit. This is a matter our scientists should explain rather than ignore the subject as they do.

I have tried in vain to get any representative of science to come and experience what takes place in this room, but, instead, everyone makes various excuses. The truth is that, just like the orthodox in religion, they don't wish their explanation of the Universe to be upset. Like the ostrich, they bury their heads in the sand and ignore the subject or try to make themselves believe that nothing super-normal can ever occur. By saying that everything is due only to imagination on the part of the Spiritualist their equanimity is not upset. My instruments show that phenomena of a super-normal nature do occur, and it is my opinion that in this way only will their hard materialist crust some day be broken.

Lastly, attached to the seat I occupy there is a switch to operate the electric light. We can have white light, red light and dull red light as we please.

As we are shut in and can hear nothing of what occurs outside the room, I have a telephone beside me so that the butler can telephone if necessary and I can also communicate with him.   It also communicates with the passage where the operator of the various instruments is in attendance throughout the séance. This brick wall which I have built is sound-proof, so that we cannot even hear the operator walking round the passage attending the various instruments and cameras.   My wife's secretary is a trained photographer.   She acts as operator, keeping everything going smoothly during the séance, and develops the films and plates after it is over.

Now, I think I have made everything clear, so I shall go down and see if the ladies are ready, as we should make a start.   Oh, here is Miss Noteall, my wife's secretary.''

Miss Noteall was introduced and then started to look round to see that everything was in order for the coming séance.

George Trueman went to fetch the others in the drawing-room and when he was away Ralph remarked : '' What an extraordinary man.   He thinks of everything and leaves nothing to chance.   I never knew a man with such a grasp of every subject he discusses,'' and then, turning to Miss Noteall, he said : '' Is it all very terrifying? ''

'' Of course not, Mr. Leader.   No more so than talking to me or any one else in the dark.   Isn't that so, Dr. Cureall? ''

'' Just exactly.   Because it is new and you have never had the experience of talking to the so-called dead, you get creepy all over.   What is unknown is mysterious. When what is mysterious is understood it becomes just like any other experience in life. If from childhood you had been brought up to speak to those in another order of existence, you would have thought nothing of it. Our grandchildren will feel like that.

Here come the ladies.''

Mr. and Mrs. Trueman, Mrs. Cureall and Hope then entered, but no one sat down, as Trueman said :

'' Each one must sit down at exactly the same time, but not till Miss Noteall has adjusted the clock under each seat. Each clock must record precisely the same time so that we know that when each one's weight alters the same phenomenon is the cause. Miss Noteall will then adjust the cameras and the voice-recording machine to the same time so that everything is recorded as occurring at exactly the same time.

Now, are you ready? It is nine-twenty-five. Please adjust the clocks to nine-thirty, Miss Noteall.

In a few minutes the instruments were all adjusted to the same time and at nine-thirty to the second all sat down. Miss Noteall then produced the two trumpets and asked the strangers to inspect them. '' Nothing inside them to make them talk,'' she said. '' Oh, yes, you can tap them and look through them if you wish. Just made of tin by the local tinsmith.''

After inspection they were placed standing upright in the centre of the circle about two yards from each sitter.

Miss Noteall then lifted the catch out of the yale lock of the door so that when shut it could only be opened from the inside.

" Everything is in order, Mr. Trueman," she said, " but I shall just test the telephone when I go out to see that it is in working order."

She then left the room, the door closing with a click and a few seconds after the telephone beside Mr. Trueman's chair softly rang.

" O.K.," he replied.

" Everything is now in order, so I shall switch off the white light and switch on the red.

Just talk as if you were round the table in the dining room.   The less tense you all are the better the results.

Now I shall put out the red and switch on the glow light.   Nothing will happen to frighten anyone.   When a voice speaks in front of you answer it as you would answer me or anyone else on earth.   I am now switching off the light entirely.

We have now done our part.   We can do no more.   We only make the conditions they require.   They on their side really do all the work.   We are the passive and they are the active participants.

After we have done our part we can only wait until they make contact with us.   Their chemists will now be busy collecting the ectoplasm from my wife, and to a lesser degree from us all, and transforming it into teleplasm.   I hope you are feeling quite fit, my dear," he concluded, addressing Mrs. Trueman.

" Quite, thank you, George.   I feel that we have harmonious conditions, which makes it all so much easier.   Oh, just one thing you novices must remember.   Don't seize the trumpet or pull it hard as each one is connected by a psychic rod to my body and any hard pull is very bad for me and would make me ill. You can hold the trumpet gently, but don't give it a wrench. If it touches you it won't hurt you. Keep quite still and just say aloud ' The trumpet has touched me '.''

'' Why must a Direct Voice séance be held in the dark,'' enquired Angela in a whisper to Mr. Trueman who was sitting on her right.

''Angela has whispered a question to me,'' remarked Trueman, ''but don't think you must talk in whispers. Just speak as you would if you were sitting in the drawing room. Stop talking only when a voice speaks so that we may hear it. Now, in reply to Angela's question, we sit in the dark because in white light they cannot turn the ectoplasm into teleplasm. White light breaks it up and keeps it from coalescing. It makes the combination of our ectoplasm and their psychoplasm impossible except under exceptional conditions. This combination, as I have already told you, we call teleplasm. We have had the voices in red light, but I shall tell you about it in greater detail another time. Let us keep to general conversation for the present.''

Thus began a momentous séance the repercussions from which did more to disintegrate a great organisation than any other event since the Reformation.

CHAPTER V.

A MOMENTOUS SEANCE.

" How do you feel, Ralph? " asked Frank.

Frank, who was sitting between Hope and Angela, replied : " Oh, all right, only rather strange. I have a kind of eerie feeling."

" Have you got the creeps, Frank? " enquired Hope. " Keep your pecker up. I shall see that no harm befalls you. Hold out your left hand and I shall give you my right hand. Now, I shall hold out my left hand to Dr. Cureall. Doctor, you take mother's hand, and she will in turn take Ralph's. Now, Ralph, give your other hand to Mrs. Cureall and she will link up with daddy, who will take Angela's hand. Angela, you take Frank's other hand. Now, we are all linked up, male and female, man and woman alternately. This order helps conditions. Now, let us unfasten. If anyone is nervous ask your neighbour to hold hands."

All unclasped except Frank and Angela.

" Never miss a good opportunity," thought Frank, " and besides, it will keep her from being nervous."

Ten minutes after the light was switched out the two trumpets began knocking against each other. They were plainly visible, as each had painted round it, at both ends, a band of luminous paint, one inch wide.

Then, with a graceful curve, one quickly rose from the floor, rising in a spiral with a swishing sound to the ceiling which it knocked with three hard raps.

"That means conditions are good; it is their sign to us," remarked Trueman. "You would notice the lights as it rose in the air. That was caused by breaking the infra-red beams. Infra-red photographs were taken on each occasion."

Then the other trumpet swirled into the air, and for two or three minutes they went swishing round the room. As they did so the lights would glow each time they crossed one of the beams. Round they went, up to the ceiling, and into every part of the room. Then they fell with a crash on the floor before the sitters.

"What an extraordinary performance," said Frank. "However does that happen?"

"Don't bother to ask questions," remarked Mrs. Cureall. "You will learn everything in good time. Just wait and see what happens."

A trumpet then softly touched Frank on the top of his head and then gently touched the two hands, Angela's and his, giving them a gentle caress.

Before he had time to unclasp, it touched his nose and then his chin, moving over to Angela and doing the same to her.

"It seems interested in you two," remarked Hope. "I wonder why?"

"Oh, we know," said a strong male voice through the trumpet.

"Wherever did that come from?" enquired Ralph.

"From Etheria," replied Trueman, "but keep quiet and we may hear what they know."

"Is it fair to tell?" came the voice, again. "These two young people are holding hands; perhaps they are frightened, perhaps not," which was followed by a hearty laugh from the speaker. "You see," he went on, "we can see in the dark."

Frank and Angela promptly dropped each other's hand and, fortunately, the darkness made their blushes unseen.

"Well, that is the limit!" blustered Frank.

"It was true, wasn't it?" enquired the tactless Hope.

Mrs. Trueman tactfully changed the subject by saying that the voice through the trumpet came from her control who was her brother Godfrey, who died some twenty years previously. He it was, she said, who was in charge on the other side, just as her husband was on this side.

Before she had finished speaking the trumpet rose again and pointed to Ralph. From it proceeded the following, spoken by the same voice :

"Please do not cross your legs, it does not make for good conditions. George Trueman will tell you why afterwards."

"Somebody seems to be present who can see in the dark," remarked Ralph. "I am sorry I did not know that I should not cross my legs."

"You will get more surprises yet," remarked Dr. Cureall. "They will tell you what you are thinking, so be careful. If you want further proof that they can see in the dark put one of your hands out and hold up a finger and see if it is not touched."

Ralph did so without mentioning it to anyone.

A trumpet rose gracefully and descended gently on to the top of his finger, which he at once removed to another place, to be followed by the trumpet and again touched. This went on some dozen times, when Hope remarked :

"Well, I hope you are enjoying your game. You can't get away from it, you see."

Then the trumpet nestled on his lap, gradually moving up to his face which it gently stroked. It then moved out from him, the small end pointing to his face.

"Take hold of the trumpet," the same male voice of Godfrey, the control, remarked, "and see if you can hold it."

Ralph did so, and it twisted aud turned, pulling all the time as if to get away.

"Don't wrench it," remarked Mrs. Trueman, "let them do that. You just hold it as best you can."

It was, however, impossible. Ralph could not hold the trumpet, and it pulled itself free and rose gently to the ceiling.

"They know the conditions," remarked Mrs. Trueman. "That does me no harm if the force comes from their side, and they tell you to hold tight. If you did the wrenching without their permission they would not be prepared for it and the psychic rods attached to me would tear my flesh. I have seen mediums with scars for life, caused by sitters discarding this warning. I think now that they have shown you what they can do with the trumpet we shall get some conversations, which are much more interesting."

As she said this the two trumpets rose and knocked each other in the air, then they went round the circle touching each person on the head, the nose, and caressing each face.

Besides these trumpet movements, glow-lights about the size of half-a-crown floated about the room, and though some of the sitters tried to catch them they always eluded their attempts, moving gracefully away out of reach.

Mr. Trueman now remarked : " Well, Godfrey, time is getting on and our friends are anxious to have some evidence of survival. Is anyone present who knows any of them ? If not, then let our regular communicators speak."

A trumpet then moved in front of Dr. Cureall and from it a voice spoke to him.

" Doctor, you have been thinking since you entered this room about your patient, Mrs. Newly-wed. We know what you have been thinking about. We have read it all from your mind. There is nothing to worry about. We have been to examine her ; she will come through her confinement safely. The child is healthy—it is a boy. Tell her that—it will please her. She wants her first child to be a boy."

" Thank you," replied Dr. Cureall. " You are quite right. I have been worrying about her and thinking about her since the séance commenced. I was fearing a premature birth. I am deeply grateful for all the help the doctors on your side give me."

While this conversation was going on, the other trumpet moved over before Ralph and a voice, clear and distinct, addressed him thus :

" Ralph, I am your father, Beresford Leader. You must have some proof that I am not dead, so tell your mother from me that when she was a girl of eighteen and I was twenty we met in London and went to see 'Cinderella' at Drury Lane. It was just before Christmas. I bought her a box of chocolates. One was a liqueur chocolate which broke and made a mess down the front of her dress. When trying to clean it up the box slipped and all the chocolates fell on the floor."

Ralph : " But how can you be my father ? You are in your grave."

Beresford : " I never heard such rubbish. I stood beside your mother at the grave during the burial of my physical body, and heard the parson saying many things about me which rather amused me. I can only look back on it as one of the strangest experiences in my life. Before she left the grave she threw a bunch of roses on to the coffin to which was attached a card on which she had written ' To Berry from Bunny.' "

Ralph : " Yes, I remember the pet names, but I have forgotten about the roses."

Beresford : " Tell your mother that when I was dying I said to her, ' Bunny, you must not grieve about me. You have Ralph, and if there is another life, then, someday, we shall be together again. If there is not, then it means oblivion, so we shall not know that we are dead.' Tell her there is another life, and I am waiting for her in a world more beautiful than the earth, where life is happier and easier. All my poor health went when I died, and I am now strong and well. Tell her also I had a mole about three inches down from the back of my neck, on my left shoulder."

Ralph : " Yes, I shall tell her if I can remember it all."

At which remark Trueman broke in : " It is all recorded, so don't try to remember. Talk to him quite naturally as, if he feels you understand, it gives him confidence.   It requires considerable effort on their part to keep their vibrations down on the earth level."

Beresford: "Ralph, my boy, come back another time. I have much to tell you but I cannot say more now as others want to speak, but remember this, that you still have my affection as you had when I was on earth, and I am just as interested in your ambitions. Give my fond love to your mother and say I would so like to speak to her also.   Tell her I got the V.C. all right.   Bring her with you when you return. Now, I must say good-bye as here is your grand-father, who wants to speak to you about something important."

Ralph : " Just tell me this first, dad, before you go.   Where are you ? "

Beresford : " Standing in the centre of this circle of eight earth people whose emanations make you all visible to us so that we see your every movement, and can read the images your minds make when you think.   But I can't keep the others waiting.   Good-bye again."

" Is the next world, then, on the same level as this one? " Ralph enquired of Trueman.

" Oh no, it is all a question of vibrations.   They come down to us.   You cannot grasp the location of Etheria unless you think of it in terms of vibrations, but I cannot go into the subject here.   The less we say the more opportunity we give our friends to speak. Let me, however, ask you this.   Did you recognise that as your father's voice?"

"Yes, that was his voice, all right," but he got no further as Godfrey, the control, spoke.

"Just keep quiet please, something very important is going to happen."

A few seconds later a precise, cultured voice spoke in front of Ralph.

"Vincent Leader speaking. I am your grandfather, Ralph. I was on earth Prime Minister of Great Britain on two successive occasions, covering eight years. Your father who has just spoken has urged me to come and deliver a message to you which we both think, after consultation with others, who have the welfare of your country at heart, should be given without further delay. The message is for my son, your uncle Edward Leader, the Bishop of Alfortruth. He has slowly come to realise the truth about communication between your order and the one we presently experience. This has unsettled him as he feels that he should speak out and not hold back any longer. He, like every educated man, now realises the false teaching on which his Church is founded and he is slowly coming into the light of Truth.

He requires some experience, such as he would have here, to make him take the step because, as he realises, it is a serious one and one which may mean his resignation from the Church. Fortunately, he is independent of his stipend, and for that reason he is the one we have chosen to take the first step in breaking up the organisation which has grown rich and powerful by gathering in the gifts of its faithful followers. This collapse of an ancient institution can

only come about slowly, but if your uncle follows out
our instructions and bravely faces the result of his
action he will have made the first break in the wall of
ignorance and superstition which stone by stone will
crumble away over the next hundred years.

Just keep quiet a minute while I gather more
power."

Again Vincent Leader spoke. " Science, to-
day, keeps most thinking people from supporting the
Church, but its doctrines, creeds and dogmas remain
intact.   The Reformation broke its power, Spiritualism will break its creeds.   We want them torn up
and scattered to the wind, as only then will its
opposition to this new Revelation be shattered.   So
long as the Church, as now constituted, remains in
being it will oppose this revelation and keep the
people ignorant of this great truth.

It will also do its utmost to keep them ignorant of
the basis of sand on which its doctrines are founded,
of its past history and the fact that the dead do not
lie, as the prayer book says, in their graves till the
resurrection day.   Whenever the people realise the
fact that they pass at once into another life somewhat
similar to the one you now experience, and that they
can return and converse with those they left on earth,
all the creeds of Christendom will be cast aside and
forgotten.

The Church authorities realise this, hence their
determined opposition to Spiritualism and all it stands
for.   So long as the Church remains the recognised
channel for religious instruction Spiritualism will make
slow progress.   Sooner or later Spiritualism will
absorb Christianity, but the Church will fight this, its

greatest enemy, to the last ditch.

It is essential that an outstanding Churchman should make the first breach in the wall of ignorance and throw in his influence to help forward the new Reformation, which is placing religious teaching on facts of the present day and not on tradition nineteen hundred years old, for which there is no historical evidence.

Now, I cannot go on longer as the power is weakening ; but promise me this, Ralph. Will you bring your uncle here so that I may speak to him face to face ? We on this side will be ready whenever he comes."

" I shall certainly tell him what you have said, grandfather," Ralph replied.

" Thank you," Vincent Leader replied, " you can do no more."

" Yes," said Ralph to an inquiry from Dr. Cureall, " that was my grandfather's voice. I remember it quite well. He died just about ten years ago, when I was about twelve."

George Trueman then remarked. " How fortunate that all that was said is recorded and can be reproduced from gramophone records. You see how important is all my attention to detail."

Frank was too nonplussed to speak while Ralph was thinking hard about all he had experienced.

After waiting in silence for a few minutes, Trueman remarked " I do not think I am exaggerating when I say that Vincent Leader's remarks constitute one of the most important pronouncements from Etheria since the first Etherian told this materialistic thinking world, nearly ninety years ago, that conversation was possible between the two worlds."

"I see they are building up again," remarked Mrs. Trueman. "The power is very strong to-night. Can you see anything, Angela?"

"Oh yes, I saw both Ralph's father and grand-father when they were speaking. I never saw them on earth. Shall I describe them?"

"I saw them also," replied Mrs. Trueman, "but wait until after the séance, as I see a cheery looking man standing in front of Frank. He is just going to speak."

The trumpet then touched Frank on the left knee and rose parallel to the floor, the small end pointing to his face. From it a cheery Scotch voice proceeded :

"Weel, Mr. Wiseman, I am glad to make your acquaintance once again. I am Sandy of Kirken-reola. Many a round we had over the Kirkenreola Links. Do you ken me?"

"Yes, oh yes, I remember Sandy the professional at Kirkenreola quite well, but I did not know he was dead."

"Hoots, man, I am Sandy. I am no deed. I am here standing afore ye, speaking to ye. Can ye no hear me?"

Frank, rather flustered, replied "What I mean is this, I did not know that you had left the earth."

"Oh aye, not so long ago, though. On the 12th of March this year I snuffed out, or that is what I thought was going to happen, but you see I shine just as brilliantly as ever."

"Though I hear you I cannot see you. Can you tell me any of your stories, Sandy?" enquired the incredulous Frank, for want of something better to say.

"Oh aye, that I can. Do you mind the story I telt ye yince aboot no copeying anything frae England?"

"Yes, indeed I do. That was one of the best you ever told me."

"Weel, it was quite true, and Jeems McTavish will confirm it."

"Yes, you told me that also, but I never saw him to ask him."

"Weel, I'm gawn awa' noo, I've had ma say : but tell yer freends whit the Laird said and how Jeems McTavish floored Donald the plumber."

The trumpet then fell to the floor.

"How extraordinary," said Frank. "I knew Sandy well and he told me that story. I must find out if he is really dead."

"He told you he wasn't. You must be careful now how you speak about him, Frank, he will be listening," said Hope. "But tell us the story. They always require a little time to build up again."

"It was about a Presbyterian Church Elders' meeting when the elders were discussing about the times of the service. Some wanted the services at eleven a.m. and six p.m., while others wished them retained at eleven in the morning and two in the afternoon. The Laird of Kirkenreola, who was also present, remarked that he had just returned from a visit to Bournemouth and there the Sunday services were morning and evening, and that he would support the change.

' That may be a' veera weel fur England,' said

Donald the plumber, 'but I wudna' like to copey onything fra' England.'

To which the Laird replied that the Church he had been to did not have a collection, when Jeems McTavish, the joiner, shouted across the table.

'Weel, Donald, ma man, you wudna' object to copey that frae England!'"

When Frank concluded, general laughter followed, but it was stopped by Mrs. Trueman remarking to Angela : "A lady is standing beside you. All keep quiet."

"Yes, I have seen her for some time," replied Angela. "She is my aunt. I have seen and heard her speak to me often before."

A gentle female voice then spoke to Angela, giving her name as Aunt Lavinia, her mother's sister, who had passed on twenty years previously.

"You are no stranger to me, aunt," said Angela. "Though I never knew you on earth, I feel as if I knew you well. I used to be laughed at when I said I saw you."

"I know, dear ; that is why I did not come back as often as I would. Give your mother my love and tell her she will never understand this great subject till she gets away from the idea our mother gave her that it was wicked and sinful. Good-bye, dear, I must leave you. Something is wrong. You are all in some danger. Listen!"

A Voice spoke before Frank, saying : "My name is Hunt. I knew your mother. My will could not be found and she never received the legacy I left her. I can tell you where I put the will, but not now—another time. Can you not smell burning?"

" Keep quiet," said Trueman, " I shall ring down to Boles." No answer came and he was about to rise when Godfrey, the control, spoke.

" You must break up this séance. Your house is on fire, George. Keep calm, all of you. Put on the red light and you slip out, George. We shall clear things up here as quickly as possible."

Trueman switched on the red light and opened the door, calling to Miss Noteall.

" They tell us the house is on fire. Come with me."

They both ran along the corridor, the smell of burning becoming noticeable, and by the time they reached the main staircase it was nearly obscured by smoke.

" Run back and bring the others," said Trueman. " I shall get down the back stairs."

He rushed along another passage, down the back stairs and into the pantry where he found Boles fast asleep. He soon had him fully awake.

" The house is on fire, Boles. Ring up the Tunbridge Wells fire brigade. Quick, man, and then tell the servants."

Then he rushed back the way he came only to be forced to stop by the thick clouds of smoke.

" This is serious," he remarked to himself. " I can only get them out of this by a ladder."

He returned to the pantry and rang up the chauffeur, telling him to rouse the gardeners and bring the long ladder, at once.

Boles had now returned from the telephone.

" Brigade coming at once, sir. I shall tell the others. Some are playing cards in the housekeeper's room. The young girls have gone to bed.''

Trueman then ran out to meet the gardeners and chauffeur hurrying to the house with the ladder, and it was not long before it was hoisted up to a window in the passage near to the séance room.

Up the ladder Trueman ran, but he could not open the window, so he called out :

'' Fetch an axe or a log ; get something quickly. I must break it open.''

An axe was quickly found, and a dozen heavy blows shattered the window. Trueman was through in an instant and ran through dense smoke to the séance room, which now was fully illuminated.

Its occupants, when Miss Noteall had returned, had tried to get downstairs, but they were trapped by the smoke which by then had filled the passage. They had then returned to the séance room and shut the door to keep it out.

'' Hurry up,'' shouted Trueman.'' You can all get down the ladder from the window here.''

One by one they safely reached the ground, and when all were down Mrs. Trueman went off to see that the maids were safe. Trueman and the others then went to see if they could locate the fire.

'' Get the extinguishers, Boles,''and addressing the chauffeur, said, '' You and the other men get out the hose, you know where the hydrant is. Come, the rest of you. Take an extinguisher each.''

The smoke, however, made the task difficult, but it was evident that the fire had originated near the staircase, which was burning furiously. The extinguishers had little effect, but when the hose was turned on the stream of water began to smother the flames.

"You may lose the staircase, sir," said Frank, "but we shall save the house. Listen, there is the fire engine."

"Go round by the back passage, Boles, and open the front door. That is the nearest access to the staircase," ordered Trueman.

Soon the brigade was at work and several lengths of hose were pouring streams of water on the burning staircase, which by now was nothing better than charred wood.

"What a merciful escape," said Hope. "We are all safe, and the worst that has happened is the loss of the staircase, some pictures, furniture and carpets burned or damaged."

"Five hundred will cover it all," remarked the Brigade Chief. "It might have been far worse. If it had happened two hours later and you had all been asleep the house would have been burned to the ground and some of you might never have escaped. How did you discover it, sir?"

"Ah, that is our little secret," replied Trueman. "Let us call it the working of Providence."

The firemen, after they had extinguished the flames, found that the fire was due to a flue, running up the wall by the staircase, which had set a beam on fire and this in turn had set the staircase alight.

An hour later all the burnt and damaged furniture and pictures had been removed and the carpets had been taken outside to dry. Many hands made light work. By midnight the firemen and the outside men had returned home, and the house party and the servants were refreshing themselves with drinks before retiring to bed.

"This has rather put the other world in the shade," remarked Ralph, "but we shall all have much to talk about in the morning."

Dr. and Mrs. Cureall took their departure and the others retired to their bedrooms. On his way up the back stairs Frank was accompanied by his host.

"Well, I have kept my promise, Frank."

"Indeed you have. You have given me an experience which is making me think furiously. Good-night, sir. I shall bombard you with questions in the morning."

CHAPTER VI.
THE NEXT MORNING.

The occupants of Sureway Court came down to breakfast the next morning none the worse for the excitement of the previous evening. The sun was shining and the trees rustled from a faint breeze. It was altogether a peaceful morning.

The household staff had made things tidy once more in the lounge where the fire had originated. The charred staircase and the absence of a few pictures which had been damaged were the only signs of the disaster, the rugs having been cleaned, dried and put back in their places.

" No more wooden staircases in this house," said Trueman, addressing his wife. " Much too dangerous. We shall have a stone one built up; a month should see everything straight again. What do you think, dear?"

" We must make this old house as fireproof as possible," she replied. " There are too many wooden beams for my liking. I don't want another experience such as we had after you left us. It is anything but pleasant to be shut in a room to get away from the smoke and not to know what is happening, or how we were to get out."

" Well, that is hardly correct, mum. We did know what was happening. Both you and Angela were told clairaudiently that daddy had sent for a ladder and we would get out by the window."

" Yes, dear," Mrs. Trueman replied, " that is quite true. These messages were a comfort, but I doubt if Frank or Ralph took them seriously."

"Speaking for myself," replied Ralph, "I don't know what to take seriously and what not. My mind is all at sixes and sevens. My reason tells me that it cannot be true and yet my senses experienced something which points to it being true. What are your reactions Frank, after you have slept over it?"

"Something like your own, Ralph, but how can you explain it all if the Spiritualist explanation is not the right one? Telepathy is now the accepted scientific explanation. From saying nothing happens our scientists now accept something not quite normal and one name is as good as another if you can't explain the cause."

"Telepathy? Humbug," blustered Trueman. "First, what do they mean by telepathy? One mind reading another, to put it briefly. Accept that first of all and any thinking person can see that it knocks the materialistic conception of the Universe into a cocked hat. On the scientists' own showing they have knocked the legs off their own idol of matter. That explanation will, however, never explain the phenomena of Spiritualism. It will never explain the direct voice. How can telepathy produce a voice which we recognise as belonging to the one who lived on earth, a voice which tells us something no one present was thinking about, something no one on earth was thinking about, something we don't know and have to hunt up to find if it is true?"

"The explanations made by those who have never been present at a direct voice séance," said Mrs. Trueman, "are far more fantastic than the Spiritualist explanation that the voices come from those who once lived on earth and are now living in a world of finer matter, having bodies of that same finer matter. Either we accept that or imply fraud ; that one of us present did the speaking. Now, who was it, I would like to know? ''

Mrs. Trueman smiled round the breakfast table at her guests.

'' Perhaps you may wonder if I took the part of the female voice and my husband took that of the male—a pair of crooks. If so, there must be hundreds like us all over the world, as the direct voice takes place in every country in the world. Why be crooked in this way only and not be known as such in ways in which we could really benefit? I don't steal the money I collect for charities, though to do so would not be difficult. George, I am sure, has had many chances in life of doing something not straight and yet there has never been a whisper against his character all his business life. Moreover, we are both accepted as truthful and honourable people. If we had not been, it would have been found out long ago.''

To this challenge, there was a general protest from the guests.

'' It cannot be hallucination because we have the voice records,'' Mrs. Trueman went on. '' We can also prove to you that we did not do the speaking, and I would like to do so to-night. I shall sit in the passage and you can prove for yourselves that I can't be heard in the séance room when the door is shut. You three novices go in, shut the door and lock it. Go over the walls and see if there is a place we can speak through. You will find only one opening in the wall on the level of the floor two inches wide by one inch high, which you can just put your fingers through. One of you, if you like, lie down in the passage and try to make yourself clearly heard in the room in which you heard the voices last night. You won't be able to, as a person speaking through it can just be faintly heard, and only if the listener keeps his ear near to the hole.

That hole is necessary for the ectoplasm from me to get through into the séance room.''

'' You are making us feel rather awkward,'' said Frank. '' If we did what you suggest you will think that we doubt your honesty.''

'' Not at all—just a sensible suggestion,'' said Trueman. '' Explore every avenue. Find a normal explanation before you resort to the super-normal. You are not the first we have asked to test us. That is why we made that hole, so as to prove that we are not responsible for the voices. Many others have gone this road before you and been forced to accept the Spiritualist explanation.''

'' It is very kind of you to put yourselves to all this trouble for us,'' said Ralph, '' but what I want to do, with your permission, is to hear what these voice records have to tell me. I wish I knew shorthand to be able to take it all down.''

'' Don't worry about that,'' said Trueman, '' Miss Noteall will have it all typed out by lunch time and then I would suggest that you start off to make your enquiries. If you can find that Sandy died on the twelfth of last March, as he said, that will be good evidence, because you never even knew that he was ill.''

'' That is true,'' replied Frank ; '' and to think

of that old story being referred to and I the only one who knew it."

"What about Frank being the culprit," said the playful Hope. "Only he knew it and pretended he was Sandy."

"But it was Sandy's voice," remonstrated the cornered Frank, "and I was not even thinking about him."

"Of course, you weren't," said Hope. "Only a joke, but you see how everyone can accuse the other. That is why daddy thought of the idea of having mum outside so that she could prove her innocence. On one occasion, every one in turn went inside, and voices spoke about things only known to the person inside. So we were all found to be honest, decent people. Pass the marmalade, please."

"At least," said Frank, "no one knew that the house was on fire. If we had not been told we might not be here now."

"How do you know it was not done on my instructions by one of the staff and that it was not all staged to impress you two?" remarked Trueman, with a twinkle in his eye.

"I don't think we are worth such an expensive production," replied Ralph, "and you, sir, don't either."

"Which proves that at least one super-normal occurrence took place last night," said Trueman.

Angela, who had been sitting listening to this conversation, which rather bored her, as she thought all this doubting so futile, broke in with the remark :

"How can you account for the trumpets moving as they did? No one present could have done that, if you exclude intelligences of a different order to ourselves, and in any case we were being photographed every time the trumpet rose, so we shall soon see that when a voice was speaking the trumpet was floating in front of the person spoken to."

" Yes, Angela, I was not forgetting to remind our young psychical researchers of all you have just said," remarked Mrs. Trueman.

" Someone might have risen in the dark and thrown the trumpet about and up to the ceiling," ventured Frank.

" Try it," said Trueman. " You both go up and see if you can do what was done last night. You will be poking each other's eyes out ; scratching each other's skins. Try it. I have done so often. I defy any person in this world to do what those trumpets did last night. Try to touch someone's finger or stroke his face gently with a trumpet in the dark— it can't be done."

" No one could even touch the trumpets without getting up, and if anyone rose he would be spotted," added Hope.

" How ? " enquired Frank.

" By the weight register and the infra-red photograph, of course. If anyone had moved out of his seat he would have cut through the beam and been photographed."

" Oh yes, we had you both under close observation, though you knew it not," went on Hope. " Just wait until daddy gets the photographs and these long strips of blue paper, giving our weights. I bet not a soul moved from his seat ; but just wait till Miss Noteall has done her work."

"Well, enough of this bantering," said Trueman. "Now, if you are all finished I shall get these weight records, and if all who are interested will go to the library I shall be there in a few minutes."

Trueman soon returned carrying a sheaf of long paper strips like elongated barograph weather records.

"Now," said he, "I shall first of all place these into this long-shaped weight record book and then we can examine them carefully."

This being done, he started explaining the first one, which was the record of Mrs. Trueman's weight.

"You will notice how much more her weight varied than that of anyone else. Angela's weight shows the next excess of alteration which proves that she is a medium. With development she could probably obtain the direct voice."

"Now, what do we find here as regards the alteration in my wife's weight? It fell as much as two-and-a-half pounds below normal and rose at times to two pounds above normal. The time all these alterations occurred you will notice on the top of the record. This paper was on a recording drum and the pointer, like one on a barograph, moved up and down as the weight increased or decreased. Now, as the voice-recording machine and the cinematograph infra-red cameras are timed likewise, we can, by comparing all these records together, find out what happened when the weight altered.

Oh, here is Miss Noteall with the photographs. Now we shall put them in the space we have left below my wife's weight chart to correspond with the time on each. There now, you see it is all quite clear. At exactly the same time all through, when the trumpet moved, breaking the beam, and the photograph was taken, her weight rose by one pound because she supported the trumpet by one or more psychic rods, so that the weight of the trumpet was added to her weight. Her increase in weight corresponds almost exactly with the weight of the trumpet. It cannot do so exactly as her weight has been slightly reduced by ectoplasm being drawn from her body.

Now, here again, when the two trumpets were off the ground, her weight increased by two pounds.

When they speak they use much more ectoplasm, and so, when a voice is speaking, her weight is reduced to the lowest point ; on this occasion by two-and-a-half pounds. When, however, the trumpet or trumpets are only floating about much less is used and her weight increases by nearly the weight of the trumpet or trumpets.

This evening I shall have everything arranged so that you can see on one screen the movement of the trumpet and on the other the convolutions of the ectoplasm. Everything is timed to the second, and I shall read out from a reading desk, with a lamp which shines on these records, the alterations of the weights as they occur.

Now you see how Angela, at one time, lost a half pound in weight and the rest of us just a few ounces each. None of us, excepting my wife, added to our weights, which proves that the movements of the trumpets were due to their being connected to my wife only. At the end of the séance it will be noticed that all weights returned to normal.

Most important of all, these charts prove that no

one rose from his or her seat during the séance.

If you wish to get more information on this subject, I would recommend you to read three books : *The Reality of Psychic Phenomena; The Psychic Structures at the Goligher Circle;* and *Experiments in Psychical Science;* all by Dr. W. J. Crawford, who was lecturer in mechanical engineering at the Municipal Technical Institute of Belfast and Extra Mural lecturer in mechanical engineering at Queen's University of Belfast.   He conducted hundreds of experiments with Miss Kathleen Goligher, a Belfast medium, and obtained most valuable information of the alteration in the weight of the medium as different types of phenomena occurred.

My records correspond very closely with his, and our independent investigations prove to my mind that what occurs in our séance room is of a supernormal nature.   Always my wife's weight has increased by eight pounds when a table of that weight has risen into the air without any physical contact.''

'' That is most impressive,'' remarked Frank. '' How vast this subject is.   If one is to study all those books you have over there it is a life's work. There is as much to learn in this science as in medicine.

'' When you learn more about it,'' replied Trueman, '' you will find, I venture to think, that there is more to learn in psychic science than in any other branch of knowledge : but I must not forget the temperature chart—that is also most interesting. Oh, you have it with you, Miss Noteall.   Now, let us see what happened.

Yes, a fall of twenty degrees Fahrenheit from

time to time during the séance, which, when we have everything joined up to-night into one complete sequence of events, will be seen to have occurred when a voice was speaking. The more prolonged a conversation the greater is the fall of temperature.''

"I have a question to ask you all and nobody will be able to answer it," said Hope. "Who was the first psychical researcher on record?"

No one could reply, so she said, "Well, as you can't reply, I shall tell you. The Apostle Thomas, who would not believe unless he could see in the hands the print of the nails, put his fingers into the holes the nails had made and his hand into the wound in the side of the re-materialised Jesus."

"True enough. I never thought of that before," said her father. "Whoever put that into your fluffy head?"

"None other than dear Angela, who said to me, 'These two, meaning Ralph and Frank, remind me of St. Thomas. They will believe nothing without proof.'"

"Quite right, too," remarked Trueman. "'Prove all things——,' to quote from the old book. There is no virtue in believing without evidence. I fought my way to my present knowledge of psychic science, proving everything step by step as I went. My knowledge has accumulated stratum upon stratum and I have undoubted facts to account for each stratum of knowledge which has been laid down in my mind."

"Let us get outside on a lovely morning like this," said Hope. "It is a sin being in the house and I am sick of the subject. Are you boys coming or do you wish to hear daddy yarn away all morning?"

"You better all go out," remarked her father, "and come back at twelve. I think you will have the voice records typed off by then, Miss Noteall?"

"I shall do my best," was her reply. "I think I can manage it. Better make it twelve-thirty."

Angela gave Frank a look and he followed her like a lamb.

The young people trooped outside and on the suggestion of Hope went off to the stables to see the horses.

"Do you hunt, Hope?" asked Frank.

"Being a dutiful daughter, I don't," she replied. "Daddy is down on hunting and all blood sports such as hare coursing, stag hunting and otter hunting. Anything which makes animals suffer he hates, and because of this he is not popular amongst the hunting crowd."

"I share his feelings," said Frank. "How any decent-minded individual can find pleasure at the expense of an animal's suffering is beyond my comprehension. My experience of hunting people is that they are bone selfish and don't care a damn for anybody or anything beyond their own pleasure. I hope some day public opinion will stop all those brutal sports just as it did bear baiting."

"I was glad to hear over the wireless last night," said Ralph, "that the German leaders have decided to abolish all blood sports, and hunting, because they are cruel and unmanly. The Church in this country supports blood sports and never denounces them, but our bishops are for ever denouncing the anti-Christian attitude of the German Government and warning the people of the danger to Christianity."

"Just as they have denounced Germany's attempt to improve the race by sterilizing the unfit and the insane," replied Frank. "Everything that has been done for the good of the race has at one time or another been denounced by the clergy, and now we find the only nation in the world, which puts the feelings of the lower animals before their own pleasures, being denounced for their anti-Christian attitude and outlook. The less Christian a nation becomes the more humane it becomes. Germany has given an example of this to the world. Its action in stopping all hunting should make everyone in this country feel ashamed. It won't be nice for us to think that Germany will now look on us in much the same way as we look on Spain, because of its bull-fights."

"Why is it sport to hunt a fox and cruelty to hunt a cat?" enquired Ralph. "Why would public opinion be shocked if I put a terrier on to hunt a cat, and why is it not shocked because a crowd of men and women, with hounds, hunt a fox, after stopping up all the earths so that it cannot get to ground? I admit that foxes must be kept down, but shoot them. To hunt them is degrading to those who do so and misery for the fox which has feelings just like any other animal."

"I saw one of the most disgusting episodes reported the other day in the newspapers," said Frank. "The 'blooding' of the ten months' old son of a member of the Quorn Hunt. Held aloft in his mother's arms he was smeared with the blood of the mangled fox. Doubtless his parents were good orthodox Christians and Churchgoers, as so many hunting people seem to be. Having heard all their lives about the blood shed by a god leading to salvation, it is easy to see how they fit their cruel sport in with their religion. A savage religion breeds savage people, or perhaps it would be more correct to say that savage people produce a savage religion. Every religion is a human production, though each one claims to be a divine revelation."

" Let us get off the subject," said Angela, " Cruelty of every kind is so repulsive to me that I hate to hear people telling about the misery those poor creatures are made to suffer to give some selfish people pleasure."

" If we don't talk about it, we shall never stop it," said Frank. " Every decent-minded person should use his influence to stop the savagery which goes on to-day under the name of sport. All who wish to see this cruelty stopped should become members of the National Society for the Abolition of Cruel Sports, whose headquarters are in London. Only by united effort will this barbarous pastime be stopped.

The other day a man I knew died. He was Lord Lieutenant of one of our counties. In his obituary, his hunting exploits were given the greatest prominence, and also the fact that he was ' blooded ' when he was five years of age."

" Such is the mentality of our age ! Such are the figure-heads of society ! " said Ralph.

" Riding is grand exercise and I love to be on a horse's back," said Hope. " Mum and I have lovely rides together. Here are the two beauties. This one," pointing to a roan mare, " is mine, the other is mum's. Yes, my precious one," as the mare poked its nose into her pocket, " I have sugar for you.   There now, isn't that good? "

After the stable had been inspected, Hope suggested a visit to a neighbouring farm.

" One of the most modern farms in England," she said.   " Mr. Farmer, the owner, always welcomes visitors.   It is only half a mile away.   It is a nice walk over these fields.   What do you all say? "

All having signified approval the party set off, and after climbing several fences and scrambling over ditches reached their goal.

" There is Mr. Farmer," Hope exclaimed. " Do you mind if we look round?   I have some friends who have come to see how cows and pigs should be kept."

Farmer was always delighted in any interest taken in his life's work, so, after shaking hands all round and expressing the hope that they were none the worse of their terrifying experience of the previous night, said that he would walk round with them.   He was a Lincolnshire man who had come twenty years earlier to Sussex, and by enterprise, thrift and hard work had become the owner of a farm he proudly declared was second to none in England.

Bit by bit the old farm steading had been replaced by modern buildings with modern equipment, and concrete had taken the place of mud.

" Yes," he replied, to a question, " every building here has been designed and planned by me. Every one was carefully thought out before it was put up.   Everything is in its right place and designed to save labour.   But come along and see for yourselves."

He led the party into a long, one-storied building.

" This is the byre, or as we call it in Lincolnshire, the cow-house.' It houses one hundred cows. Concrete floors and stalls. Good light, which is important when you start milking at five in the morning.

Oh yes, there is electric light in every building. We need it in the winter, starting as we do when it is dark. Then the milkers get a few hours off at mid-day and milk again till six. We milk twice a day, morning and afternoon."

" Well, I never saw such a place in my life," said Ralph, " and I was brought up in the country."

" You will see no place like it anywhere," was the boastful reply, " though, to be honest, there are cow houses like this here and there ; but what I mean is that the entire lay-out of the place cannot be beaten. No time lost in carrying the hay or straw, and the manure is run out to the heap here and lifted every day."

The visitors had by now walked the entire length of the cow-house, when the proud owner, instead of going on outside by the large double door, beckoned them to follow him. Going along a passage he led them behind the stalls, where a passage ran right down next to the windows.

" There is a passage on the other side just like this ; it is called the feeding passage. Instead of feeding the cows from behind they are fed from here, their troughs being easy of access ; and you will notice that water is laid on for each cow."

" What quaint halters, or whatever you call them," said Angela.

" These are tubular, made of steel. The cows just put their heads into them and then they are closed in a second—see, like that. Saves labour and gives them more room to move about and lie down. The less the men have to do in tying them up the more time they have for what is essential."

" How many cows can a man milk? " enquired Ralph.

" Sixteen both morning and afternoon, and bed them down at night in winter. One man sees to the feeding of the lot ; that is an expert's job, and must be carefully done. The least change in the rations affects the milk supply. I am sorry that they are all out. Being summer they sleep in the fields. They come in from five till nine in the morning and again from two till six."

" What cows do you keep? " enquired Frank.

" Mostly shorthorns, but also about a dozen Guernseys. They add to the quality of the milk and make it creamy looking."

" Do you supply Sureway Court, because I noticed how good the milk is there? " enquired Angela.

" Indeed I do. They take two gallons a day. My best customers, Miss Hope, and I hope I shall always give you satisfaction."

" How large is your herd? " enquired Frank.

" Two hundred head from calves upwards. I must always keep about seventy coming on and then about thirty are always dry for about three months before calving, so to keep a hundred milkers I need two hundred of a herd. A dairy farm is just a factory for manufacturing milk. The cow is the machine which is supplied with water, hay and other food-stuffs, which it turns into milk. It is a machine which wastes away and on the average does not produce milk for more than eight years, so provision must be made for a proportion to be replaced each year. Now come and see the pigs.''

At every stage in the pig's career a different kind of house was used. Rows of houses for farrowing, houses for pigs from 4 till 8 weeks, after which they left their mothers, when they spent a joyous free existence in the neighbouring woods, in specially prepared houses and runs, till five months old, when they were moved into a large house for a month to be fattened.

'' Yes, this is the fattener,'' said Farmer. '' See how clean they are. The pig is a very clean animal if things are arranged as they are here. A manure channel runs behind their pens, to which they get access through that opening. A pig will never dirty its bed if it can help it. Aren't they a lovely lot ? ''

'' I hope you kill them by a humane killer? '' enquired Angela.

'' Oh, they are not killed here, but don't be afraid. Before I started to have pigs, I got the Rural District Council to make the humane killer compulsory in this district for all animals. The pity is that it is optional for each district to make it compulsory, and not the law in England, as it is in Scotland, that every animal must be killed instantaneously. These will be electrocuted and never know. I have seen some horrible sights in my life. Man's cruelty to animals in the past is too shocking for words.''

" We were just saying, coming along," said
Hope, " how daddy is down on hunting."

" Your father, Miss Hope, is a noble soul.   I
wish there were more like him.   Many farmers hate
the hunt.   They are a selfish, cruel lot, leaving gates
open and caring for no one and nothing but to have
a day's fun.   Farmers have to spend thousands a
year to wire off their poultry.   All unnecessary
capital expenditure if foxes were not preserved to be
hunted ; and we have to compete with foreigners
sending in eggs and underselling us.   My private
opinion is that hunting should be made illegal.   It
does no one any good.

Oh, yes, I have three thousand hens, and they
are kept just like the cows and pigs, clean and comfortable.   Every device for saving labour.   Would
you like to seem them ?"

Frank and Ralph, however, were anxious to
return to see the typewritten records of last night's
séance, so they remarked that Mr. Trueman was ex-
pecting them at twelve-thirty and that they would just
have time to get back by then.

Thanking the genial farmer and again compli-
menting him on his wonderful farm, they said good-
bye, but he called after them—

" You have not seen half there is to see.   How
the milk is bottled and everything it touches is
sterilized, and how it is delivered every day.   Two
thousand bottles go out daily in vans ; but you must
come back again, and remember to tell your friends
that you have seen the finest Grade A milk farm in
England."

The promise was readily given and the party set off for Sureway Court.

Miss Noteall had everything carefully typed out in triplicate by the time she promised, and she, Trueman and the two young men sat down in the library to read and discuss what the records revealed.

Frank was the first to speak : " Well, I must track down Sandy. That is easy. I shall write to the proprietor of the Golf Hotel at Kirkenreola—he will be able to tell me if Sandy was telling the truth or not. This about the lost will, is, however, much more important. Hunt said he had left money to my mother which never reached her as the will was never found. The only Hunt I have ever heard her speak of was one, Alfred Hunt, who died about ten years ago. He inherited the old family place in Essex from his father and then retired from the Army. The present Lord Kilforfun is his brother. He inherited such a large fortune from Alfred that he was able to buy his title. I think £50,000 to the party funds got a peerage, £25,000 a baronetcy, and £10,000 a knighthood. So I have been told by those who have managed to procure these titles."

" That's about right," remarked Ralph.

" That's all I know about him. It is unfortunate that he had to stop speaking because of the fire."

" Well, you will get another chance," said Trueman, " but you amuse me by the way you have slipped into talking, as if you had missed a good chance of hearing something you wish to know. Your mother does not know where the lost will is, you don't, I don't, my wife doesn't, and no one you know does, so who is going to tell you?"

Frank smiled, and without replying lit a cigarette. He rose from his chair, and standing before the fireplace he was just on the point of speaking when Ralph broke in with the remark :

"My advice, Frank, is this. If you find that Sandy died on the twelfth March, then take this will seriously and ask Mr. Trueman if he will ask you back to another séance when you may hear from the voice where the will is. It may still be possible to find it unless the present owner has found it and destroyed it, then that is the end of the whole affair."

Turning to Trueman, Ralph went on :

"Are you going to be so kind to ask my uncle so that he may hear what his father has to tell him?"

"Certainly," replied Trueman, "I was just coming to that, but you had better approach your uncle rather carefully. I don't know how much he knows about this subject, and he may be rather touchy, and take it all as either humbug or imposture."

"Oh, that will be all right, sir, Uncle Edward is one of the best. He and I are great friends. He has no pomposity or cant about him. Very broadminded. But for his clothes you never could believe he was a bishop."

"That being so," remarked Trueman, "ask him what day would suit him best. Has he a wife? Well, I shall ask my wife to send her an invitation which you can take with you."

"It is very kind of you, sir," said Ralph. "I shall make a point of getting in touch with him as quickly as possible. It means a visit, as a letter or telephone call could not explain all I want to tell him.

I wonder, sir, if I may use your telephone. I would like to ring up my mother and I shall be sure to get her now. Lunch time is generally the best time for getting people in."

Permission being given, Ralph went off to the telephone. Miss Noteall, who all this time had been listening, then remarked :

"I am sure you don't realise, Mr. Wiseman, what a great work is going on in this house. My entire time is taken up with what is called rescue work and comforting the bereaved. On an average, at least twenty letters are replied to by me every day. Mrs. Trueman employs me for this alone."

"Miss Noteall," Trueman remarked, "is an expert in this work and has been trained in it for years. You are perhaps not aware that in London there are Societies with large memberships which specialise in mediumship. One has four thousand members or associates. Each has its own head-quarters, with a secretary and staff, where both the members and the public can go and sit with mediums. Rooms are specially set apart for these private séances and the mediums go there by appointment. Thus, only the genuine ones are employed and no one is imposed upon. If any of those societies ever find a medium defrauding he or she is never employed by any of them again because the information is passed round. Miss Noteall was secretary of one of these societies for ten years so she knows all about medium-

ship and what can be considered good evidence and
what should be discarded as worthless.''

"It is just as much a specialised training as any
other in life," Miss Noteall remarked. "It requires
tact, the understanding of human nature, and above
all the critical faculty fully developed.

Mr. Trueman offered me this work some years
ago, and I have been very happy working in conjunction with Mr. and Mrs. Trueman. I have an
office of my own, a bedroom and a sitting-room in the
west wing. Come along and see them.''

"You see," she remarked, when they had
reached her suite, "how business-like I am. This
is my office. I get to my sitting-room through this
door. Isn't it a delightful room, looking on to that
lovely park, with its stately oaks and beeches.

Please sit down, you have a quarter of an hour
before lunch—it is not till one-thirty. I want to tell
you what an unselfish life Mrs. Trueman leads. She
gives up so much of her busy life to helping those in
sorrow. Three times a week she sits with me for
two hours each time. She finds that more than this
tells on her health, so she must be careful. She gives
out so much vitality each time, and if she were not
well looked after by the doctors on the other side,
who revitalise her after each sitting, she never could
continue doing what she does year after year.

What I am going to tell you now will show you
that the only explanation for it all is that intelligences
beyond our sight, but still with us, are responsible for
the voices.

People write to Mr. and Mrs. Trueman, and the
letters are handed over to me. They contain stories

of bereavement and a request that a good medium be recommended. In such cases, I send them the name of the society of which I was secretary. Often, however, they ask if contact can be made for them, so I reply asking for the person's name and where he or she died, as with this information I have enough to enable me to give the group working with us on the other side information enough to track down the person in Etheria and bring him or her to our séance."

" How extraordinary," said Frank. " You don't mean that they have an organisation over there for bringing people back to earth."

" Yes, that is what they tell us. There is an Information Bureau over there where people register their names and whereabouts. From time to time they call to find if anyone they are interested in on earth is attending séances. Every night at precisely eleven o'clock I read over a typewritten list of those names I have been given by my correspondents who wish me to get into touch with someone on the other side. Each list contains the full name and address at which the person died. The group working with us details off someone each night to be present at eleven o'clock. This person stands behind me when I read over the list and photographs my mind. As our mind pictures everything we see, hear or think, they thus obtain a photographic record of the list which the messenger takes back with him.

This is posted up at the Information Bureau and, from other information they have, the people wanted are tracked down. Remember, the other world is a well-ordered state, and as we have our directories and registers of everybody in this country, so they have

also.   Although the surface on which the recently-
departed live is larger than the earth surface, yet
nationalities there live together.   So the British live
mostly together, just above this country, and thus
they can quickly make contact with any place in
Britain.   In fact, they can move about at great speed.

The people there who are wanted by their earth
friends are generally quickly found and hardly ever
do they fail to turn up.   I get them to tell me all
about themselves, their families on earth, the nature
of their last illness, and what their work was on earth.
Everything I can get helps to make their friends
recognise that they have come back.   The most
trivial remarks are often the most evidential.

Everything said is recorded on the soft gramophone records, which I then paint over with a solution
which hardens them, when they can be run off on the
gramophone you saw in my office.   As this goes on
I type off in duplicate what I hear, one copy going to
the enquirer and the other I file away for reference.

Hardly ever is there a mistake because my correspondents reply confirming what has come through.
Thus they get the comfort and knowledge that their
friends still live and that they will join them some day.
One of the strongest evidences we have that the
voices which speak are those of people who lived on
earth is that often we hear from those who have just
died in Australia, New Zealand or South Africa
asking us to let their friends in England know.   They
give the address they wish us to write to in England,
and our letter is often the first news of death, as our
message has arrived before the letter from abroad containing the news.   Never have we made a mistake

as sooner or later they hear from their friends abroad that their friend has died as and when he told us."

" What a wonderful work," said Frank. " Is this the only place such work is being done?"

" Oh no," Miss Noteall replied. She rose and went over to the bookcase and took out a book : " Here is a carefully compiled record of work done which is similar to what I am doing. The book is written by Sir Oliver Lodge's Psychical Research Secretary, Miss Nea Walker. It is called *Through a Stranger's Hands.* Take it with you but let me have it back. You will find enough evidence of survival within these two covers to keep you thinking for many months to come, and, what is most important of all, this work we are doing eliminates the theory of telepathy as the cause. Neither Mrs. Trueman nor I know anything about the people except their names and where they died. All these masses of details about them are furnished by those on the other side, and we don't know whether they are true or not till I hear from my correspondents. Seldom have we had a disappointment.

I have not time to tell you all about our rescue work as there goes the gong, but they bring to our séances people who don't know that they have passed over and we talk to them and waken them up to the fact. Often they can't get low types of mind to understand that they have made the great change, and it is only by bringing them back to earth that they can make them understand.

Again, people of gross mentality are sometimes too earth-bound for the Etherian missionaries, who work amongst them, to be able to raise their thoughts and aspirations to a higher level.   Thus, these people of low mentality herd together and make their conditions like their thoughts, as they did on earth. We here can influence them in a way they cannot do over there.   Because our conditions on earth are more material we can help them by advice, which, owing to their gross conditions over there, the Etherian missionaries cannot do.   Take the name of this book, *Thirty Years amongst the Dead*, by Dr. Carl A. Wickland.   That will show you the work that we and others are doing to help to raise these degenerates who need our help as much as those of a similar type need it on earth.''

Frank ran into Ralph coming away from the telephone.

'' Well, any luck ? '' asked Frank.

'' Yes, it is all true—every word.   Come into the library—they must be waiting for us—and I will tell you and the others.''

'' Yes, it is all true,'' replied Ralph to the questions which met him on entering.   '' Everything told me is true.   Most extraordinary.   All that happened in the theatre before my father and mother were engaged to be married.   The roses she threw into his grave and the message attached to them. Also what he said when dying.   The mole on his back ; and last of all—what I thought was rubbish— about him getting the V.C.''

'' Was he a soldier ? '' asked Mrs. Trueman.

'' No, never in his life,'' replied Ralph.

'' Well, you can't get the V.C. unless you are a soldier,'' said Hope.

'' It wasn't the Victoria Cross he got.   When

he was dying, mother said to him : ' Be brave, you
have suffered much. You will get the Victor's Crown
in Heaven.' .To which he replied : ' I shall get the
V.C. for suffering bravely.' That is what he meant
when he asked me to tell her that he had got the
V.C. all right.''

"All goes to show that there is only one explanation to it all,'' said Trueman, "which is that
the dead have never died.''

" How did she take it ? " asked Mrs. Trueman.
" I don't suppose she ever imagined you would be
attending a séance here.''

"Well, from her voice, to say the least, she
seemed more than surprised at all I told her. The
more she thinks it over the more this is likely to
increase.''

After lunch the party separated to spend the
Sunday afternoon as each liked best.

Frank and Angela went off to meet Dr. Cureall
as arranged and heard from him about the cures his
patients had obtained through attending psychic
healers. They were so absorbed in their talk that
they did not realise that after an hour's walking they
were approaching Sureway Court by another drive.

" Oh, there is the house,'' said Angela. " However have we got here? ".

" I took you a round ; we have had a three mile
walk,'' replied the doctor. " Now, I must be off, I
want to look in to see Mrs. Newlywed and give her
the message I got for her last night. She is one of

my converts.   Good-bye to you both, and good luck,
Wiseman, in your quest.   You will be a convert also
before long if you go through with it, but go slow,
taking step by step and some day you will know that
it is all true, just as true as that you can talk to and
hear your fellow man."

After tea, Mrs. Trueman suggested the experi-
ment of her sitting outside the séance room in the
passage.   Ralph and Frank, accordingly, went upstairs with her.

Mrs. Trueman sat in the passage, in front of the
small opening, in the chair Miss Noteall usually
occupied, and after each of the young men had tried
to make his voice heard through the hole to the other
one in the séance room, with but slight effect, she
proposed that Frank should stand beside her and
hold her hands while Ralph went into the séance room
and locked the door.

As the séance room had no window, all he had
to do to darken it was to switch off the light.   He had
been told to stand about three yards from the wall,
to hold the trumpet in his hand, and keep the small
end to his ear, pointing the larger end towards the
place where Mrs. Trueman was sitting on the other
side of the wall.

"There won't be the same power as at the
séance," Mrs. Trueman remarked, "as they have
to take the ectoplasm from me through the hole, and
the further they have to take it the less they have to
work with.   However, see what you can get."

During the time Ralph was in the room, Frank
and Mrs. Trueman carried on a continuous conversation, he telling her about his talk with Miss Noteall.

In ten minutes Ralph returned, looking rather astonished.

"Well, what happened?" asked Mrs. Trueman.

" A man I knew at Cambridge, who died a few months ago as the result of a motor accident, spoke to me, giving me his name, and told me something that only he and I knew."

" What was that? " asked Frank.

" Well, he once confided in me that his father would have taken him into his business but for the opposition of his partner, who said that it meant, sooner or later, his father would want to have him made a partner, which would mean less to divide all round. My friend was rather sore about it as he wanted very much to enter his father's business. My friend lost his mother some years ago. Both his father and partner died last year, and then a few months ago he himself was killed in a motor smash. Thus, I suppose, I was the only one on earth who knew the meaning of his words to me just now."

" What did he say? " asked Frank.

" Well, I heard his voice through the trumpet saying : ' Well, Ralph, old man, it doesn't matter now about me not getting into my father's business. I am your old friend Jim Lamond—L A M O N D, not L A M O N T.' He spelled out letter by letter both Lamond and Lamont, and, funnily enough, nothing annoyed him more when on earth than to have his name spelled Lamont."

" Now you go in, Frank," said Mrs. Trueman, " and see what you can get. Ralph, you stay here with me. Frank may hear more about the lost will. Lock the door."

Ten minutes passed and Frank came out.

"Yes, he spoke again about the will. This is what he said : ' The will I told you about last night is in a secret chamber at Huntingham, my old home. You can only get it if you go in to the Gothic Room and press————.' "

" Press what? " asked Ralph as Frank stopped.

" That was all I could hear as the voice became so faint and then trailed off to nothing."

" How annoying," said Mrs. Trueman. " Don't bother about it, however. He is evidently anxious to tell you, so he will tell my control Godfrey to let him know when you come to the next séance and he is sure to turn up. This just proves that the voice does not come from me. Ralph and I have been talking all the time you have been away."

" Was Huntingham the name of his old home? " enquired Ralph.

" Oh yes," Frank replied, " and I don't suppose anyone here knew that except myself."

" Just one thing more," said Mrs. Trueman. " Before we go I would like you to get an apport. Don't bother to ask me what that is. I don't want to waste time telling you now as our friends in Etheria are here ready to do their part, which means that we provide the article and they do the rest. Have either of you a cigarette case? "

Frank produced his.

" Can it go through that hole? " she enquired. " Try every possible way. Well, it can't, so put it on my lap. Ralph, hold my hands—don't let go, whatever you do."

" Now, Frank, go into the séance room, put out

the light and stand a few yards on the other side of this wall, facing me. Hold out your hands in front of you."

Frank did so and in a few minutes appeared with his case.

"It was put into my right hand," said he, rather sheepishly.

"Well, Ralph never let go my hands and you left it on my lap," she replied. "That is what we call an apport."

"Matter passed through matter," said Trueman when Ralph and Frank arrived down stairs in the library, "but it is too long a story to tell you now how it is done. Your cigarette case is just a swirling mass of electrons and protons whose movements they accelerate and then bring back to normal. They tell us that by this acceleration they dematerialise the object and then rematerialise it when they get it on the other side of the wall. But I am busy just now helping Miss Noteall to fix up everything for to-night. We are just putting everything in position."

After dinner all the party, Dr. and Mrs. Cureall and a few friends from the neighbourhood, who had also been asked, assembled in the library and for over an hour George Trueman demonstrated on the screen what had taken place the previous night in the séance room, showing how everything harmonised, how, when the trumpet rose, Mrs. Trueman's weight increased, the temperature fell, and how, when the voice spoke, her weight decreased. The gramophone records were played recording the voices which they had registered. Everything that occurred during the séance, second by second, was thus again recorded on this occasion.

Frank was especially interested in seeing the ectoplasm pouring from the orifices of Mrs. Trueman, and to a slighter extent from Angela. This was seen to accumulate on the floor and change from a vapoury substance to that of a solid material during the time the voices were speaking.

Mrs. Trueman and Angela then both described the appearance of those they saw speaking. Not only did these agree in detail but, though neither of them had ever seen the people in life, those present who knew them on earth recognised the descriptions as correct.

The next morning the two men left with Trueman for London, Ralph promising to let Mrs. Trueman know when the Bishop and his wife could come. Frank arranged to keep in touch with Ralph so that he could also come on the day suitable to the Bishop.

Thus ended Frank and Ralph's first introduction to Psychic Science.

At Charing Cross the three separated, and Trueman, when saying good-bye, remarked to Frank : " I think I have put your foot on a new ladder of knowledge, the rungs of which you must now climb yourself. You are only on the first rung and your immortal existence will be occupied in climbing this ladder of knowledge which some day will lead you into the realm of reality. You now have something tangible on which to base your opinions when talking to John Matterson."

" The light seems to be breaking through," said Frank to himself on the way to the hospital,

'' but how to work it in with our present knowledge of nature is the problem. However, I shall be seeing mother at lunch. She may be able to tell me if she has ever heard of a Gothic room at Huntingham, and if so if she knows anything about a secret chamber. After that I must find out about Sandy.''

CHAPTER VII.

IMPORTANT DEVELOPMENTS.

"How very extraordinary! Most extraordinary! Very strange indeed, to say the least! Just let me get your aunt in. She must know, and I have every confidence in her judgment."

The speaker was none other than Edward Leader, Doctor of Divinity and Bishop of Alfortruth. He was speaking to his nephew, Ralph Leader, and this was taking place at the bishop's residence, Alfortruth Palace, on the Tuesday evening following the events recorded in the previous chapter.

"Well, uncle, I felt it was my duty to come and tell you. You, of course, must judge for yourself. Here is Mrs. Trueman's invitation, and now that I have given it to you I feel that my responsibility ceases. Shall I go for Aunt Katherine?"

"Yes, please do so. You will probably find her in her boudoir."

During Ralph's absence the bishop paced up and down his study. He had rather a slight figure and was of medium height. He was clean shaven with an attractive round boyish face, from which peered two blue eyes. His face shone with kindliness, and when he spoke it lit up with a smile. He was highly respected by all who knew him and he and his wife were devoted companions. "Most interesting and evidential," he muttered. "Most interesting," but these words were cut short by Mrs. Leader entering with Ralph.

"Well, my dear, what is your trouble? Ralph

says you need my advice about something. Let us all sit down and hear about it."

Mrs. Leader took after her husband in build ; rather short and thin, with a sweet, gentle face. She was beloved by all, and on her sound judgment and common-sense her husband relied, never taking an important decision without consulting her.

"Well, my dear," remarked the bishop, "I must tell you what has happened. Most interesting and evidential when we consider what has gone before."

"Now, Edward, please don't beat about the bush. Have you been offered an Archbishopric?"

"My dear girl, I have been asked to do something which, if I do it, will mean my resignation from the Church."

"How terrible," she replied, "and you need my advice to help you to overcome some great temptation. Ralph, whatever have you been saying to your uncle? I never imagined that you would take up the role of sister Eve."

"I have only given him an invitation to Sureway Court from a friend of mine, Mrs. Trueman," replied the half-truthful Ralph.

"If that were all, my dear," remarked the bishop, "I would not seek your aid, but Ralph has asked me, and you also, to go there to attend a séance, at which my father wishes to speak to me."

"Well, that is nothing very dreadful," remarked his wife. "It won't be the first séance to which you and I have been, though I admit if we do go, it will be the first time anyone except ourselves will know of it."

"You have now let Ralph into our little secret,

but he will be very discreet, I am sure.   You understand, Ralph, it is next door to heresy for a bishop
to attend a séance or show any leaning towards Spiritualism, and so both your aunt and I have kept the
fact private that we have attended séances from time
to time in London.   Quite incognito, of course.
Quite incognito.''

"Don't worry about me, uncle, I shall do nothing
to blacken your character, but I had better tell Aunt
Katherine all I have told you and then she will know
how you are up the pole, so to speak.''

" Yes, yes, do so, Ralph, but keep off slang.
Up the pole, indeed !   Not a bad simile, all the
same, and we can add that if I do what my father
suggests I shall never be able to come down.   I shall
have to learn the Indian rope trick and disappear.
That is rather apt, isn't it, Ralph?''

" Then you believe that it was your father who
spoke to me,'' enquired Ralph, with a grin.

" Will you both come to the point and remember
I know nothing about what you are speaking of,'' said
Mrs. Leader.   '' Now, Ralph, tell me everything
from the beginning.''

Ralph then told his aunt all he had previously
told his uncle, not only what Vincent Leader had said
and the message he had sent to his son, the bishop,
but also all his own father, Beresford Leader, had told
him which he had found out to be true, concluding
by handing his aunt the typewritten copy of the
various conversations.

'' Did all this you are telling me take place in
the dark?'' his aunt enquired.

'' Oh yes, the room was quite dark except for

the occasional dull red and violet glow from the lamps when the infra-red and ultra-violet photographs were taken.''

"Well, if it was dark, Ralph, how did you get this?" she enquired, holding up the verbatim remarks typed on the paper. "You could not have taken all this down word for word, and carried on a conversation at the same time."

So Ralph had to describe the séance room to his astonished listeners, and concluded by saying: "Now I have told you everything that I can remember. Why not come and see for yourselves, and if you want to keep it dark, you can come as Mr. and Mrs. Snooks? I shall tell Trueman not to make any pointed enquiries and accept you just as my friends. He will let you both in, I am sure."

"Don't be silly, Ralph; this is too serious a matter to joke about," replied his aunt.

"I am really quite serious, aunt, but of course uncle couldn't very well go as Mr. Snooks in these togs—that would be too funny for words. Mr. Snooks in gaiters, an apron, black coat with braided buttons, a dog collar and bishop's hat."

"This question of clothes and name does not enter into the question," remarked the bishop. "If I go I go as I am and under my own name. I could never lend myself to any kind of deception. I am sure you agree, my dear."

"Oh, quite. I am afraid Ralph must have got the idea by our telling him that we went to séances incognito."

"Oh, that was quite another matter. That was in London and we were not the guests of anyone.

We went to have our sittings in one of the private rooms of a well-known and highly-respected Spiritualist Society which particularly asks that no name be given.   We always telephoned beforehand to the secretary, and gave our names as Mr. and Mrs. Quest.   I told the Secretary that it was not my real name, in fact he asked me not to give my name, as that was their regular practice, so that no one could turn round afterwards and say that what they obtained at the séance had been told the medium beforehand. Now, that was quite honourable," he concluded, turning to Ralph.

"If you never do worse than that, uncle, you may be an archangel some day, but never an archbishop."

"Well, you can understand," the bishop went on, "it gave us confidence that there was no dishonesty.   Because if the secretary didn't know who we were, the medium could not know, as the mediums are just told to expect someone and given the time.   I always dressed in layman's clothes so that my calling could not be known to anyone."

"So you went as a wolf in sheep's clothing—and I don't blame you.   You must have been thankful to get out of that get-up even for an hour or two. I always think that nothing is too much to pay a bishop when in return he must go about in medieval dress, retain his pomp and dignity, and never be able to give the glad eye to some saucy wench."

"Try to be serious, Ralph," broke in his aunt. "I am the only saucy wench your uncle ever gave the glad eye to, and if I remember right it was I who gave the first to him.   He was not easy to bring up to the scratch. You see how you have infected me with your slang ; but let us return to the business under discussion. You want my advice, I suppose, as to whether we are to accept Mrs. Trueman's invitation."

" Yes, my dear," the bishop replied, " I know what I would do, but I would like to hear your decision."

" Go, of course, and I know your opinion is the same as mine, is it not ? "

" Yes, it is. There is nothing to be ashamed of. If my brother bishops like to bury their heads in the sand they must take the consequences. I don't mind your knowing, Ralph, that we have had most extraordinary evidence of survival through the lips of several trance mediums, whom we have come to look on as our friends. Their honesty is undoubted and they are performing a noble work. It is now ten years since we both entered on our enquiry and though I remarked that what you told me was strange and extraordinary, to us it really is nothing of the kind. I have become a keen and deep student of Spiritualism, so has your aunt, and what you tell me does not surprise me any more than it surprises her. You see that I have now thrown off my cloak of reserve, and I may say that I am more than glad that you have had the experience you have told us about, as you will now have a compass which will keep you on your course through life and help you to face what you will experience after death. My earnest advice to you is to study the subject deeply and you will get a new outlook, a new philosophy which the world to-day sorely needs."

"You look surprised, Ralph," remarked his aunt, "and I don't wonder.   Our position has made it very difficult to speak about the subject to anyone, and in a Cathedral town it is not only difficult but almost impossible. Anything tainting of heresy in a bishop, in the direction of Spiritualism, is looked on by the clergy as something too dreadful for words."

"Personally speaking," replied Ralph, "I would rather not be a bishop and be confined to a mental prison.   I much prefer my freedom and being able to speak my own thoughts, unafraid of what my neighbours may say."

"Just what your uncle feels, in fact he longs for freedom of speech. I know it only too well ; not only as regards Spiritualism but as regards the creeds and dogmas of the Church.   You don't know how much he would like to speak out and tell the truth, instead of being confined to beliefs held sacred by our ignorant ancestors who knew little more about the world in which they lived than does a child."

"It is too bad to give the poor boy so much to think about," remarked the bishop.   "To have told him that we both believe in the claims made by the despised Spiritualists is enough without burdening his mind about our heterodoxy.

However, the time has now come when I must make my position clear.   I pay lip service to honesty. I always lay great stress on honesty and uprightness, while all the time I am a living whitened sepulchre. The time has now come for me to declare my position and my philosophy.   The old creeds are not for this age, they are too narrow, too cruel and barbarous. We have advanced beyond the beliefs of our savage ancestors with their revengeful god, who would not be satisfied unless blood was shed, by another god who was the same god, yet not the same. No person who really thinks can accept the doctrine of the Trinity and all the dogmas and beliefs the early Church Fathers wound round it. Scholars know to-day where all these doctrines originated, and what they know to-day the people will know to-morrow."

" You do surprise me, sir," said Ralph. "What heresy ! What would your brother clergy say if they heard you ? "

" We parsons speak about these things amongst ourselves, and so long as we do not give an unortho- dox opinion in public we are not thought any the worse of amongst ourselves. Most of the bishops and the intelligent clergy know quite well that modern scholarship has destroyed the entire foundation of orthodox Christianity. The policy of the Church is, however, to say nothing and discourage the people in every way from finding it all out for themselves. This they are doing slowly, with the result that fewer and fewer are attending church services.

What, however, the Church authorities fear more than anything else is Spiritualism. That is the real rival to Christianity, and it is because of that my brother clergy, now that their old authority has gone, and they are no longer obeyed by the people, take every opportunity to frighten the people from what they call dabbling in the subject. The devil has been a very useful agent, used by the Church to frighten the people and keep them faithful believers in what the Church teaches, so some of my brethren continue to make use of him by calling Spiritualists ' Servants of the Devil.' I saw only yesterday a parson reported as saying that 'Spiritualism is the damnedest lie ever vomited out of the mouth of Hell.' Well, that may be his honest opinion and it will certainly frighten the unthinking individual. Thus, by bluff and frightening them, the clergy keep many people from becoming acquainted with the greatest truth God has ever given to mankind.''

'' I am sure you do not approve of these terrible admissions, Aunt Katherine,'' said Ralph. '' If I had made such remarks in a bishop's palace, in a bishop's study, to a bishop, I would not have been surprised if I had been shown out of the door.''

'' Your uncle has always had advanced views. He joined the Church under a wave of enthusiasm during the Moody and Sankey revival and like many others regretted the things he said and did when the wave receded. What happened then is happening again to-day. The Oxford Group Movement has carried many emotional people on its crest to saying and doing very foolish things, which some must now regret and others will regret. Your uncle entered the Church against the advice of his father who, as you know, was a very shrewd and far-seeing man. But for his influence he never would have become a bishop as he never has been a loyal churchman. Only those who put the Church first, and all else last, make headway and obtain the plums of office.''

'' Though I have never been a churchman as your aunt says,'' continued the bishop, '' I have always had deep religious and philosophical leanings. My religion has been more universal than parochial. My special study has been philosophy and this has been my standby in my religious work. I came to look on all the creeds of every religion as merely symbols of the greater truth behind. It is this truth which philosophy reveals. It was not, however, till I became acquainted with the truths of Spiritualism that my philosophy came to rest on a firm basis and then all that was dark became clear.

The fact of survival and continuous progression of the individual is but the first step. What impresses me is the revelation Spiritualism gives of Mind working throughout the Universe, which raises our thoughts above material things and shows how true are the words of St. Paul, ' For this corruptible must put on incorruption, and this mortal must put on immortality. The things which are seen are temporal, those which are unseen are eternal.' These words sum up in my mind the foundation of true religion. They focus the cause which, when properly grasped, explains this urge in all of us to seek deeper into the mysteries of the Universe, to increase in knowledge and wisdom and thus attain greater at-onement with the Divine which we call God. That is true religion and in my opinion only in Spiritualism can it be found in its essence. Spiritualism is the only revelation which has come from a higher order of existence than man himself.

Every other religious system, including Christianity, is but man's speculations about the unknown in nature, about God, and the hereafter, based on a glimmer which our greater knowledge to-day turns into a shining light. We, with the increased knowledge, should not be tied to these ancient speculations and we would not be if the clergy were more honest.

and less ignorant. It is, however, not in their interest to enlighten the people or themselves that it is possible to get into touch with the hereafter through mediumship because, when this means is employed, the medium takes the place of the parson, who has always claimed, and does so still, that he only is the one appointed by God to reveal his will to man."

" I think," replied Ralph, " that my mind does not run on religious or philosophic lines. My interests in life are politics and that will be my life work. All the same I quite follow your argument, and I quite see how important it is to let the people know that survival is a fact. My job, however, concerns this earth, to make the people happier and more contented, better educated, and richer in this world's goods. I hope some day to enter Parliament and follow in the footsteps of my illustrious grandfather."

" You have our heartiest good wishes, Ralph, dear," said his aunt. " It is a great and noble work which your uncle would be the first to acknowledge, but he has the philosophical mind, the enquiring mind of the seer, and I believe he still has a great work before him in raising the people to a greater consciousness of the magnitude of their inheritance, not only in this world but in the one we shall all one day reach."

Talking thus, the evening sped by, and Ralph left the next morning with the knowledge that his mission had not been in vain, Mrs. Leader having written and posted a letter to Mrs. Trueman accepting her invitation for the Wednesday of the following week.

When saying good-bye, his uncle shook him

warmly by the hand, saying : '' Good-bye, Ralph, my
boy. You have been the messenger I have been
waiting for. My father has spoken to me from the
other side from time to time and what he has said was,
I now see, just leading up to this. It will mean a
break but I am prepared for it, because I know that
if I declare myself I shall have to stand before my
fellow bishops and explain my position. This will
end in my resignation from the Church.

I have, however, made up my mind to make my
stand for truth. The time has now come for me to
speak out regardless of the consequences, and speak
out I will.''

Mr. and Mrs. Trueman gave the bishop and his
wife a warm welcome to Sureway Court. They
arrived just before dinner, so after words of welcome
were spoken they were shown to their bedrooms.

At dinner the bishop sat next to his hostess and
Mrs. Leader beside her host. The others round the
table were Frank, Angela, Hope, Ernest Keen and
Grace Loveall.

Grace and Hope had become friends at Turnberry and in a letter Hope had received a week ago
Grace had told her of her engagement to Ernest Keen,
who had recently lost his mother. Knowing the
interest Hope's parents took in Spiritualism she had
mentioned how devoted Ernest was to his mother and
how nothing on earth would please him more than to
have an opportunity of again speaking to her. Could
Hope tell her of a reliable medium in London to whom
he could go ?

This letter being shown to Mrs. Trueman resulted in both Grace and Ernest being asked to Sureway Court for the same evening as were the bishop and his wife.

Ernest was a young London stockbroker and he and Grace hoped to be married in a few months' time.

Frank was also present at his particular request as he was anxious to hear more about the lost will, and Mrs. Trueman, in the kindness of her heart, asked Angela, also knowing, as she did, the growing affection between these two young people. Frank had tried to persuade his mother to come but without success. She could not bring herself to believe that it was right, as she put it, to disturb the dead, and took the advice of her parson who expressed his opinion to the same effect very strongly. His father said she could please herself but he for one believed it to be all humbug and not worth bothering about. These two adverse opinions made her, therefore, decide not to accept Mrs. Trueman's invitation.

Ralph had also been asked, but owing to an important engagement he could not accept, much to Hope's disappointment.

" I see," remarked Frank, looking across to Hope, " that there are nine of us to-night and there are only eight chairs in the séance room. How are we going to manage? "

" Oh, Angela can stop out and you can hold my hand instead."

" Try to be serious, Hope, " chimed in Angela.

" Well, we have other similar chairs which can be brought in to the room ; in fact, the extra chair is already in its place."

Mr. Trueman, during a pause in the conversation, addressed Hope :

" My dear, neither of your two friends who are here to-night for the first time probably know much about what they are likely to experience. After dinner will you take them to the séance room and explain things to them and what they may expect to happen? To be forewarned is to be forearmed. Isn't that so, Mrs. Leader?"

" I would like to be forearmed also," she replied, " and so would my husband, so perhaps you will take us up beforehand and explain to us your wonderful séance room."

" Delighted," replied Trueman, and, leaning across to Hope, remarked that as both the bishop and Mrs Leader wished to come they would all go up-stairs together, immediately after dinner.

Resuming his conversation with Mrs. Leader he explained : " It must be by the back stairs. We had our main staircase burned out about ten days ago and the new staircase is not yet ready for use."

This remark led him on to telling her of the experience they had during the séance when her nephew was present.

" Yes, Ralph told us. How terrifying ! and yet how wonderful to know that your escape was due to our friends on the other side who were watching over you and protecting you against danger. It reminds me of the words, ' He shall give his angels charge over thee to bear thee up in their arms lest at any time thou dash thy foot against a stone.' "

" Very true," replied Trueman. " How little do we realise how often our friends come back to us,

but we cannot go to them.   Only by our creating the
conditions on earth can we make ourselves aware of
their presence and then only if they care to come
back.   Everything really rests with them.   If the
desire exists to come back, and they know how to
do so, then they take any chances we give them to
speak to us.   If this is not so, then they don't, which
explains how people on earth are sometimes disappointed and wrongly conclude that, as their friends
never return to them, when they sit with mediums,
then communication never takes place."

      After dinner was over the four strangers followed
George Trueman upstairs to the séance room where
he explained the reason for everything and the duties
each instrument performed.   During the explanation
Miss Noteall put in an appearance and was introduced.
      " Now I think I have explained everything,"
said Trueman.   " Miss Noteall will now have things
adjusted and we shall return in a few minutes.   Let
us go to the drawing-room, and bring the others."
      The séance commenced punctually at nine-thirty
to which time all the clocks were set, and Miss Noteall, after placing the trumpets in the centre of the
circle, closed the door and took her seat in the
passage beside the voice-recording machine to which
she always gave close attention, as it was quite the
most important instrument under her charge.
      " The door when closed locks itself automati-
cally," remarked Trueman.   " No one can get in
from the outside, so when you hear voices speaking

they are produced either by those present in the flesh or by other beings outside the flesh. Everyone must be his own judge as to where the voices you will hear originate. All I would ask you to do is to reply to them in the same way as you would reply to voices on earth. They don't want to carry on a one-sided conversation. If they do not give their names then ask who is speaking and they will tell you."

The white light was switched off and the red light put on.

" Frank, did you find out anything about Sandy?" asked Mrs. Trueman. " You were going to write and enquire."

" Yes, I got a letter a few days ago from the hotel proprietor at Kirkenreola. It was all true. Sandy died on the twelfth of March of this year, just as he said he did."

" Well, who should know better than he as to when he died," remarked Hope, which remark caused general laughter.

" Well, I never knew he had died," replied Frank. " No one in this house ever knew of Sandy, and yet Sandy's voice spoke to me and told me that he (Sandy) had died on twelfth March of this year. I enquire and find that the voice spoke the truth. I can only conclude that the voice was really Sandy's voice and that Sandy, or the intelligence I knew on earth under that name, still continues in existence and can still produce the same voice as he had on earth even though his body was buried. That is the difficulty. How can anyone speak without a body?"

" Frank, my boy," said Trueman, " you have not yet mastered the first principle of Spiritualism, that we have a duplicate etheric body which carries our mind, intelligence, memory and character, all combined, with it into another order of existence. Till you get that firmly into your head you will never understand how it is possible for those who die to come and speak to us in the presence of a medium, by gathering teleplasm round their etheric vocal organs and thus again vibrate our atmosphere. Now I shall put out the red light and switch on the glow light for a few minutes."

" By the way, Frank," asked Angela, " did you find out if there is a Gothic room and a secret chamber at Huntingham ? "

" Yes, my mother faintly remembers a room called by that name, but she never heard of a secret room. It was when she was a girl that she stayed there, in the time of Alfred Hunt's father. Alfred and she were good friends, but when he was about twenty-five his regiment was ordered to India. Then she married dad, and she saw Alfred only occasionally on his return home. He lived a bachelor's life at Huntingham, which he inherited when he was thirty. He died at forty, about ten years ago. I hope we shall hear more about it to-night."

The glow light was now switched off and all sat in silence, broken only by the faint hum of the electric vibrator.

" What is that hum," asked the bishop.

" That," replied Trueman, " comes from the atmospheric vibrator which vibrates the atmosphere. They speak better if the atmosphere is in vibration."

" To understand this great subject we must have a considerable knowledge of physics," replied the bishop. '' When I hear my ignorant colleagues condemning Spiritualism, as if they knew all about it, I think often of the blind leading the blind, whereas a man like yourself, Mr. Trueman, who has made a life-long study of both physics and psychics will doubtless admit that you are only on the threshold and that, like Newton, you have only picked up a few pebbles from the shore of knowledge.''

'' Well, the clergy condemned evolution and every other important discovery made over the last four hundred years,'' replied Trueman.

'' Keep quiet,'' broke in Mrs. Trueman. '' I see a form building up in front of Frank.''

A minute later a voice spoke.

'' Here I am, Frank. I shall tell you everything now. Conditions are good, so listen. My name is Alfred William Charles Hunt, the owner, when on earth, of Huntingham in the county of Essex, where my ancestors lived for over four hundred years. I never married, but I greatly loved your mother. If my regiment had not been hurriedly ordered to India I would have asked her to be my wife. The news of her marriage to your father was a great blow to me, as I was contemplating coming home to ask her to be my wife.

I left a large fortune which my brother inherited. In my will I instructed my trustees to pay over to your mother the sum of fifty thousand pounds. I also left her a diamond necklace and a sapphire ring which belonged to my mother, but she never received the money nor the jewels as the will could not be found after my death. Now, here is the point. The will can be found because I kept it in a secret room

leading off the Gothic room. I found this room by
accident and foolishly kept my papers there, and
bonds worth thousands, also valuable jewellery,
without telling anyone how to get into it. Being a
bachelor I had no one I could trust with the secret.
Owing to my sudden death the secret went with me.
Now take a careful note of what I am going to say.
In the Gothic room above the fireplace is a large
mantel-piece, beautifully carved. It is as old as the
house. It is supported on either side by two square
pillars. Each is clustered in front with bunches of
grapes. It is the pillar on the left as you enter the
room I now want to speak about. Push with your
finger on the fourth grape from the bottom of the top
bunch, and at the same time with your left hand push
inwards the disc you will find on the side of the pillar
nearest the window and the pillar will swing open if
you use a little strength with your left arm. The disc
is the shield of the man carved on the left side of the
pillar. Is that clear?"

" Quite," replied Frank.

" Well, once the pillar has opened like a door
you will see an entrance. Go in and you will find my
will inside a black japanned deed box, on the top of
the other contents, also the ring and necklace, in a
small box, addressed to your mother. That is all.
Now, I must go. Good-bye!"

" Just one question before you go," said Frank.
" Why have you only told us this now?"

" Why have you never given me the chance to
tell you before?" came the reply. " I was present
when you told your mother that you were coming here
to a séance, so I have taken the first chance you gave

me. Au revoir, until we meet here. Give your mother my love and say that it has made me happy to see her so happy with your father.''

'' Now you know,'' said Hope, '' that dead men do tell tales. I hope when you come into your fortune, Frank, you will remember a poor girl whose dress allowance never meets her needs.''

'' The money is not mine,'' replied Frank. '' Even if it is all true, how we are to get this will is the problem. My mother knows Lord and Lady Kilforfun only slightly and even if she did know them well we could not very well go and stay with them as guests and then commit a robbery.''

'' It is not robbery to find a lost will,'' said Hope.

'' We shall discuss this afterwards,'' remarked Mrs. Trueman. '' Someone wishes to speak. Keep quiet, please ; I see a form building up.''

A woman's voice spoke before Mrs. Trueman had finished speaking. It was opposite Ernest Keen, and because of Mrs. Trueman speaking he did not catch what was said.

'' Someone spoke to me,'' Ernest remarked, '' but I could not make out what was said.''

He had no sooner finished this remark than the same voice, but stronger, again spoke.

'' Ernest, darling, I am your mother : Madre you called me, your father called me Mousie, because I was always calm and placid. I am so pleased to be able to tell you that I am well and happy. It was such a wrench leaving you both. My poor health had gone. I am well and strong again. Such a lovely place this is. I live with Edith. Such a lot of friends met me when I arrived here, and some are here with me now."

"Oh Madre, is it really you?" enquired the incredulous Ernest. "Tell me something I can tell the pater so that he may be sure it is really you."

"Tell him, Erny, that after dinner last night he went into the drawing-room, took up my photograph and kissed it, saying : 'My darling, some day may we meet again. You were always my treasure. I don't know how I can live without you.' I was beside him and gave him a kiss."

"Yes, go on."

"Tell him this. He is not to take his own life. He must wait till his time comes. He went into a chemist shop the day after my funeral and bought some laudanum, telling the chemist that it was to put a dog to sleep. I am glad he was brave enough to throw it away. We need not be separated ; he can speak to me anytime he likes if he will go to a good medium. Now I must go, darling. I am not used to this, but if you come back I shall be able to speak longer the next time. Bring Pussy with you."

Then there was silence broken by Grace, saying : "Why bring Pussy with you the next time?"

"My mother did not much like being called Mousie so she called my father Pussy when he called her Mousie."

"Who is Edith?" enquired Mrs. Leader.

"Edith is my sister, who died three years ago."

"Well," said Trueman, "you have something to tell your father. I don't doubt it is all true though he may not like to admit about the laudanum. Was that your mother's voice?"

"Yes, it was mother's voice, all right," replied Ernest. "It seems too strange to be true, and yet who knew these pet names but our three selves?"

Then something strange happened.

Angela said: "I see the form of a Chinese woman—it is standing before Grace. It came over to me first of all and looked into my face as if looking to see if I were the person she wanted. Then she moved over to Grace. Such a kindly face."

Just then from the trumpet proceeded what can only be described as gibberish, which ended in a soft, melodious song.

Grace, instead of replying in English, spoke back in the same language, and this went on for a time. When the conversation finished a chorus came from the others : "Whatever was that? What language was that? Did you understand her, Grace?"

"Oh yes," replied Grace, "that was Chinese. My old Amah. She told me about something that happened to both of us in China."

"What is an Amah?" asked Hope.

"A Chinese nurse," replied Grace "That song she sang is what she used to sing to me—a lullaby."

"I never knew you lived in China," went on Hope. "Was that really Chinese she spoke to you?"

"Oh yes, the Canton dialect which was spoken where we lived. My father was head of one of the big banks there. I came to England to school when I was fourteen, but I have never forgotten the language."

This conversation was interrupted by a voice speaking to Ernest :

" Ich bin Karl.   Erinnern Sie sich meiner noch?
Wir waren Studenten zusammen in Bonn.   Ich
verunglückte tödlich auf meinem Motorrad.

Sie haben mir immer gesagt dass das einmal
geschehen würde.

Ja Karl, ich erinnere mich ihrer sehr gut.
Erzählen sie mir mehr sodass ich sicher sein kann dass
sie es sind.

Als ich in England war besuchte ich sie.   Sie
waren Älle sehr freundlich zu mir.   Ihre mutter ver-
anlasste mich mit ihr hierher zu kommen aber ich bin
dies nicht gewöhnt.   Ich habe nie gewusst dass dies
möglich wäre.   Teilen Sie es meinem Vater und
meiner Mutter mit.   Ihre adresse ist Kaiser Fried-
rich Strasse, Zwei, Frankfurt."

" Ja, Ja," replied Ernest.   Then came silence.

" Very interesting and evidential," said the
bishop.   " You should write to the address given
and find if he was killed on his motor cycle.   I
suppose everything else he said was true."

" Oh yes, we were both at Bonn together.   I
told him often that he would be killed on his motor
bicycle, and he did stay with us in England."

" Well, the address of his parents is likely to be
true also," remarked Trueman, " though if you do
write to them be careful how you put it to them.   Germany, speaking generally, knows very little about this
subject.   They killed off thousands of witches in the
old days, and this went on till the eighteenth century.
Mediumship is consequently at a very low ebb over
there, as it is an hereditary gift.   The witches were
just what we to-day call mediums.   Does anyone
here know German?"   To which question the reply,

'No' came from everyone except Ernest and the bishop.

"Now, bishop," remarked Mrs. Trueman, "I think someone wants to speak to you, so all keep quiet."

"Edward, I am your father, Vincent Leader. I have spoken to you before from this world in which I am now living. I have been leading you up to your present line of thought. If you want proof as to who is speaking then what does this mean to you?—

'Those who so act and so live as to give proof of loyalty and uprightness, of fairness and generosity, who are free from all passion, caprice, and insolence, have great strength of character.'"

"You quoted that to me," replied the bishop, "when I told you I had made up my mind to become a parson. You were grieved————."

"Stop; let me tell you!" interrupted Vincent Leader.

"Yes, I was grieved and I said, 'I am sorry a son of mine is mixing himself up with an ancient superstition and with those who lived by deluding the people into believing it is true.' If you must go back to the past I told you that you would get enough in Cicero's definition of a good man. Is that not so, Edward?"

"Yes, father, you were right and I was wrong; but I am not too old to make amends. I have decided to speak out."

"Speak out you must. The Church will stifle this truth if it can, but it is so shaky now in Protestant countries that it only needs a prominent Church leader like yourself to speak out to make an immense impression on the people. You can do so, as you have plenty of money and are not dependent on your stipend. Make a bold stand ; but they will make it impossible for you to do otherwise than resign. Be another Ridley or Latimer. They made a stand which you can do more easily to-day than they could in their day. The Church cannot now burn you. Break the wall of ignorance and arrogance and the disintegration will become more rapid. The truth must break through some day. You make the first opening and accept the consequences like a man.''

Vincent Leader paused for a second and then went on :

'' Be another Erasmus. Though a priest he did not hesitate to expose the errors of his Church's teaching. The Pope offered to make him a Cardinal if he would keep silent but he refused to do so. Four hundred years ago that was a dangerous thing to do. He was a brave man and the greatest scholar of his age. Be as brave, as honest and as candid as he was. He undermined the edifice of superstition and in the interval between then and now its walls have cracked, its stones have crumbled, and it is now ready to be razed to the ground. It only needs knowledge, courage and effort.

When the people realise that Christ is a mythological creation of the ancients, who lived only in the imagination of those who worshipped him, the foundation on which Christianity rests has gone, and the entire collapse of all which rests on this false idea is sure and certain. The man Jesus was used by the Church Fathers as a prop to wind the Christ idea.

round, so as to materialise it sufficiently to enable the people to accept it.   Thus, what was never more than a theological speculation was identified with a human being who came to be worshipped as a God-man.   It had all been done before by the priests of previous religions, and it was done for the last time by the Pagan priests who called themselves Christians.   It will never be done again.

I know of no one who has been able to trace the Jesus of the Christian religion in this world in which I now live, but if he ever lived on earth he was an obscure Jewish martyr.   At his death he would arrive here like everyone else, no special notice being taken of him.   He became famous on earth only by the miraculous stories told about him, years after his death, by the founders of the Christian Church who made use of him in order to propound the doctrine that the God Christ had become man and suffered for the sins of humanity.

Whether Jesus ever existed or not is quite unimportant.   The knowledge that you now have of life after death, which comes from communication between the two states of existence, is, however, all important.   This will satisfy all religious desires and give everyone a foundation on which to build a firm and lasting philosophy to help them on earth and here where I now live.

You, of course, understand that the Christian religion means nothing to us here.   After we forget what we were erroneously taught on earth we cease to be Christians, Jews, Hindoos or anything else, these being only earth labels, which mean nothing to us here.''

Vincent Leader paused a second and then slowly, enunciating every word, in measured tones, he said :

" My message to you to-night from the world in which I live is this—Edward Leader, you must speak out and be an honest man."

" Yes, father, I will.   I have made up my mind to do so, and I am glad to know that you approve—it gives me strength to do the work which is before me."

" Well, I need say no more.   You must make your own plans and carry them through as you think right.   It is most fortunate that your dear wife approves of your decision.   I heard all you and she said to Ralph at the palace.   Go forward, then.   You will help to light a torch of knowledge and truth which will never be put out.   Good-bye, and remember, I shall come and speak to you any time you give me the opportunity."

Vincent Leader then moved over to Mrs. Leader and said : " Katherine, my dear, it is unnecessary for me to ask you to give Edward all your help and support, but I did not wish to leave without just giving you my greeting and love."

" Thank you, Mr. Leader.   Edward will get all my help and support.   Accept my thanks for your kind greeting and give my love to your dear wife."

Thus ended the first act in what became the most outstanding case of its kind.   The public became aware of the second and following steps, but only a few of the bishop's intimate friends knew what led him to take the line he did.   To the public, the first act in the drama commenced by the issue of a Diocesan letter to his people.

" Well, Edward," remarked his wife, " the die

is cast.   That means good-bye to the Palace.''

" It is better to have my mind a palace than for my body to live in one," he replied.

From now till the end of the séance various friends of the Truemans spoke, but, as what they said was personal and not of public interest, it is unnecessary to repeat the conversations.   Godfrey, the control, was the last to speak, saying that the séance must now end as the medium could not stand more.

The next morning George Trueman asked the bishop to come into his business room.

The two men sat down, the bishop accepting a cigarette while Trueman took out his pipe and filled it.   When he had it going to his satisfaction he enquired : " If you are in a position to tell me, may I ask how you propose to proceed, as you will realise as well as I do what a momentous step you are taking? ''

" I have it all planned out," the bishop replied. " I shall issue a Diocesan letter telling my people that the Dean has asked you, and that you have kindly accepted his invitation, to preach in Alfortruth Cathedral on, ' Our Life after Death and the Teachings of Spiritualism.'   I shall tell them how I have become convinced of the truths of Spiritualism and that the Church must accept them or finally perish. On behalf of the Dean will you accept this invitation? ''

"Are you speaking with the Dean's authority ?"
"Yes.   Before I came here yesterday I told him

that I proposed giving you this invitation and he readily concurs. He may have to leave the Church also, but he doesn't mind. His wife has money. He, like myself, has had some remarkable evidence of survival and is determined that the people should know about it. As things are at present no leading parson dare stand up in a pulpit and declare that he has been to a medium and received conviction of survival. One or two defy their bishops who pass them by as they are not prominent men. It is considered better policy to leave them alone than make their opinions public.

With a Bishop or Dean it is different, and up till now the Dean and I have kept silent in the pulpit on these matters, but our consciences will not permit us to do so any longer. Both the Dean and I have decided that the time has now come for us to speak out."

"That being so," replied Trueman, "I have much pleasure in accepting the Dean's invitation, and will you give him my congratulations? I have never spoken in a Church of England place of worship on this subject but I have done so in a Congregational Church and in a Presbyterian Church. In these denominations more latitude is given to the parson, though I know that it is discouraged by the leaders of both Churches. What date would suit you best?"

"That," said the bishop, "must be left for the present, but I shall give you ample time to prepare your remarks and, at the same time, I shall give you a choice of dates."

"You need not worry about giving me time to prepare my remarks. I speak regularly to far larger audiences than your Cathedral will hold. I am speaking, for instance, in the King's Hall next Sunday evening. When leading Spiritualists speak, the largest halls available are filled to overflowing. The public is only too anxious to hear what the Church is keeping from them. I can promise you a full Cathedral when I speak, not because of the speaker but because of the subject."

" Yes, I have heard of these large meetings, but I have never been to one. I must go some day."

" When you leave the Church I can promise you an invitation not only to the platform of the King's Hall for the Sunday evening service but an invitation to speak from the platform. In fact, I think I can go further and say that the invitation will be, not for the King's Hall, but for the Royal Albert Hall. The Spiritualists in London fill the Albert Hall every Armistice Sunday, and on other occasions, and will do so again whenever you are ready to accept the invitation to be the speaker."

" Are there regular Spiritualist meetings all over the country? " enquired the bishop.

" In every town of any size there is a Spiritualist Church. In the large towns there are many, some holding nearly a thousand people, and they are always filled to the door. In London on Sunday evenings there are many Spiritualist services, the one in the Queen's Hall being the largest."

" How very interesting. I see I have much to learn," said the bishop, " but I think the time has come for us to leave. I told my chauffeur to be at the door at ten and it is that time now. I thank you for all your kindness to us. I wonder where Mrs.

Trueman is—I must thank her also. You have been more than kind to two strangers, though I am glad to say that is a word that no longer applies to us.''

Mr. and Mrs. Trueman and the rest of the house party were on the front door steps to see the bishop and his wife depart, and when good-byes were being said the bishop gave Mr. and Mrs. Trueman a warm invitation to Alfortruth Palace.

'' Your husband has promised to speak in my Cathedral,'' remarked the bishop to Mrs. Trueman. '' We shall be delighted if you will spend that week-end with us. The country around is beautiful and we shall show you the principal places of interest. Thank you for your great kindness to us and for your wonderful mediumship. It was all too wonderful for words.''

This invitation having been accepted the car moved off, and so ended the beginning of the Bishop of Alfortruth's stand for truth.

CHAPTER VIII.

THE SECRET CHAMBER AT HUNTINGHAM.

Lord and Lady Kilforfun were seated in the Gothic room at Huntingham on the Saturday following the events recorded in the previous chapter. Breakfast was just over. He was reading the *Sporting News* and she was going through her morning correspondence.

"Diana Hunter can come, and so can Tony Goodenough," she remarked, "so we shall have two guests in the house for the week-end. I am asking a few people in for dinner."

Just as Lord Kilforfun was about to reply the butler opened the door and announced : " My lady, a young man has called in reply to your advertisement about the vacancy for a footman."

"He has not been long about it," she replied. "He must be a local boy. What is he like, Glen? Will he suit, do you think?"

"A nice, well-mannered youth, just the height and build of the one that has gone," Glen replied. "Will you see him, my lady, as he can come at once? He is in the housekeeper's room."

"I shall come just in a minute," she replied.

The result of the interview was that the young man was engaged. He was recommended by his parson, who spoke well of his character, and gave further information to the effect that he knew him and his parents, and that he came of a very respectable family.

"Have you been in a situation before this one?"
Lady Kilforfun enquired of the applicant.

"No, my lady, I have not been in service before,
but I shall soon pick up the work. I am quick at
learning and if the butler shows me once what to do
I won't make a mistake."

"Well, I am having people to dinner to-night,
and your build will fit the last footman's livery; so,
as we are alone at lunch, Glen the butler will tell you
what to do. Now try and do not make any
mistake."

She got up and rang the bell.

"Glen, I have engaged—ah, what is your name,
again?"

"Frank Wiseman, my lady."

"Well, Glen, take Frank and show him his
room. He starts at once."

Frank, with his bag, was taken out by the back
door to some outbuildings, up a stair and introduced
to his bedroom—quite comfortable and roomy.

"Now, here is your livery, my boy," said Glen.
"Change at once, and I shall get you into your work
as quickly as possible."

"Well," said Frank to himself when he was
alone, "that is the first step. How fortunate I saw
that advertisement in the local paper—a chance in
a thousand. But I don't like this room being outside.
How am I to get into the house at night, and it is
only at night that I can be sure of finding the Gothic
room empty. Luck has favoured me so far, and it
will, I am sure, to the end."

Huntingham was a large Tudor mansion situated
in a spacious park, the main drive being nearly a mile

long. It had four castellated towers and many chimneys of the twisted pattern usually associated with this type of architecture. It was built as a square, enclosing a courtyard. On one side was an archway through which one passed to reach the main entrance door in the courtyard. This door led into what was once the dining hall but was now used as a lounge, from which a door at either side led into the other apartments of the house.

Frank had no difficulty in picking up his duties. Having to go into the Gothic room to fetch something he took the chance of examining the mantel-piece, which was just as the former owner had described it at the séance. The grapes, beautifully carved, were prominent, and on either side was carved the figure of a man holding a shield.

He had time to carefully examine both the grapes and the shield but could not find anything to reveal the secret they so carefully retained. He then put his finger lightly on the fourth grape from the bottom of the top bunch but it was just like the others, nothing to show that it could be moved. An examination of the shield revealed the same master workmanship.

He turned away with a sigh. How much he would have liked to test it without further delay, but it was too dangerous. The Gothic room which had been used by the former owner as his business room was now the private sitting-room of the master and mistress who were continually in and out of it.

" Well, I have found my way about and everything so far seems o.k.," he mused, " but how I am to get into the house at night is a puzzle. It is much too dangerous to try to get at the will during the day."

Lunch passed off well and Glen was delighted with the new footman, who seemed to understand very well what was expected of him.

"You will do all right," he remarked. "Why! there is the bell ; one of them already. Now, come with me."

The guest proved to be Diana Hunter, a tall, bright, good-looking girl, who was received by Glen as no stranger to the place.

"Well, Glen, it's nice to see you again. All well—your wife well? That's good. You always look the same and give me the same hearty welcome."

"Always glad to see you, miss, and so are the master and mistress ; that I know."

Glen had no sooner shown her into the library and announced her arrival to his mistress than the sound of another car was heard. He hurried back to the entrance door. Frank ran down the steps to open the door of a car when, instead of waiting for the occupant to descend, he rushed to the back of the car and began unstrapping the luggage.

"What is he thinking about?" muttered Glen, who ran down the steps and stood by the door.

"Glad to see you, sir. Yes, we shall get all your luggage out. Just come this way, please."

"Well, I am done for now," quoth Frank. "None other than Tony. He must spot me sooner or later. I'd better make a bolt for it now before he sees me. It was fortunate I saw him first."

But this way out of the difficulty was not to be, because Glen just then appeared.

"Take Mr. Goodenough's things up to the Jacobean room, and remember when guests arrive to wait at the car door till they get out. What way was that to receive a guest?''

Frank muttered his apologies and lifted the luggage.

'' It is the room straight in front of the main staircase—you will find it easily. Start unpacking and laying out his evening clothes. Put the rest in drawers or in the wardrobe. I shall be up in a few minutes to give you a hand.''

Frank had no sooner started to unpack than he heard Lady Kilforfun's voice outside : '' Yes, Tony, this is your room. I think you will find everything you want. Oh, I see Frank is putting out your things. He will look after you.''

Frank, fortunately, had his back to the door and had enough presence of mind to pretend to be doing something.

'' Come down when you are ready,'' she went on. '' You will find us in the lounge,'' and with these words she went out and closed the door.

'' I must tell him and trust he will not give me away—it is the only way,'' Frank decided, and no sooner had this been done than Tony said :

'' Have you seen my pipe? I can't find it anywhere.''

Frank turned round and faced him.

'' Frank !'' ejaculated Tony, '' whatever does this mean, old man?''

'' Lock the door, Tony, and I'll tell you, and for my sake keep quiet. I am here under false pretences, as you may gather.''

'' Tell me, old man,'' said Tony ; '' you can trust me implicitly ; I won't give you away.''

"It started at Turnberry," Frank commenced. "You remember the Trueman's? Well, I went to his house and we had a séance."

"A séance! By jove! Babbling with spooks, eh! Has some wizard turned you into a footman? Well, that is great! Tell me about it."

Just then a knock came at the door.

"Yes," said Tony, "who is there?"

"It is Glen, sir."

"Oh, Glen, I am changing, I can't let you in. Everything is all right. Don't wait."

"Well, I must hurry," said Frank, "or he will find out that I am missing."

Frank then quickly told Tony about the lost will, the secret chamber, and his reason for being at Huntingham as the footman, without, however, giving any details.

"It was the only way, old man," Frank concluded. "We talked it over the next day and thought of every possible way. I got a fortnight's leave from Guy's and came down to Bishop's Stortford yesterday to take a look around, hoping I might get a job on the place. Yesterday evening in the dark I prowled around the house to see if I could slip in, but it couldn't be done. I went back to my hotel rather nonplussed, but just before going to bed I picked up the local paper which had been issued that evening and I caught the heading ' Situations Vacant.' Running my eyes down I saw that a footman was wanted here, so this morning I paid my bill, packed my bag, and took a taxi to the entrance gate nearest the house. I did not want to carry my bag up the main drive, which is a mile long.

I presented myself before anyone else could possibly get in before me and, fortunately, I got the job. Lady Kilforfun asked me some rather awkward questions about whether I had been in service before, but fortunately my mother's parson gave me and my people a good character. As I came under my own name the parson did what I asked, just saying that he had known me and my people for years and that we were respectable, decent people. The old boy, I am sure, wondered what I was up to."

"Well, Frank, old man, trust me, I won't give you away ; but you had better open the door in case Glen comes back. He will be looking for you."

As Frank opened the door, Glen was coming up the stairs.

"Where have you been ?" he enquired. "I have been looking for you everywhere."

"Oh, that is all right, Glen," said Tony. "He has laid out my things to perfection. He knows his work well."

Meanwhile Frank slipped downstairs to the pantry.

Dinner that night was a lively meal. Frank did his duties to the satisfaction of both mistress and butler.

Lord Kilforfun confided to Diana that the footman had just been engaged that day : "You know," he went on, "it was beastly awkward ; we were without one for a week. I had to sack the last man for insolence."

"Well, you have made a good change," remarked Diana, whose eyes followed Frank as he went about his duties.

"Yes, quite a bit of luck getting him so quickly. We only put the advertisement in last night's local paper ; but what I was going to tell you is this : I took the last one out otter hunting with me, but he was too chicken-hearted. He hated to see the kill. This is what happened : We walked up stream with the hounds and soon struck the ' drag,'—the scent, you know—left by the otter. The pace quickened till we came to the reed and osier beds where there are deep pools and shallows. The hounds got well away in a deep pool and soon the otter was dislodged. I spotted him when he came up to breathe ; he was just in front of the hounds, going for all he was worth."

"How exciting," said Diana. "I wish I had been there."

"' Keep him on the move,' yelled the master. ' He is under that bush there. Someone over there beat him out. Now he is going for the shallows.' ' Watch that ditch,' shouted someone.

The water had become muddy by now but we soon spotted him again and then the shout went up, ' He's over the shallows.' Immediately we were all in after him to keep him from getting back to deep water."

"Yes, go on," said Diana.

"By now he was hard pressed in the shallows. Every time he came up to breathe he was beaten back. Oh, it was great sport. At last, choked with mud, and, in desperation, he took to land in an effort to get cover in the osier beds.

We tried to stop him and I shouted to Jim—he was the footman I sacked—' Run ahead of him, Jim. Follow the hounds.' And what do you think the impudent blighter said?''

'' No, tell me,'' said Diana.

'' ' Go and do your own dirty work ; I'm off. I can't stand any more of this fiendish sport.'

'' ' Fiendish sport,' I replied. ' If that is what you think, then off you go and don't let me see you again. Ask Glen for your pay and clear out.' ''

'' Quite the right thing to do with soft muffs like that,'' agreed Diana.

'' Then I went after the hounds,'' continued Lord Kilforfun. '' Everyone present had gone mad with excitement. The hounds had got the otter and were tearing him to pieces, worrying him, and pulling him this way and that. He was screaming and took a long time to die because of his thick skin.

When he was dead I blooded two kids who were out for the first time, smearing his blood over their faces, and presented to each, as a momento, the 'pad' cut from his mangled body.''

'' What a day you must have had,'' said Diana. '' The best sport I ever had was otter hunting once in Sussex. I was in at the kill. I shall never forget the fun. Were you at the Waterloo Cup meeting?''

'' No, I haven't attended it for some years,'' he replied. '' Have you?''

'' No, not recently, but I was at a Coursing meeting last week,'' replied Diana. '' The ground was enclosed on three sides by a deep, wide ditch, the fourth side being open country. One by one the hares were driven in by the beaters.

Two greyhounds waited on leash for the hare to be driven in.   When this happened the hounds yelped like furies and the crowd went mad with excitement.

When the hare realised that it was trapped on three sides it made for the open country.   It was given eighty yards start, when the hounds were released.   It was all so exciting.   Everyone was keyed up and after a moment's intense silence up went a mighty yell.

Gradually the hare got weaker and the hounds nearer.   They snapped and missed : snapped again and got it.   Then they started to chivy it.   It lay wriggling and squealing, crying like a child.   It was a good show that day.   Only one of the dozen got away ; but that disappointed some, as I heard one man say that he considered it was a bad show.''

'' Well, we get good sport here coursing hares,'' said Lord Kilforfun, '' but I can't attend as often as I would like as I am out fox hunting four days a week. When I was at Eton I did a lot of beagling.   Not many hares got away, I can tell you.   We were all very keen.   Once so keen that we got into an awful row because we went out coursing on Good Friday. So long as we kept off holy days the College authorities encouraged the sport, and long may they do so.

It is good for those kids to get blooded young. The parsons like to get the kids young to make them Christians—quite right too.   I am a strong supporter of the Church.   I read the lessons every Sunday. Blood them young, I say, and it will make them good sportsmen all their lives.''

'' No Christian would ever think of hunting on a holy day,'' said Diana.   '' I have never heard of it being done.   It would be a sin to do so.''

Tony Goodenough, after listening to his partner telling of a fox which had taken refuge in a chimney of a disused house, only to be burned out by the South Durham Hunt, related how it had climbed on to the roof from which it fell to be torn to pieces by the hounds, then went on to tell his latest experience :

'' I was in Leicestershire the other day and had one of the best runs I ever had.   Off we went at the very start as we found quickly.   The fox was a nippy one.   On he went for ten miles without a break. He tried to get to earth several times but they were all stopped up.   On he went, but we saw he was getting done.   The hounds got closer, the excitement increased, and at last we thought we had him, but no—he got to earth at last.''

'' I saw an article in *The Field* of January last year,'' replied the lady to whom he was speaking, '' that hit the nail on the head.   I can't quite quote what it said, but something like this—

' No fox can be hunted as a fox should be if the country is not properly stopped up.   If everyone would work together we would not hear so much of hounds being deprived of blood as they are to-day.' ''

'' I quite agree,'' said Tony, '' and that is what I thought when this one got to earth.   Well, we tried to bolt him with terriers but that was no use so we started to dig him out.   He was done to the world, his heart and lungs practically burst.   He was too far gone to dig himself further in so we nabbed him all right, and the hounds got their blood lust satisfied.''

'' I always say,'' said a weedy-looking youth sitting on the other side of Diana, '' that you should always keep a terrier in at the fox, for if you don't he may gain ground and dig himself in further. When the hounds are in want of blood, stop all the holes round the earth and keep him in. If the hounds want blood and have had a long run it is the best way to kill the fox when he earths, but if they have had a short run it is better for the hounds to turn him out upon the earth. Let them work for him, I say. It is the blood that will do them most good."

" I quite agree," said Diana. " They must be blooded regularly or they will lose taste for their work."

" I remember," went on the weedy youth, " when I was hunting with the South Knotts Hunt. One day we chased the fox into a field near some houses. It had taken refuge in a drain and two terriers were sent in after it and we began digging him out. When we found him the huntsmen started pushing their whips into the drain, one getting the fox from behind and the other from the front. This went on for twenty minutes and we could hear the fox and terriers fighting underground. At last his head appeared. He had a fearful look in his eyes, with his face red with blood. A few more prods with the whips and he was forced out. He made a vain attempt for his life, but he was scarcely out before the hounds pounced on him."

" I can imagine your excitement," said Diana.

" The hounds were yelping," went on the narrator, " and for a minute or so we could not see the fox. Then the hounds wheeled round and we caught a glimpse of the fox quivering as it was being torn limb from limb and its inside was being torn out.

Soon it was a mangled carcase. So ended one of the best day's sport I have had this year."

"Digging out a fox is cold work," replied Diana. "I always take a gallop after it is over to get warmed up. After a dig out the other day the hounds got hold of a badger. If those badgers are not protected they will all be killed, as they have no chance against the hounds."

Then the conversation turned to stag hunting; one guest telling of a particularly good day's sport in the New Forest, and the fine kill after an hour's hot pursuit. Another capped this by recounting a day's sport he had when the stag took to the sea and swam for hours, only to be torn to pieces when it came near the shore.

Then Frank overheard Lady Kilforfun describe the visit of an artist to Huntingham who had objected to the numerous prints hung all over the house depicting hunting scenes.

"'They are not true art,' he told me. 'No real artist would paint pictures showing animals in such pain. It is neither ennobling nor beautiful.'"

"Why?" said her companion. "If he had seen a good run of the hounds he would have seen the prettiest picture in the land."

"Oh, he saw us all out in our glory," she replied. "He even saw the kill which took place here in our park. He walked home alongside of me and I was telling him of the glorious day we had had, the risks we had run, when he said:

'All to kill a little fox. One would think you were all starving when you put yourselves to so much trouble and risk to get him.'

" ' We don't eat him,' I told him.

" ' Why then do you hunt the poor little animal?' he enquired.

" ' Just for the fun of chasing him,' I told him. ' It is the best way I know to build up our characters and make us men and women.' Can you imagine what he replied? He then asked me why I did not hunt a cat or a dog, seeing hunting was such fine sport for building up the character. Why not chase and kill every cat and dog you see, and thus never miss a chance several times a day of becoming finer and more beautiful characters, instead of doing so only four times a week?"

" These sentimental fools have always been the curse of all true sportmen," came the response of her companion.

Lady Kilforfun then told of how somebody had stuck up a poster near the Church before morning service a few Sundays back, reading :

WHY IS IT CRUEL
TO SET A DOG
ON A CAT
AND NOT CRUEL
TO SET THIRTY DOGS
ON A FOX?

" The vicar, like a true sportsman," she went on, " took it down at once " : ' I can't offend my congregation,' he told me, ' with sentimental sob-stuff like that.' "

" Good fellow," replied her neighbour. "I saw, the other day, that the railway companies refused to allow their advertising agents to put up this same poster on the railway stations. It will be a bad day for England when these soft-hearted humanists stop blood sport. We have always had the Church with us, and always shall. The railways are evidently also our friends, and so we may take it that the backbone of England is behind us. Whatever would we have to do if there were no huntin' or shootin' or fishin'?''

Frank was heartily sick of it all and his thoughts ran thus :

'' I suppose that people, who can believe in a God who sacrificed and shed the blood of his Son, and who have a regular weekly cannibalistic ceremony for the purpose of eating their god and drinking his blood which was shed, think that they have every right to treat animals in the same cruel way. Is cruelty of every description not particularly encouraged and prescribed in their Holy Book? For nineteen centuries Christendom has been nurtured and fed on sacrifice and bloodshed as a requisite to salvation. The people make their God in their own image, and the Christian God just typifies the mentality of Christian people. Throughout the Christian era there has been more cruelty, war and suffering than in any other period of history. Give me Trueman's religion, whatever the clergy may say. Parsons have never condemned blood sports, and often have been their ardent supporters. I suppose this kind of talk will go on the whole evening, and they will get on to shooting next. I imagine that they are all good Christians, while Spiritualists, who believe that animals have souls and should never be made to suffer, are the servants of the devil, according to the Church.

The mental level of these Christian people is so low that, instead of reaching Heaven as they expect to do when they die, through the shedding of the precious blood of the Lamb, it is more likely that they will grovel in darkness, to be helped by Miss Noteall and Mrs. Trueman at one of their rescue séances.

I suppose, however, that it would be incongruous for the Christian Church to go against blood sports when their chief God, that barbarous fiend Jehovah, is worshipped and ' His Holy Word,' or ' God's Holy Word,' as the people call it, which advocates far worse slaughter and cruelty than animal killing, is looked on as sacred, and kept in every Church in the land.

What a God to worship, who is believed to have written that cruel, degrading story about a poor helpless woman, as given in the nineteenth chapter of Judges.   Professor Laski in his book, *A Century of Municipal Progress*, remarks that ' the state of English towns a hundred years ago was surely a condition of barbarism that would have put a citizen of the Roman Empire to blush.'   Was this astonishing when the mental level of the people was so low that they could believe in their God being the author of the Holy Bible?   All the progress we have made over the last hundred years has been accomplished by those who ceased to believe such blasphemy.

Jehovah wrote many another cruel and revolting story, but that one in Judges was certainly his *chef d'œuvre*. They are translated by Christians into every language in the world, and millions of copies are circulated by Christian money every year in the attempt to get the 'Heathen' to become Christians.''*

Thinking thus he started cleaning up and when this was finished he went off to his room to make his plans for recovering the will. '' The sooner I get out of this blood-thirsty house the better. What a difference there is between the mental level of the occupants of Huntingham and Sureway Court.''

When alone in his room Frank turned over in his mind what his chances were and came to see that they were not bright. '' Here am I,'' he thought to himself, '' shut out of the house, just as much as if I were not on the staff. If I had known that I was to be put here to sleep I would have made other plans.

---

* Frank's soliloquy was very much to the point because the author, just before the publication of this book, read in a newspaper the following by the Rev. J. Price, Vicar of Talley. This man of God, in the course of his argument in favour of cruel sports, wrote as follows :—'' The supreme example of suffering was shown to the world on Calvary. Why should animals be exempted from the operation of this law or principle? Is it not in accordance with this great principle that animals should play their part by sometimes suffering and dying to help in keeping Britons hardy, healthy and brave? ''

According to Lecky, the historian, '' Countries where Christianity has most deeply implanted its roots are even now, probably beyond all other countries in Europe, those in which inhumanity to animals is most wanton and most unrebuked.'' From the explanation for this state of affairs, as given by the Vicar of Talley, it follows that cruelty is the natural outcome of the Christian religion. Because Christ suffered for us so animals must be made to suffer to make us hardy, healthy and brave, and the Vicar might have added, to give us pleasure and enjoyment. This is typical priestly reasoning, but it is as false as the religion he professes.

The right way to think is that man by his carnal nature is cruel and the lower his mentality is the more cruel he is. Because he is cruel his religion is cruel. Christianity, which appeals only to those whose minds are undeveloped, is consequently a cruel religion, a religion based on suffering and vengeance. The lower the mental level the more cruel the people are and the more ardently they accept its cruel creeds and dogmas. Not because Christ suffered must we be cruel but because man is cruel he has evolved in his mind a cruel God, and a suffering victim, which he has made into a religion. The more we develop mentally the less carnal we become and thus we rise beyond the cruelties of our carnal nature to the realm of the virtues which are related to this higher order of thought.

I shall wait until midnight and then go to explore. If only I had asked Tony to help me, I could have told him how to get into the secret room. It's too late now, and I heard him say that he was going off to-morrow. Anyway, it is safer to keep the secret confined to as few people as possible. He might have let it out, and then all chance of getting the will would have gone."

When midnight came he slipped out and first tried the kitchen door, which he found locked, then he went round to the front door, to find it also firmly closed. He tried the windows but all were closely barred and bolted.

"No use," said he. "I wonder if I should let one of the staff into the secret—Glen, for instance," but he ruled that out. "Much too risky. He might help, but on the other hand if he refused the first thing he would do would be to tell his master."

Thinking thus, Frank returned to his bedroom at one o'clock, having made up his mind to try to get into the secret chamber when the household was at Church, the day which had just commenced being Sunday.

Tony left immediately after breakfast, and with a grin pressed five shillings into Frank's reluctant hand.

At 10-45 Lord and Lady Kilforfun and Diana started for Church, followed by Glen and some of the staff.

"Now is my chance," said Frank. He walked cautiously to the Gothic room, making sure that no one was about. All was quiet as he entered and closed the door. First he locked it and then decided that that would be unwise, so he turned the key back again.

He crossed the room, going over to the mantelpiece. He then counted the grapes on the left hand pillar and pressed the fourth grape from the bottom of the top bunch, at the same time pressing inwards the wooden shield on the left side of the pillar. As his pressure increased the grape slowly receded until he could push it in no further. The shield had likewise yielded to the pressure of his left hand, and then with a pull towards himself the entire pillar swung out like a door.

Frank peered in and saw a narrow opening leading into a dimly-lit square chamber about six feet long by six broad. He was just about to enter when he heard a knock on the Gothic room door and had just time to slam the pillar into position when the door opened and Agnes, the second housemaid, entered.

"Hullo, Frank. What are you doing over there?" she pertly enquired.

"Oh, just admiring the beautiful mantel-piece," he replied.

"You would not think it beautiful," she remarked, "if you had to dust it every morning. The dust gets so into these 'ere gripes. It makes me fair distracted. But you were more than looking at it. I heard a bang when I opened the door."

"Oh, I may have kicked my foot on the pillar," he replied.

"A funny kind of kick—it sounded like a door slamming. Anyway, it doesn't matter. Sit down here by the window. I come up here at this time every Sunday when his lordship and her ladyship are

at Church and read the Sunday paper.   All these
sporting papers don't interest me."

Frank stood still, saying nothing.

"Come here," she said.   "If you sit by the
window you can see them coming back—it is quite
safe.   Don't be frightened.   I do this every Sunday."

Frank sat on the window seat beside her, turning over in his mind what best to do.

"I'm leaving in a month's time," she went on.
"I'm sorry, now that you have come, but it is that
lonely.   I am accustomed to service in London.
Where do you come from?"

"From London, also," Frank replied.

. "Well, just think of that—and we have never
met before," she smilingly remarked.

Agnes was a tall, handsome girl, and Frank, had
his position been different, would doubtless have been
less backward in coming forward.   As it was, he was
thinking hard if he could trust her.

"If I asked you to do something for me, would
you be so very kind?" he asked.

"It all depends what it is," she cautiously replied.

"Well, will you not tell anyone if I tell you,"
Frank continued.

"Oh yes, I promise that.   But how very mysterious."

Frank then said, very diffidently, and it was perhaps this diffidence as much as anything else which
made him misunderstood :

"Will you leave the back door unlocked to-
night?"

Had Frank stated boldly his wishes the effect on the girl might have been different, but her reaction was quite unexpected.

"Oh, is that the sort you are. I never could have believed it. What do you take me for, I should like to know. I am a respectable girl, I am. No, I won't, and that's flat; and I shall tell the housekeeper, that's more. That is why you sleep outside, so that you can get into no mischief in the house."

And with these words she tossed her head and sailed out of the room before Frank could get in a word of explanation.

"Now I'm done for. She will tell the housekeeper and that will mean my dismissal. I won't go through that indignity, so I shall get into my own clothes, pack my bag and get out. I am not going to have my character ruined over an old will."

He changed quickly, slipped away and cut across the park in the opposite direction to the Church, so that he would not be seen by the congregation on its way home, it being just the time the service was about to end.

"At least I have found that Alfred William Charles Hunt told the truth, and if he did he must be alive, and if alive he is not dead. If he is not dead, then we don't die when we are dead." His thoughts wandered on : "He must be alive because only he knew the secret—at least, so he said; and here again he must have told the truth, as no one else seems to have known it. The present owner doesn't—at least if the will is still there that will prove that he doesn't—because he would either have announced the find or destroyed the will.

It is impossible to imagine that the Truemans or Ralph or Angela or the Curealls knew about the secret room. None of them have ever been inside Huntingham. If the will is found inside the black japanned deed box that will settle the matter, because only Alfred William Charles could know what the will contained and where he put it. Everything points to no living person knowing anything about the secret chamber and the will being there. Moreover, all this happened more than ten years ago. If the will is there, Trueman will have given me proof of survival, beyond the shadow of a doubt."

With these thoughts coursing through his mind, Frank, after what seemed miles of walking, reached Bishop's Stortford and took the first train to London.

CHAPTER IX.

THE BISHOP'S BOMBSHELL.

A fortnight after the bishop's visit to Sureway Court the Dean of Alfortruth wrote to Mr. Trueman inviting him to speak at the morning service in Alfortruth Cathedral on the Sunday ten days hence, and enclosing at the same time the proof of the Diocesan letter the bishop intended to issue to his clergy and people. Trueman read it through, and just as he had finished doing so his wife entered the dining-room.

" I hope you have not yet finished breakfast," she remarked. " I am rather late."

" Not yet," he replied, " but listen to this. The bishop has burned his boats behind him for good and all. Let me read to you his Diocesan letter, which starts off with :
' My dear people,

I have decided to take a great step which may lead to my parting from you, my people. If this parting takes place it will only be as a bishop parting from his flock, not as a friend leaving his friends, because whatever happens I trust that you will always look on me as your friend, as I shall always look on you as my friends.

Over the last ten years I have become convinced of the truth of the claims made by Spiritualists, that communication is possible with the blessed departed, and that they in turn can communicate with us on earth. This great fact, which I personally have proved for myself, has led me a great step forward in

my religious life.   It has also made quite clear to me
that the eschatological beliefs of the Christian Church
about death, the resurrection, and the last judgment
are wrong and founded on an incomplete knowledge
of the facts of nature.

If we can speak to our beloved dead, it means
that they are not dead, in the Christian sense of the
word, but very much alive.   They moreover tell me
that they know of no resurrection of the dead, or the
last judgment—that in fact at death they have made
their resurrection and that they are their own judges,
as what they have sown on earth they either reaped
here or are reaping now where they dwell.

Each one of us is therefore his or her own judge,
as our character determines in the hereafter where we
dwell, the good keeping company with the good and
the bad with the bad.   Each one is consequently his
own saviour because now, and after death, exactly
as we develop our sense of right and wrong, we
determine our fate here and hereafter.   If we have
been selfish or if we have been unselfish here so shall
we be there, and our only punishment is regret for
former wrongs done here on earth.

There is always, however, opportunity for
advancement for all, as mistakes can be atoned for by
effort to do right, this effort training our mind into
the way of truth and righteousness.

All this being so, the creeds and dogmas of the
Christian Church have no bearing on our present-day
life.   Moreover, it is becoming more than ever
apparent that those creeds and dogmas have no relation to the teaching of our Lord and Master Jesus,
whose simple teachings have been overlaid by the

early Church Fathers' theological doctrines, all of which were taken from the Jewish or Pagan religions, believed in by the people surrounding Palestine in the days when the Christian religion was becoming crystallised into an organised faith.

I am aware that this heretical letter may mean my resignation from the high office of Bishop of Alfortruth, and that I shall be called upon by my brother bishops to account for my heresy. I shall then have an opportunity to make my opinions more clearly understood, so I shall not enlarge on this subject further in this letter.

With the consent of the Dean I have invited my friend Mr. George Trueman, the eminent Spiritualist, and well-known man of business in the city of London, to give the address at the morning service in the Cathedral next Sunday.

His address is entitled—

" Our Life after Death and the Teachings
of Spiritualism."

I trust that all those who are unfamiliar with the discoveries of psychic science will attend and hear what this well-known authority has to say on this vital subject.

Your sincere Friend and Bishop,

Edward Alfortruth.'

" Well, dear," Trueman remarked after finishing, " we are living in very interesting times. For ages the mind of man seems to remain stagnant, and then as if with a surge it rises to a higher mental level within a few short years. China, Babylon, Egypt, Greece, Rome and Europe took these successive jumps upwards after running along the flat for centuries.''

"I suppose you will accept the invitation," she replied. "You always put what is your duty first and never miss an opportunity to help where you can in raising the mental level of our fellow countrymen. England may now be getting ready to make another jump upwards as you put it, and lead the world away from its crude and superstitious beliefs to a rational and humane religion. You and others may not be recognised during your lifetime, but you will be remembered some day, and your work appreciated, when those to-day who are looked on as great are forgotten. Thomas Paine, Voltaire, Rousseau, Bradlaugh, Ingersoll, and many others who helped to raise the mental level are now remembered, whereas the so-called religious leaders of their time are forgotten and the orthodox opinions of their times are now derided and scorned.''

"Yes, dear," Trueman replied, "you may be right, but you will deserve remembrance as much as any one. If it had not been for you I should have lived and died an outstanding chartered accountant and there it would have ended. If George Trueman is remembered in after years as one who helped to give the people a rational religion, he has his wife to thank for it. and no one else. That, however, is off the point. I have already promised the bishop that I would go to Alfortruth. As the date the Dean has given me suits me I shall do as he asks and telegraph my acceptance, which will enable the bishop to have his Diocesan letter printed and published in

ample time before the date of my address in Alfortruth Cathedral.''

Mr. and Mrs. Trueman arrived by car at Alfortruth Palace on Saturday, just before lunch, and the
afternoon was spent in visiting various places of
interest in that old-world cathedral city.

The Dean and his wife came for dinner in the
evening and as all had interests and an outlook on life
of much the same nature, the evening passed
pleasantly.

The next morning the vergers of the cathedral
were preparing for a large congregation. Usually a
hundred seats in the nave were sufficient for all who
attended morning service, but to-day seating accommodation was available for a thousand.

'' If the talk that is going on in the town about
this Spiritualism is any guide, the whole of Alfortruth will want to be here to-day,'' remarked one of
the vergers.

'' Well, we haven't more chairs, and they can
just stand. They won't all see the speaker, nor hear
him either, but they can at least sing the hymns.''

By ten-fifty Mr. and Mrs. Trueman were ready
to leave with Mrs. Leader. They strolled through
the precincts and entered by a side door which led to
the palace pew. The bishop had gone on before.

What a sight met their eyes ! The nave of the
huge edifice was packed from wall to wall, and right
back to the entrance. The seating accommodation
was quite inadequate to the occasion, and the majority
had to stand.

" Our cathedrals," remarked Trueman, " were built for these large congregations, but year by year the doctrines taught in them have appealed less and less to the people.   So, though the population of our cathedral towns has increased the congregations have decreased."

The service commenced at eleven o'clock and, after the usual preliminaries, which occupied about half-an-hour, Mr. Trueman rose from his seat and walked up the steps to the pulpit.   He was dressed in a well-cut lounge suit and, with only a few notes scribbled on the back of a postcard, stood before his audience, as one well accustomed to such a situation. Placing his hands before him, on each side of the reading desk in front of him, he spoke in a strong, clear, pleasing voice, which carried right back to the entrance.

" My friends," he commenced, " everyone here to-day in this vast cathedral must at some time or other have given thought to the great question— What happens when the clock strikes and each one of us has to leave all his earthly friends and possessions and go out into the unknown alone?   When we stand at an open grave do we not ask ourselves—Is this the last of my friend?   Shall I ever hear his voice or touch his hand again?   Is life but a narrow vale betwixt two barren wastes, or on the other hand, is death not a wall, as it appears, but a door—the beginning, and not the end, of a day?   I am here to answer this great question to the best of my ability,

as it is a subject to which I have given many years
of serious thought and investigation.   I now speak to
you not as one who hopes, but as one who knows.
Not, believe me, as one who claims to have solved
the mysteries of the Universe ; by no means.   What
I do claim is this, that what past generations have
hoped for, I and other similar investigators have
proved to be true.

This great truth, which in the past has been the
cause of all the world religions, is that we each
individually survive bodily death and, with our
memories and our characters intact, we continue our
lives in another order of existence, in proximity to
this earth of ours, but separated from it by what the
poets of the past have termed a veil.

I, however, as a scientific man, could put it somewhat differently, but as this would mean entering into
an abstruse explanation of what really constitutes existence on earth, I shall confine my observations on
this point to stating the case in a few simple words.

Our life consists of our experiencing something.
If we experienced nothing we would be in truth dead.
Life is just a variety of experiences.   Many believe
that it commences at the cradle and ends at the grave.

If our physical body were ourselves, that would
certainly be true, as there is nothing more sure on
earth than that what we call our body dies and disin-
tegrates.   Some day your body and mine will be dust ;
it will have mingled with the soil and become uncon-
scious clay.

My argument for survival is not concerned with
the physical body, which is but a house for the mind
and the etheric body—a house to be left to crumble

and decay when the time comes, as it will come to everyone, at death. Death is the parting of the etheric duplicate from the physical body. This etheric duplicate is the structure which holds the physical body together. When it leaves the physical body the individual cells of that body separate and fall apart.

Let me give you one reason why we may conclude that each living thing has an etheric duplicate body. For instance, cows, sheep, horses and all kinds of animals feed on grass, but a calf always becomes a cow, a foal a horse, and so on, though all eat the same food. Why? Because each has inherited from its parents the mind and etheric structure of its parents. The grass only goes to produce and nourish the cells of the physical body. The shape, form, colour, etc., and all the idiosyncrasies of the type, come from the etheric structure which produces the type the individual mind images.

If we take the next step and consider this etheric duplicate, what do we find? It also is not ourselves ; it is but another house or habitation. For what?— for ourselves.

Now, what are we? That is the first question for consideration, because if you do not know what you are, you will have great difficulty in accepting what I am about to tell you.

We are mind—nothing more, nothing less. What then is Mind? Mind is that which experiences, that which thinks. Without mind we should experience nothing, we should be dead. We should not be. Now, let me put it to you this way :—

I have already said that life is just a series of experiences, but before you experience anything each one of you requires a mind to experience it. Keep clearly before you this great fact that I am mind and mind only. Each one of you is mind, and mind only. Now, what is mind? And if we answer this correctly we reach the explanation of existence. In the past, mind has rarely been accorded its proper place. In future years, with our increased knowledge, mind will receive its due.

Mind is that substance which makes images.

Now, how do I know this? The answer is simple. I have proved it on numerous occasions, but to prove it for yourselves you must attend a séance. Outside the séance room it is impossible to obtain this proof.

I have proved it in this way. I think of something, and my friends in Etheria then tell me what I am thinking about, because they can see the image of it in my mind. They can see imaged my slightest thought and feeling, and never have they made a mistake. I have tested them over and over again, and only by accepting the fact that my mind images my thoughts can I explain their consistent accuracy in reading my mind. I can only accept their explanation because they always prove themselves to be right. But this is not difficult to believe when you remember that physical matter does not exist to them, as its vibrations are too slow for them to appreciate.

In the same way they read our books. They see imaged each page we read, which they photograph, and thus they have the entire book which can then be printed and published in Etheria. So they obtain our literature, if they wish, and those books, for instance, dealing with Survival are thus reproduced in Etheria for the benefit of those who arrive there without any knowledge of the subject.

I have been told what is true and what is untrue in books I have read dealing with Etheria, because someone there has read the books along with me and criticised them when next they spoke to me at one of the séances I hold twice a week at my home, my wife being the medium.

This must seem new and strange to you, but let me explain further.   Cicero wisely remarked that 'all things that think are divine.'   Each thinking, living thing is to a greater or lesser degree a part of that divine essence, or substance permeating the Universe, which thinks, and so far as each individual sentient being is concerned that thinking consists of image-making.   Image-making is experiencing, which experiencing, constitutes existence.   If you stood behind me and had the power, as they have in Etheria, to penetrate my skull by your sight you would see more or less what you see on the screen at a cinematograph theatre.   Let me tell you what a being with this capacity would tell you if he saw through my skull at the present time, if he confined his attention solely to looking into my head.

He would see everything as I see it.   He would see registered my slightest emotion ; my every thought.   He would see every colour I see.   He would sense whether something I lifted was heavy or light ; whether something I touch is soft or hard. Everything I heard would be imaged according to the words used.   If I heard someone speak the word 'table,' a picture of a table would appear, and so on.

Everything I see, touch, feel, smell and hear is imaged by my mind, the image-maker. This all comes about by the vibrations of substance which are picked up by my sight, hearing and nerves, and conveyed to the physical brain, thence to the etheric brain and thence again to the mind, which immediately turns them into images of the object sensed.

Now let us take the next step. Mind to be able to image requires a place prepared by nature in which to image. You can get no picture on a cinematograph screen if you do not provide a camera to project the image. So you can get no mind-images without a place suitable for the mind to image in. That place is the etheric brain, which is part of the etheric body, which in turn is an exact duplicate of the physical brain and body.

You now see how you can exist apart from your physical body, because you yourself, which is your mind, the image-maker, is housed and can function in the etheric body. That is your mind's real home, the physical body being merely a temporary covering for the purpose of housing the etheric body and the mind during existence on earth.

Here, then, lies the answer to the materialist who asserts that there can be no survival after death because the mind, which he contends erroneously is a function of the physical body, dies with it at death.

During the mind's tenancy of the physical body it sees physical things, hears physical sounds, thinks about the things of this earth, but this is only a transitory experience for the mind, which appears from all we can learn to be immortal.''

Here Trueman paused for a few seconds, and

his hands found their way to the lapels of his jacket.

"I have now briefly considered what we really are
—mind. Without mind we should experience nothing ;
the Universe, so far as all thinking beings are concerned, would cease to be. We can, however, con-
ceive another state of affairs, and that is a Universe of
Mind only. What would that bring about? Precisely
the same state of affairs as if there were no mind in the
Universe. Why? Because there would be nothing
to stimulate Mind to make images, and if that were
so it would be static—dead. Thus, to experience
life, which consists only of thoughts, we require two
substances—the Mind which makes the images, and
the substance which acts on Mind through our sense
organs. Mind and matter are the pre-requisites of
thought. No mind without matter, no matter without
mind, sums up the position as we find it, in a few
words.

Now we come to the next consideration. As
our physical body is only our earth body, is the
physical world the only world?

How I would like to take you into the realm of
physics, use technical words, and explain what matter
really is, all of which are necessary for a proper understanding of this great problem ; but to do so here
would be out of place, so I shall confine myself to
statements of facts which I have proved to be correct.

I ask the question—is the physical world the
only world? No ; because around this earth there
are globes of finer and finer matter. Imagine that
fascinating wooden ball children play with. You
unscrew the outer covering only to find a smaller ball

inside, and so on till you come to a tiny ball in the centre. Imagine this earth as the centre ball. Around it is another and another, and so on, each increasing in size. Each has a surface. That is a crude description of what the real world is like.

Above us in space is another surface of finer matter which we cannot see, but it is real for all that. Above that is another, and so on. How many there are we need not trouble about at present. If there is only one my argument still stands.

Here on earth we experience physical things because our mind is for the time being housed, or to be more correct my mind has housed itself, or we have housed ourselves, in physical matter. We are in tune, in harmony, with things physical.

What, then, happens at death?

The physical body is discarded—thrown aside to decay. But what we call ' death ' is the name we give for the release of the mind from the physical body. The mind carries with it the etheric body and so we are still ourselves in form, thought, and desire, just as we were before death.

But here comes the question : Where is mind— which is the individual—now inhabiting only this finer body, going to live? It must live somewhere. Remember, no mind without matter, which is one of nature's cardinal laws. The answer is that it rises in this finer body to the first finer surface above the earth, with which it is in harmony, and there finds a habitation similar in many respects to the earth. This finer body is now related to the finer matter. A being composed of a substance like water would find water solid ; a being composed of matter which forms, let us say, a cloud, would find a cloud solid.   Like to like ; each in its own order.

We of the earth are related to the earth because of our earth body.   In the etheric body we are related to the etheric, but with this difference.   Mind is not now trammelled with a gross physical body, which cramps our thoughts and movements.   It is freer, it does not suffer from the afflictions of the physical body, as the etheric body is a more perfect body—it is more permanent.   Our physical body is continually wasting away and being renewed.   Were it not for the etheric structure we would all disintegrate very quickly.   In Etheria there are trees, flowers, houses, and everything we have here, all solid to the touch, just as is our etheric body, because there it functions in matter of a similar density.   The earth is solid to us because it is of the same nature as our body.

Now I have told you what we really are.   Mind we now know is the real self.   We now know that mind and matter are inseparable.   We now know that there is a place awaiting each one of us in this Etheric World, which will be in harmony with our etheric body, just as earth is in harmony with the physical body.   The earth-made body inhabits the earth, which is solid to it because it is of the earth. The etheric body inhabits what I call Etheria because it is of Etheria.

Now you will ask me how I know that this land awaits us all?

The answer is that those who die come back to earth and tell us so.   We cannot go to them till we die, but they can come back to us and talk to us.   I shall now tell you how this happens. We all have in our bodies a substance we psychic students call ectoplasm ; some have it more than others, some less. This, I think, is the connecting link between our two bodies during their partnership on earth.

Those people called mediums have this ectoplasm in fuller measure than others. It is often seen and photographed at séances coming out of the orifices of the medium's body. It also comes through the pores of the skin. What it is I shall not take time to tell you now. The substance is there and has been photographed, touched and handled hundreds of times.

This substance our friends in Etheria use in conjunction with a substance of their own to re-materialise their vocal organs, lungs, etc., to such a degree that they can again vibrate our atmosphere, talk to us and hear our replies.

So it is that I, who have been fortunate in having a wife abundantly supplied with ectoplasm, have been able, with the help of those who have died, to make conditions which have enabled me to carry on conversations for hours at a time with those we call dead.

Any of you here to-day could be present and do the same as I have done. Hundreds of different voices my wife and I have heard in our séance room at Sureway Court—children's voices, men's voices, women's voices. Almost every language of importance spoken on earth has been spoken to people present, who understood what was said to them, and answered back and were understood. Information is continually being given to us which only those who have passed over could have given. Information is being regularly given of things no one present knows anything about, but afterwards they are found to be true in every respect.

We are taught by the great thinkers over there how best to live, and how we should look on life and existence so as to obtain a truer and fuller understanding of the Universe.

Moreover, my wife's sight is beyond the normal, and she, with others similarly gifted, see these etheric beings standing before us speaking to us, and can describe correctly people she has never seen on earth.

Only by accepting the facts I have given to you can all this be rationally explained. Each year the evidence accumulates to support the fact that we live on in our etheric body and can come back and again converse, by means of our own voices, with those we left behind on earth. There is always only one condition necessary and that is that a medium must be present who is endowed with the connecting link called ectoplasm.

The fact of the mind's survival of physical death and its return to earth, clothed in an etheric body, naturally raises in our minds the question—

This all being true, what then happens to all the old theological beliefs regarding life and death? ''

Here the speaker again paused, and placing his arms behind his back continued :

'' Firstly, we now find the reason for all the world's religions, namely, man's instinct that earth does not constitute his entire existence. That is the first great discovery and refutes the explanation of the materialist that all religions originated through man's fear of death and the unknown.

Secondly, finding mind to be something super-physical, which does not decay at death, and judging from the qualities of mind as revealed in man, we can believe more readily in mind directing and governing the Universe. If man is something above and beyond a physical being it is not unreasonable to believe that the Universe is something greater than what we sense on earth. Mind need not be limited to life on earth. Why limit so wonderful a substance? To do so would be foolish.

Mind in man reveals a supreme directing substance in the Universe. We have come close to the essence of reality by our discovery that there is this vital substance in each living thing, because survival after death is by no means limited to man. I do not say that all living things are immortal. I do not say that we human beings are immortal. Who can possibly penetrate the infinite and make such an assertion?

If, however, mind can be accepted as something super-material, then it is reasonable to accept the contention that this super-material substance is in operation throughout the Universe. The Universe we now know is not just bricks and mortar, stone and rock, flesh and bones, so to speak.

Now we know that mind is the directing force in each of us ; it moves our bodies, it is the thinker, it is the cause of all we are to-day, our houses, our railways, our ships, and all our comforts, our clothes, our food, and so on. All such things were just mental images, first conceived in the mind. Thus mind is responsible for everything produced by man from this earth.

Finding, as we do, in man and all that lives this constructive substance, it must be something appertaining to the Universe. If individual man can fashion and mould matter, is it not equally possible for universal mind to fashion and mould the substance of the Universe, not only the physical but the etheric besides?

The answer is obvious. Such is not only possible but probable; and so we come to realise that it is not unreasonable or unnatural to accept a guiding principle in nature, which in the past for want of a better word we called 'God.'

Pain, suffering and disease are due to ignorance of nature's laws. How much these have been mitigated in civilised countries! Man is his own saviour and cannot look to a power higher than himself for aid. It is the individual mind which suffers, but when it advances in its development it learns to overcome its suffering. Are not pain, suffering and disease just character-forming agents, in this the early stage of life's evolution? When we look back on these from the vantage point of Etheria we shall realise then, in a way we do not now, how what we experienced on earth merges harmoniously with the greater knowledge we shall have there.

It is impossible, logically, to believe in a personal God because a person must be limited and God cannot be. So let us postulate the Infinite as boundless as the Universe, without beginning and without end, eternal, just as is the Universe.

God or mind manifests to us through the

Universe. It is the Divine essence and the Universe is but an expression of this thinking infinite mind. In other words mind is the fundamental reality and because we are each part of this Divine substance we are related to the Infinite, our evolution being determined by the closeness of the relationship.

In all living things this relationship exists, but the more we develop the more real it becomes. Thus we progress towards greater harmony with the source of our being till the time comes when we have outgrown the limitations of matter, both physical and etheric, of time and space. Thus we attain reality when to each of us the Universe will become comprehensible. That, I believe, is our destiny."

Mr. Trueman paused for a few seconds. In the vast, crowded cathedral absolute stillness reigned. The congregation had followed him word by word, and even when he paused the magnetic link between the speaker and his hearers remained unbroken. The spell remaining he continued in his strong, clear voice to bring home to his listeners the conclusion each must logically draw from his remarks.

" Thus we come back by logical thinking to the basis of religion, to the idea of a directive intelligence guiding the Universe ; but only by accepting the claims of Spiritualism is this logical conclusion possible.

We can now take a further step. If survival is a fact, as I assert it is, the true meaning of religion becomes apparent.

Let me first of all tell you what the great thinkers in Etheria have told me. Our death on earth is but the first step on our journey. We go on from stage to stage, over the æons, experiencing finer and finer matter. Mind development in each of us increases until the time comes when we are able to appreciate the real Universe. We reach reality. Here on earth everything is upside down, topsy-turvy, the opposite from what it really is. Just two instances may serve to indicate this, the fact that the sun appears to go round the earth, and that death seems to be the end of life. I could give you many more examples to prove to you that what seems real is not so, and that our world is largely one of illusion.

Death is one of nature's greatest illusions. It appears as if the individual ceases to be, whereas the reverse is the case. The individual at death begins to live a life of such intenseness that we are unable on earth to understand what a blessing death really is to all who have lived their allotted span on earth.

Now, this being our destiny explains the urge in the human race to reach out to higher things and to attain to greater knowledge and wisdom. At times this urge seems to be static, but as it always re-appears it is evidently part of us. We all have within us, whether we know it or not, this latent urge to reach out to higher things, to greater and better thoughts.

This urge can obtain satisfaction, by freedom for development, only when the mind is unshackled from the tyrannies of State or Church. Much better is it to be free, to forsake the battlements behind which we shelter through fear. Far better is it to stand erect and take the consequences of our own deeds, and not lean upon some authority as our guide, or look for some saviour to accept the punishment for our sins. Thus by so rousing ourselves to do all useful things, to reach out for greater knowledge, each can attain the ideal of his mind. Thus can we give our fancies wings. Thus can we confront facts without fear or shame. Thus can we some day hope to join the subtle threads which on earth seem such a tangle. Thus can the riddle of the maze be solved. Thus can we increase in knowledge and wisdom.

And by this freedom we are able to speak honest thoughts, develop the sense of justice, and give to others every right we claim for ourselves, to take the burdens from the weak and help those less fortunate than ourselves. By serving others our minds develop. Thus by justice, honesty and service our minds can exchange a condition of grossness for one of greater refinement ; a slum for a palace.

This then is real religion. This then is true worship. This then is the source of the religious instinct in man ; this urge to reach out, shall I say, for the want of a better word, to the Divine in nature, to the essence of thought, the core of the Universe, to the guiding principle in nature, which is called God.

Our discovery of the facts of survival and communication not only reveals to us another world but also the cause of the religious instinct in man. Moreover, it likewise proves the accuracy of humanity's instinct of mind guiding the Universe. That our ancestors individualised mind into one or more beings superior to man and gave him, or them, the term God or Gods, with the likes and passions of man, does not affect the argument. The fact remains that man has always accepted an overruling mind or minds guiding the Universe.

Thus the teaching of Spiritualism strengthens all that is true in religion, whilst equally demolishing what is untrue. Spiritualism is a universal religion while all the other world religions are parochial, having their own individual gods, saviours, doctrines, and dogmas.

The fact that our conduct on earth determines our place in Etheria shows the futility of particular forms of belief, as it is not what we believe that counts but what we do, think and say. It is character, or what we are, that determines our place and those we shall live with in Etheria ; the good with the good and the bad with the bad. All wrong-doings on earth which have not been cleansed from our minds by regret will be remembered there, and we shall see more clearly our shortcomings than we do on earth. Remorse is the penalty for all wrong-doing. After we have cleared our conscience by right living and right thinking we start our life of progress so that there is no eternal punishment or place of punishment as taught by Christianity.

Spiritualism unites, creeds separate. We all, irrespective of race, colour or nationality, have the same destiny and will reach this future habitation just as naturally as we reached this earth at birth.

Thus it is seen how foolish it is for this earth to be divided up into different religious sects—Christians, Jews, Hindoos, Buddhists, Moslems. These religious sections in the human race have come just as naturally as have languages, the reason being that in the past communication was not possible between the different parts of the earth, and each tribe or nation developed its individual religion as it developed its individual language.

Therefore it is wrong to hold up one religion as the only true one and denounce all others as false, or one holy book as ' The Word of God ' and all other sacred books as naturally produced.

All religions and holy books were produced naturally, never super-naturally, by the same cause, namely, mankind's religious instinct, based as we have now seen on the instinctive belief that he survives death. This developed into the erroneous opinion that his theological beliefs determined his happiness or unhappiness hereafter.

The sacred books of all religions contain similar teaching, the same beautiful thoughts mixed with cruel and savage instructions from the god or gods the people worshipped, because they were all naturally produced from minds which were either kind or cruel. There is nothing in Christianity that was not taught thousands of years before its birth. Its myths and legends are but copies of older and similar beliefs held sacred long before the birth of Jesus.

Spiritualism gives us the knowledge which enables us to unwind the drapings of myths and legends of the past from the truth beneath, which those myths and legends have hidden. Those myths and legends were just symbols to express a great truth, but the people forgot the reality beneath and worshipped the drapings.

Thus we have to-day the people of all creeds and races worshipping and holding sacred that which is unessential while neglecting the essential in their religious life, which is to develop character, acquire knowledge and wisdom, and live unselfish lives. They have imagined sins which are not sins, and forgotten that the only sin is selfishness.

The past is interesting only as history, but we should not be guided by it nor worship it. Our knowledge to-day is greater than that of our ignorant and cruel ancestors, and to be guided by their religious or philosophical opinions and speculations while neglecting and condemning the discoveries and knowledge of the present is not only foolish but wrong.

Let me, therefore, urge you to discard all ancient superstitions in your religion and cleave only to that which our present-day knowledge proves to be true, relegating to the historian the speculations of our ancestors on God and the Universe, which have only academic interest.

If you do so you will enlarge your minds, increase in knowledge and wisdom, and cease wasting your time on religious forms and ceremonies which, however much they may have been necessary in the days when the world was young, are not now in a community which has absorbed the knowledge of the present.

This then is the message Spiritualism brings to a world torn by war, and ignorant of the meaning of existence and the destiny of the race. It is a great and glorious message. It gives comfort to the mourner by practical means and not by empty words taken from ancient documents whose origin no one knows.

I can only give you the message ; I cannot make you accept it. This, however, I can say, that those who do accept it, who come to know by direct evidence that survival is a fact, just as you know that you are sitting listening to me to-day, rise to the heights and leave all earth's trivialities far below. They at once attain a philosophy which puts this earth in its right perspective and in its true relationship to the individual. They rise to a higher mental level, as far above their neighbour relying on faith or having no knowledge of this other life, as he who is literate is above one who is illiterate. The one who has solved the mystery of death, as I and others have done, is to be envied far more than kings and princes, than those having titles, honours, or wealth, and yet we are the very ones the world despises. How everything on earth is topsy-turvy.

The acceptance of this message takes the mystery from existence and places mankind's religious longings on a practical and sure basis, so that we no longer need to count as religious and sacred those things which are not so, while on the other hand we can build up a philosophy and religion which helps us in life, and strengthens us in death, without outraging our reason, as does orthodox religion to all thinking people to-day.

I therefore look forward to a quickening in the mental development of the race, now that closer contact has been made with a higher order of intelligence. This raising of the mental standard will bring to an end war and all cruelty to man and beast, thus achieving that which has been hoped for by the greatest minds of the human race.

When this time comes all this world's Cathedrals, Churches, Mosques, Tabernacles and Pagodas will not be occupied, as they are to-day, by those of different creeds and beliefs, performing different ceremonials and rites, but by humanity with but one common thought and ideal.

The Church of the future will embrace the Universe in its teaching ; its members will be all mankind, and within its precincts the two worlds will meet.   Its worshippers will consist of all the teachers, all the uplifters, and all the healers of humanity.   Its altar will be dedicated to love and service, and its priests will be those precious beings called mediums who will perform the service to humanity, hitherto confined to the priesthood, by being used to effect a bridge between the two orders of existence.   This has always been nature's plan, and would by now have been effected had it not been for man's ignorance in destroying the channels naturally provided.

I am looking far ahead, but at least we, as intelligent people, can help forward this, my vision of the future, by giving earnest thought to those things which are beautiful and true while discarding those things which are cruel and false.   By doing so we shall raise ourselves mentally.   Thus we shall attain greater at-one-ment with the Infinite.   Thus we shall approach more closely to reality.   This and this only is true religion.   This and this only is true worship.''

Mr. Trueman thus concluded his remarks.   He then turned round and came down from the pulpit, resuming his seat beside his wife.

The service came to a close in the usual manner.

On their way back to the palace the Dean came hurrying on behind and overtook Mr. Trueman.

" Have you found any cracks in the walls of the cathedral, Mr. Dean?" enquired Mr. Trueman.

"Well, I did not stop to look," replied the Dean, "but if there is no crack in the walls after all you said there never will be.

I once remember hearing of a church in Scotland where it was decided that the people must kneel at the prayers instead of stand, as had been the custom. This caused so much discussion that the congregation was nearly divided on the subject, and the difficulty was only settled by having different services to suit the kneelers and the standers. The minister, after the first kneeling service was over, found the village wag carefully going over the walls of the church and inspecting the structure.

' Anything wrong, Andrew,' he enquired.

' Oh ! no, nothing so far as I can see,' was the reply, ' but after all the bother I thought I would like to fin' oot hoo' the kirk had stood it. I thought that this innovation wud at least ha' made a crack in the wa.' "

" It is easily seen or I should say heard," remarked Trueman, "where you come from, my friend. Only one from across the border can tell a Scotch story with the right accent and intonation."

"Well," the Dean replied, "I come from Aberdeen, the home of amusing stories. I shall tell you some good ones another time ; but it is much more important that I thank you for your illuminating address. I feel that you have a great message to give to humanity. To the countless numbers who cannot accept our doctrines it must come as a new revelation. I believe that there is more than one path to Heaven, though I am afraid that most of those professing my faith do not agree with me.

I would like to be walking behind each one of to-day's congregation and hear the comments made. All you said is so new that it is bound to cause controversy. You must well know that some of the greatest saints have been regarded as the greatest heretics."

" I am not setting myself up as a saint," replied Trueman, " so you must not liken me to one. All I am trying to do is to give the people the truth as I see it, and leave it to them to think the matter out for themselves."

" Yes, that is what the orthodox find so difficult to understand," went on the Dean. " Do you remember that our Lord was termed ' Beelzebub ' by the religious people of his day, and they asserted that he performed his miracles by the help of the powers of darkness ? "

" That term," replied Trueman, " has been given by the orthodox to everyone who has brought forward something new and hitherto unknown, but intolerance is not so bitter to-day as it was forty or fifty years ago. Education, which then had hardly begun to make its mark, is now having its effect on the minds of the people. In religious matters they have been spoon-fed and have never been taught to think for themselves."

" Quite true," replied the Dean, " but to be told, as you have told them to-day, that Christianity developed out of paganism and was not a new revelation but naturally produced will bring consternation to many poor souls."

" Well," Trueman replied, " that comes of just

accepting and not thinking, and, to be honest, I must say that history will put the blame on you parsons. You have looked on yourselves only as preachers and never as teachers. You have never sought truth for truth's sake, and what you taught the children in Sunday School you have preached to youth, the middle-aged and the old. You have never encouraged the people to think, as that would mean that your teaching would be doubted. Doubting leads to enquiry and enquiry to the throwing over of all the false doctrines of the Church. That is why the Religious Committee of the B.B.C., which is run by parsons, will not allow my philosophy to be expounded by means of the Radio. How you priests have kept back and still keep back all progress and reform!"

"Well, it is hardly in the parsons' interest to make the people think, to educate them," replied the Dean. "The parson is the priest, and the priest is the medium between God and man."

"He is the man-made medium," remarked Trueman, "the bridge between heaven and earth, so naturally he dislikes competition from nature's mediums—my wife, for instance."

"Naturally," replied the Dean, "that is what the priests think, but time will show them their error. Many people think, as we do, that the days of the priest are numbered. He has had his use in the past. I suppose that all that has been is the result of cause and effect, but his days may now be numbered if the Church does not enlarge its vision. In Christendom he has still a firm hold in the most backward Catholic countries; elsewhere his grip, I must admit, is slackening."

" Well," said Trueman, " the sooner his grip goes entirely the better it will be for the people, as the priest in the past has kept back nature's mediumship from developing by burning all the mediums, while at the present time he uses his position as a religious leader to misrepresent and frighten the people from accepting this great and elevating truth. He opposed all education so that, when the Church ruled, Christendom was illiterate, cruel and ignorant. Only as his influence has disappeared have the people developed mentally and morally."

" Only too true," replied the Dean, " but there are priests who are now living lives of self-sacrifice in the slums. As to the failings of the Church I can only admit them to you privately. When I resign, or what is more likely, when I am compelled to resign for to-day's doings, I shall then join the staff of some newspaper, as other retired Deans have done, and be able to express my honest thoughts untrammelled."

They had by now reached the palace door and the Dean, when shaking Mr. Trueman warmly by the hand, remarked :

" Again, many thanks for your brave words ; words which, if the people only knew more, would make them shout for joy, because of the knowledge which has now come to the world. They have, however, been so long used to creeds as crutches that they cannot bear the thought of now being well enough to discard those unnecessary incumbrances and walk erect."

The bishop was delighted with Mr. Trueman's

address, and after lunch they both seated themselves
in his study and discussed the future.

"I've burned my boats, my friend," the bishop
said, "but to make assurance doubly sure you have
filled them with your oil of heresy and made their
destruction all the more certain."

"You gave me a free hand," replied Trueman.
"I came on the understanding that I was permitted
to speak the truth as I understand it."

"You did well," remarked the bishop. "You
carried into that building the Torch of Knowledge.
You spoke up and said things that no parson dares
to say. The priesthood is a close corporation, and we
clergy must keep to the old grooves, never depart-
ing from the ancient tradition. The Church is not
an open platform for the purpose of promoting truth.
It asserts that it, and it only, has had the truth since
its inception and always will have it. That is why
you, by outlining a universal religion to-day, and a
way to heaven outside the way laid down by the
Church, will cause so much controversy. That is
why I now await my trial knowing full well what the
result will be.

The clergy dare not open to discussion the
various subjects considered by you to-day—that would
be fatal. They must stand or fall by the creeds of
the Church. If they admit the slightest crack in the
structure of the edifice, so loosely built and put together by the Church Fathers in the third and fourth
centuries, their doom is sealed."

"I agree," said Trueman, "and I for one have
never expected the clergy to hang themselves. What
will happen is that the people will hang them by

refusing to attend Church services. That will bring the Non-conformist Churches in time into line with modern thought, but with your denomination it is quite different. The Established Church of England is a wealthy institution and so is the Roman Catholic Church. Both can remain in being unchanged because both can snap their fingers at the people. The parsons in the Church of England, to consider only your own sect, as that is the one that interests us, are always sure of their stipends and their vicarages. Whether the people attend Church or not does not affect their livelihood. You will always find some who put an easy living before honest thinking, eager and willing to obtain part of the income your organisation enjoys."

" Yes," replied the bishop, " I fear my sacrifice for truth will not change the teachings of the Church. I wish it would, but at least I am following my conscience. It must make people think and talk and wonder ; and the more they do so the less the teaching of the Church will appeal to the people. Perhaps some day it will be shamed into coming into line with present-day knowledge, but that day is a long way off. No ! my colleagues are safe for many a day to enjoy their livings. Little wonder that they hold on to what they have and drown their consciences as best they can. I, however, have made my decision and I shall never regret it."

The bishop, having a service to attend, left his guest, who spent the afternoon quietly engrossed in a book taken from the extensive library.

After tea, the Truemans and Mrs. Leader went out in their car to see some of the surrounding country and did not return till dinner-time.

The next morning Mr. and Mrs. Trueman returned home and as they came in sight of Sureway Court Mrs. Trueman remarked : " Perhaps some day Sureway Court will be remembered as the place where a Bishop finally decided to put the dictates of his conscience before his palace."

CHAPTER X.

THE MISSING WILL.

Frank, on his return from Huntingham, went to his home in London and told his father and mother all about his adventures.

Both had been rather opposed to his doing what he had done, but he had made up his mind to find out if what he had been told at the séance was true or not. Moreover, he had reminded his parents of all the money which was due to his mother if the will was found to contain the legacy, which the voice, claiming to be that of Alfred Hunt, said it contained. He asserted that every effort should be made to find if this was true, and this could only be done by producing the will. It was a sporting chance and he would run no risk. His parting words before leaving for Huntingham had been :

"At least, mother, Alfred William Charles told me something I never knew—which you say was right—that he went off to India without proposing to you as you had expected." To which she had replied : "Yes, Frank, that is quite true."

Thus they had parted a few days previously and now he met them again, empty-handed, but having made a great step forward in proving that the message was genuine as regards the secret chamber at Huntingham.

When he told his parents about his discovery of the secret room and that he had found it by following out the instructions he had received at the séance, his father was much impressed, though his mother still held to her opinion that dabbling with the occult, as she called it, was wrong. All the same, she was very much interested in what he had to tell her and sympathised with him in his disappointment over his failure.

" Better luck next time," said his father. " We must make other plans. That housemaid Agnes who spiked your guns said she was leaving. Could we not find a girl to take her place who could get into the Gothic room during the night and explore the secret room ? "

" Rather an impossible procedure," said Mrs. Wiseman. " No girl we could trust would risk being discovered. Much too risky."

" Well I don't know but that the pater's idea is a good one. It is one that occurred to me. I shall talk it over with Angela. She is a sport, and might do it for us. In any case I shall be seeing her soon. I am going to ask her to marry me and I hope she will do so. You will increase my allowance if we get married till I am fully qualified to get started on my own, won't you, pater ? She has some money of her own, so if you gave me another hundred a year, we could manage splendidly."

" Oh, Frank, how pleased I am," remarked Mrs Wiseman, and turning to her husband she said : " Of course you will, Jim, won't you ? I have never met Angela but from what I have heard of her she seems just the girl for Frank."

Colonel Wiseman smiled but said nothing.

" Well, I am glad you both seem pleased, but I am not going to ask her to help us yet. We shall become engaged first of all and then perhaps she

would help us as one of the family. I want her for
her own sake, not for helping us in our difficulty.
If I waited and asked her after she had found the
will she might think I did so out of gratitude.''

'' Frank,'' said his mother, '' if the will is
found and I am named as one of the beneficiaries I
shall give you both as a wedding present half of all
I get. Now, that is fair, is it not? I did not encourage
you to do what you did and I don't advise you to
pursue your adventure, but if you do so and are
successful, then all I get will be due to you, so you
are entitled to half. Don't you agree, Jim? That
is only fair.''

'' Quite fair,'' he replied, '' and I shall increase
your allowance as well, so you will have something
substantial to marry on if all we hope for materialises.''

Frank went over to his mother and kissed her.
'' You are a brick, mater,'' he said, and laying his
hand on his father's shoulder, said ''and you also,
pater. I never thought about myself. I only wanted
the mater to get her due. But thanks awfully for
your generosity, both of you. I shall never forget
it. The mater has gone the wrong way to stop me
following this up to the end. What she should have
said, if she really thinks it is all so wicked, is that I
would be cut out of her will if this will is found through
my efforts. I am going to ring up Angela now and
ask her to come up to London for the day. Where
is a good place, pater, to ask her? What about a
picture house, during some sentimental love scene?''

'' Oh, you will find no difficulty about the place,''
his father replied. '' What is important is how you
lead up to the subject. You must think this out

beforehand and step by step lead her on and then you will find that when the crisis is reached she will fall for you just like a ripe cherry."

"Now, Frank," said his mother, "don't be like the man I heard the story about the other day, who was walking out with his girl. For a mile he never spoke a word. Then in a moment of inspiration he said ' Annie, will ye marry me?' 'Of course I will, John,' came the ready reply. Then there was silence for another mile, when Annie ventured to remark ' Have you nothing more to say, John?' 'No, I haven't,' came the reply, 'I've said too much already.' "

"Cautious lad," replied Frank. "But I went one better. You know I am very thorough in everything I do. Well, after I had made up my mind that I loved Angela I put down on a piece of paper all her good points and all her bad points, and then I weighed up the good with the bad. Ah, here it is, but never tell her that I shewed this to you. I shall burn it, but as you don't know her you can see it first."

Frank handed a sheet of note paper over to his mother, his father getting up and looking over her shoulder. This is what Mrs. Wiseman read out :—

FOR	AGAINST
Decidedly pretty.	Sees things.
Gentle and attractive manner.	Hears things.
Sympathetic.	May be temperamental.
Seems good-tempered.	Only medium height.
Seems affectionate.	Dreamy eyes.
Good figure.	May not be practical.
Seems intelligent.	Perhaps casual.
Reads good literature.	Lacks sense of humour.

FOR	AGAINST
Talks intelligently.	Straw-coloured hair.
Soft musical voice.	Lacks dress sense.
Enjoys good health.	
Seems domesticated.	
Hates blood sports.	
Not dancing-mad.	
Doesn't paint or powder.	
Hasn't long nails.	
Doesn't paint nails.	

" That sums her up well," said Frank. " I couldn't think of anything more to put down."

His father and mother were so amused at the businesslike way of going about a most unbusinesslike affair that they could not restrain their mirth and both laughed aloud.

" You always were a queer fellow, Frank," said his mother. " Not like other boys. Always asking questions about things nobody would ever think would interest a child. You never would accept statements. Always wanting to know the why of everything. It was painful to go with you to church. After the sermon it was always an argument over what the clergyman had said and why he said this and then something quite different."

" What do you mean by Angela seeing things and hearing things? " said his father.

" Oh, she is a medium," replied Frank. " I told you so before. She sees people who are dead and hears them speak. I have given her bad marks for that, not that it makes me love her the less, but it is not what you expect in a wife; that's all."

" She surely doesn't show her peculiarity," said his father. " She won't, for instance, when sitting talking to me stop and say, ' Oh, there is my great-grandmother. Excuse me, I just want to have a chat with her for a few minutes,' and I have to sit and listen to a one-sided conversation.''

'' Well, I can't be sure,'' replied Frank. '' So far, I have never heard her going on like that. It seems to come over her at times when everything is quiet. She appears quite normal, but the fact remains that she has far more good points than bad and it wouldn't matter a button if it were the other way about. I love the girl and am going to marry her if she consents.''

'' You have our best wishes,'' said his mother, '' and from this list here of her good and bad qualities, I think you have made a very good choice. Beauty palls if you have not intellect behind it. No, I would say, taking girls as they are to-day—light-headed, painted-up creatures—that Angela is the very girl for you.''

'' Well, we all think alike,'' replied Frank. '' Give me that paper, please. I shall now tear it up and burn it. Never tell Angela. Too like going over the points of a horse. Now I am going to telephone to her.''

Three weeks after this conversation took place Frank and Angela were walking down Regent Street. Angela's engagement ring did not quite fit so they had both been to the jewellers to have it put right.

'' Oh, there are Ralph and Hope coming towards us,'' exclaimed Angela.

Thus the four friends met, and as it was just lunch time Ralph suggested lunch at a delightful place he knew off Lower Regent Street.

" You get a topping lunch there," he went on. " Will you join us ? "

This being agreed the four were soon seated round a table with the menu before them.   Matters between the waiter and the guests being fixed up to the mutual satisfaction of all concerned the conversation turned to Frank's escapade at Huntingham.

" Dashed   hard   luck,"   remarked   Ralph. " Agnes was a saucy wench.   You said she was leaving in a month, so her time is nearly up.   Lady Kilforfun will soon be looking out for another— doubtless is so already.   What about having a shot for the place, Hope?   Your domestic economy training would stand you in good stead."

" I would be scared stiff," replied Hope.   " No, I wouldn't have the pluck to walk about that house in the early hours of the morning.   Angela, why don't you do it?   It is always an education to see all sides of life.   You would be killing two birds with one stone."

" How's that?" Angela enquired.

" You could tell your friends that you had plumbed the depths of life and reached its heights, had been a burglar and conversed with angels.   You would find the housemaid's work most interesting. Remember that the custom is to go to the Gothic room every Sunday when the master and mistress are at church."

Angela kept quiet during this bantering, then turning to Frank she said :

" Frank, dear, I shall go if you think it would be wise."

" You are a sport," said Hope, " but why Frank, dear. Are you two engaged. Where is your ring, Angela ? "

" Right first time," replied Frank. " We have just been to the jewellers to get the ring altered—it did not quite fit."

" Congratulations ! " both Hope and Ralph exclaimed in chorus.

" I am so glad," remarked Hope. " When did it happen ? "

" About two weeks ago," replied Angela. " We both went to a picture house, and Frank could not miss the chance. We were sitting alone and no one was near. If you want to get engaged, Hope, go with your boy to a cinema."

" Your advice, my dear girl," Hope replied, " comes rather late. Ralph and I became engaged yesterday at Sureway Court when we were out in the woods. Except mum and daddy, you are the first to know about it."

Again congratulations were expressed, but this time by Frank and Angela.

When this diversion had passed, Frank turned to Angela and said :

" You are a brick, Angela. Will you really take on the job ? "

" Yes, of course I will, if you wish me to, Frank. If I am caught then all we have to do is to tell the Kilforfuns that they have the will hidden in their house and that your mother demands it, as by keeping it they are depriving her of her inheritance."

"Well, that would be our last move. If they got to know about the secret chamber and how to get into it they might destroy the will and we never could prove that it was there. We must try every other way first, and you won't be caught, Angela. The housemaids have a room each. I found that out when I began to realise that I hadn't a chance of getting into the house at night. My thoughts turned then to you getting taken on as a housemaid or kitchenmaid."

"Well, now that is decided," Angela remarked, "we must make our plans as the chance may not come soon again of there being a vacancy. How about a character?"

"Oh," said Hope, "I can get mum to say she knows you and that you bear an excellent character; been well-trained, and are a good housemaid. You were at whats the place—some grand name—for the purpose of educating and training young ladies in every branch of household economy."

"Yes," replied Angela, "Cookem House, Cleanemwell."

It was then arranged that Hope would obtain this on her return home that evening, post it to Angela's aunt's house, where Angela was staying in London, and that Angela would go to-morrow and have an interview with Lady Kilforfun.

"Will she not smell a rat?" enquired Ralph.

"Why?" said Hope.

"Well, she would wonder how Angela knew that the situation was vacant."

"That's easily got over," replied Frank. "Ten to one there will be an advertisement in the local paper. Anyway, that is easily found out. I shall telephone to the newspaper in the morning. To-day is Thursday ; it will be published to-morrow."

" Well, good luck to you, Angela," said Hope, when saying good-bye. " Remember the fourth grape from the bottom of the top bunch, and press the shield with your left hand at the same time ; then the trick is done. As easy as falling off a tree."

Just as Frank had expected, Lady Kilforfun was advertising for a second housemaid, so Frank and Angela took an early train to Bishop's Stortford and the bus from there to Huntingford village which was just a mile from Huntingham House. Frank parted from Angela at the entrance gates, promising to return to the same place in an hour. During Angela's absence he disappeared from human ken by taking a side road in the opposite direction to the mansion.

" Someone might spot you, Frank, so do be careful," were Angela's parting remarks.

" Well, that is settled," remarked Lady Kilforfun. "You will be here to-day week, when Agnes will be leaving. I shall now ring for Ruth, the head housemaid, and she will tell you what your work will be. Arrange with her the time you will arrive."

Angela and Ruth, after a few minutes talk, went into the servants' hall and each had a cup of tea, during which time Agnes looked in and sat down beside them.

" I was just telling Miss Bridge," said Ruth, " about Frank disappearing three weeks ago and never being seen again. Nothing taken, so he was quite honest. Such a nice young man, too. We were all so sorry he went off like that.''

'' Him and me got on quite well together,'' remarked Agnes, who had entirely forgotten all about the cause which had led to Frank's disappearance. '' I was real sorry when he left in the way he did.''

'' Anyway, you are going soon, so if he had stayed it would only have made the parting worse,'' remarked Angela, in all solemnity.

'' Yes, but we might have met somewhere, or I might have stayed on,'' replied Agnes, to which opinion Ruth remarked :

'' You and your boys, Agnes. Ever running after them. That is not the way to get married. Do as I do and wait till they come to you.''

'' I would have to wait a long time if you are any example,'' replied the pert Agnes.

'' Perhaps it was a ghost who frightened him away,'' said Angela, casually.

'' Now, that's funny,'' replied Agnes. '' That is what cook said happened.''

'' Is there a ghost, then, at Huntingham?'' enquired Angela.

'' So it is said. A man with clanking chains, carrying his head under his arm, who walks up the front staircase and then disappears.''

'' That's not the story,'' broke in Ruth. '' I've heard it from Glen—he's the butler. A man, said to be the brother of his lordship, who died about ten years ago, is seen walking across the Gothic room and disappears into the left side of the fireplace. Isn't that odd?''

'' I don't believe a word of it,'' said Agnes.

" Do you believe in ghosts, Miss Bridge ? "

Angela now thought that the time had come for her to go. The talk was getting too near home to be pleasant, so she casually remarked :

" Yes, I do. Life would be rather dull without them." She then took her leave and met Frank at the entrance gate.

On their way into Bishop's Stortford she amused him by relating the conversation she had had with Ruth and Agnes.

" So you can go back, Frank ; she has quite forgiven you."

" Never again," he replied. " Once is enough for me ; but isn't it strange to hear that Alfred William Charles Hunt should have been seen ? This will business must be keeping him earthbound, as Miss Noteall calls it. He can't throw off the regret that mother never benefited owing to the lost will. This fixed idea seems to bring him back to earth, and some clairvoyant has evidently seen him."

On arrival in London they went off to get Angela a print dress for the morning and a black dress for the afternoon, also a cap and apron.

" Now you do look smart," Frank said, with real admiration in his tones. " You must get nippy and be home soon or the footman who is my successor will be falling for you."

A week later Angela presented herself at the back door of Huntingham and was met by Ruth who showed her to her room, told her to change, and then come down and have a cup of tea with her in the servants' hall.

Angela's room was small but comfortable. She quickly put on her black dress, apron and cap and came downstairs to join Ruth.

When the tea drinking was finished Ruth took her over the house, into all the bedrooms, the public and private rooms and told her the ones for which she was responsible.

As the housemaid's work in a large house is mostly done in the early part of the day Angela found little to do in the afternoon of her arrival, everything having been done before she had arrived.

In the evening, after having gone through her rooms to close them up, she was invited by the cook to her private sitting-room, there to hear all the gossip of the place and just exactly what was thought of everyone, including the master and mistress.

Angela had previously discovered the Gothic room, and had made a point of walking from it to her own bedroom and back again. The distance was not so very far, as by coming down a back stair near her room she found herself on the ground floor, in the corridor, along which she had to go only twenty yards or so till she came to it. Frank had provided her with an electric torch so that she would not need to remember where the electric light switches were placed.

Angela had decided that the sooner she carried through her task, the better, especially as Frank had taken up his quarters at Bishop's Stortford for the week-end, hoping that by Monday at latest Angela would have returned to him. He wanted to be back at Guy's by Monday morning.

The maids retired to bed at ten and Angela read a book she had brought with her till one o'clock in the morning, when she slipped on a pair of rubber-soled shoes and crept quietly downstairs, along the passage, and into the Gothic room.

The house was death-like in its stillness. The night was calm ; nothing stirred ; all nature was asleep.

She quietly unbolted the Gothic room door and then closed it behind her. With quiet, steady step she moved across to the fireplace, pointing the torch on the fourth grape from the bottom of the top bunch. She placed her index finger of her right hand on it, transferring the torch to her left hand. Then she found the disc representing the shield.

Remembering its place she then put the torch in her apron pocket. After doing so she replaced her left hand on the disc and commenced to push, at the same time pushing the grape inwards with the finger of her right hand.

Slowly the grape and the disc gave to her pressure, and when she could make no further impression on them she pulled with her left hand and the pillar swung out like a door, revealing a small passage about eighteen inches wide, and just as high as the pillar which she had swung open.

" So much for that. Now, what is there to see ? " she thought.

She flashed the torch into the passage and cautiously entered. After six steps she found herself in the secret chamber—a small room covered over with dust ; airless and stuffy.

In front of her stood a black japanned deed box, placed on a wooden trestle. She moved over to it and tried to lift the lid, but this she found impossible as it was locked.

"Well, that ends to-night's adventure," she thought. " I must come back to-morrow night with a hammer and a chisel. Where I shall get them is the question."

She tried again, but the lid wouldn't move. The box was too heavy to lift and there was no key anywhere. She turned to go, creeping sideways carefully along the passage, when her shoulder came with a bump on something hard.

Directing her torch on the place she was horrified to find that the pillar had swung to and closed her in. She tried to find an inside handle and came across a rusty ring fixed into a rusty bolt. This she pulled and it came away in her hand, it having rusted through.

" That is my only chance gone," she remarked in desperation, " I should have been more careful. The ring is evidently the other end of the bolt which is pressed inwards when the grape is pushed and then returns by means of a spring. Yes, and here is the bolt which the disc moves. This unlocks the door but can't be moved till the grape is pushed inwards. This also returns to its place by means of a spring. The door is evidently made to swing to for the sake of safety. To open it from the inside, the ring is pulled, the bolt moved to the left, and with a push the pillar swings open."

She tried to get at the end of the bolt from which the ring had broken away, but it was impossible.

She could get no grip as it was too close to the wood-work.

After vain attempts she gave it up, philosophically saying to herself, " Well, Frank will know by Monday that I am missing. I won't starve till then ; and he will come and find me, even if he has to tell the Kilforfuns."

So Angela, being a brave girl, sat down on the deed box to await her long vigil.

Then she seemed to feel as if someone were present beside her, and turning round she saw her Aunt Lavinia.

" Don't fret, darling," her aunt said, in words which Angela heard clearly and distinctly, " the True-mans will be told in the morning and they will tell Frank. Keep your courage up and be brave."

" Yes, aunt, I shall. Thanks for your en-couragement ; I shall be brave. Tell Frank, please, to bring something to open the deed box."

Then she lay down on the wooden floor, resting her head on the bar of the trestle supporting the deed box, and fell asleep.

Mrs. Trueman awakened as usual about seven-thirty on the morning of the day Angela had become imprisoned in the secret chamber, and while dressing heard distinctly a voice repeating :

" Angela is locked in the secret room. Sit with the trumpet after breakfast."

" George," she called out, " something is wrong with Angela. It was yesterday she went to Hun-tingham, wasn't it ? "

"I'm not sure, my dear, but Hope may know. We shall find out at breakfast."

Then she told him of the message she had heard clairaudiently.

"Very strange. However can that be?" he remarked.

"Well, I am told," she replied, "that we are to sit for a séance after breakfast; so we shall find out."

At breakfast Hope confirmed that yesterday was the day that Angela was due at Huntingham as second housemaid.

"Well," said Trueman, "will you please go when you have finished and tell Miss Noteall to come to us in the library after she has finished her breakfast."

Miss Noteall duly appeared and it was arranged that she, Hope, Mr. and Mrs. Trueman would go upstairs at once and hold a séance.

There was no need to adjust the various instruments, and all Miss Noteall did was to start the voice-recording machine and place the trumpet in front of Mrs. Trueman.

Then they all sat down and the lights were put out.

In about ten minutes Mrs. Trueman said: "There is a form building up before you, George," and shortly afterwards a strong voice through the trumpet spoke:

"Mr. Trueman, I am Alfred William Charles Hunt. Things at Huntingham have gone wrong. The girl got in and found the box but the door panel swung to and closed her in. I should have warned you of the danger. In my time this happened but I could always open the door from the inside. The mechanism broke off in her hand—rusted through. Tell Frank to go at once—he is in the neighbourhood. Remember to take a hammer, chisel and tin-opener. I forgot the box was locked. That's all ; goodbye.''

'' Well,'' said Trueman, '' the sooner we find Frank, the better. Hope, please ring up his mother and enquire where he is, and when you find him let me know, as I want to speak to him.''

In about a quarter of an hour Hope called to her father : '' Come on, daddy, Frank is waiting.''

'' Oh, Frank, this is what has happened,'' and Trueman then went on to tell him all that they had been told. '' Remember the hammer, chisel and tin-opener. What do you propose to do ? ''

'' Well,'' he replied, '' I would rather slip in and wait somewhere until night, but I cannot keep the poor girl waiting—she will be in misery. This is Sunday. I shall get in when the family is out at church. Fortunately I know my way about the house and what goes on at church time. Agnes is away now so the Gothic room will be empty. Goodbye, and thanks so much for your trouble.''

Immediately this conversation finished, Frank set about to find the tools required and had no difficulty in obtaining the loan of them from the hotel porter.

It was now ten-thirty so he ordered a taxi and within fifteen minutes of receiving the message he was at the main entrance gates to Huntingham. He walked smartly up the drive, being sure that he would not meet the church-goers from the house as they walked to church through the park by a private path.

He arrived at the front door unseen and finding it unlocked stepped in. He was just about to cross the entrance hall and open the door leading to the passage, from which access to the Gothic room could be obtained, when he heard a voice in the passage calling to someone.

"Well, I've looked everywhere and I can't find her."

Frank was trapped; He looked round like an animal at bay and his eyes fell on a long wooden chest. He rushed across to it, found it empty, jumped in and lay down just as the door opened.

Ruth and the cook came through.

"Well, her ladyship told us to look everywhere," Ruth was saying, "and this is the last place. I have been in every room in the house."

"There is something wrong with this place," replied the cook. "First, Frank disappears all of a sudden-like and now it's Angela. That 'ere ghost is at the bottom of the trouble. It is the first place I've been in where goings on like this have taken place."

"Well, we shall have a look round here," replied Ruth, "and then we can go off and have our eleven o'clock tea. No, nothing is in there," she remarked, slamming a cupboard. "Well, that's that; come on."

The two women turned to go and Frank gasped with relief, but it was only momentarily.

"What is in that chest?" remarked the cook. "Let us have a look." She walked over to the chest in which Frank now lay hardly daring to breathe and had just put her hand on the lid to open it when Ruth called out to her :

" Come on ; its full of rugs. I'm sick of this and must have a cup of tea."

The cook, who had by then lifted the lid an inch, dropped it, remarking as she did so : " You are right ; the girl has bolted. She is not in the house, that I bet."

Frank breathed again and after waiting a few minutes lifted the lid and stepped out.

" Well, those two are now in the servants' hall so they are out of the way. Glen and the others will be at church. Now for it."

He opened the door, slipped quickly along the passage, opened the Gothic room door and, greatly to his relief found the room empty. Remembering his last time in this room he took no chances on this occasion, so he took the key from the other side of the door, put it in the inside, and locked the door.

" Now," said he, " I won't come out of here without Angela and the will. They can beat the door down, but this job will be finished before anyone gets in."

He walked quickly over to the fireplace, pushed in the grape and the shield and swung open the panel.

Angela had wakened from her sleep in a rather dazed condition. The smallness of the room and the want of proper ventilation had produced a heavy atmosphere. Instead of waking in a normal way she remained in a semi-conscious state and only became aware of Frank's presence when she felt his touch and saw him bending over her.

" Are you all right, darling ?   You are not ill,"
he enquired.

" Oh no, Frank, my darling, just sleepy.   The
atmosphere is so heavy."

" Well, let me help you up, and then we shall
open the box.   I have the necessary tools."

Frank set to work with the hammer and chisel
and easily made a hole in the tin lid.   Then he inserted
the tin-opener and slowly cut through the lid, right
round the top of the box.

The excitement of the two was intense.   Would
the will be found or had it been already taken ?   Perhaps this place was known to Lord Kilforfun and the
will had been found and destroyed long ago.

Their anxious thoughts were, however, soon put
to rest as there on the top, just as they had been told,
lay a legal-looking document on which was written in
neat copy-book writing, peculiar to a lawyer's clerk—

W I L L

of

Capt. ALFRED WILLIAM CHARLES HUNT, M.C., J.P.,

of

HUNTINGHAM.

" At last !   Our work has not been in vain,"
exclaimed Frank, " and this must be the packet containing the jewellery.   It is addressed to Gertrude
Eva Edith Cuningham, now Mrs. James Wiseman ;
but we shall leave it here till we see if it is referred
to in the will.   Now let us go."

Frank went first into the narrow passage, which
he could only negotiate by walking sideways, but he
was no sooner in it than he exclaimed :

"Angela, the door has closed again! I can't see any daylight." He pushed on only to find his fears realised. "What a fool I was. I was in such a hurry to find you that I forgot all about that confounded door always swinging back into its place and locking itself. Whoever conceived such a death-trap I would like to know."

"It is for reasons of safety," replied Angela. "In the old days it could be opened from the inside but when I tried to do so the ring attached to the bolt broke away. It was rusted through."

"Have you the torch I gave you?" enquired Frank.

"Yes, here it is," replied Angela.

Frank examined the inside of the door and found, just as Angela had told him, that the only way now to open the door was to get hold of the bolt, pull it, and at the same time move the bolt attached to the disc towards the left. He found he could not move the latter because the bolt, from which the ring had come away, could not be moved, each bolt locking the other.

"Well, our only way to open the pillar," said Frank, "is to cut away the wood round the bolt attached to the grape till I can get my two fingers on it and then to pull it inwards. Hold the light on it, please."

The task was more difficult than Frank imagined. The oak was old and hard, like iron. The chisel was blunt and his position made working difficult. Besides this, owing to him taking up the entire width of the passage Angela found it almost impossible to direct the light on the required spot.

Bit by bit, however, he enlarged the hole until it became big enough for him to grip the bolt, but his fingers could not get a sufficient hold to enable him to pull it inwards.

" Hold these tools, Angela.   I shall wrap my handkerchief round the end of the bolt.   That will grip it.''

This plan succeeded and as the bolt came inwards towards them Frank pushed to the left the other bolt.

Then with a push the pillar opened and both saw daylight again.

" Now, have we got everything?'' enquired Frank.   '' The tools, torch and above all, the will.''

" What about the other contents of the box?'' enquired Angela.

" They don't belong to us unless the will says so.   The will is all that we can legally take away with us.''

" I know that,'' replied Angela, '' but should we not look through them to make sure that nothing is removed?''

" That's all right.   Lord Kilforfun will only go in here along with me and we shall go through the box together if the will makes out that anything in it belongs to mother.''

" Now let us go off,'' remarked Angela.   It is after twelve so they will soon be back from church. I can't, however, go like this.   I can run up to my room, pack my bag, and get my hat and coat.   You wait here.   I won't be a minute.''

She unlocked the door and peered out to see that the way was clear.   Out she slipped and soon was back again with Frank.

Angela had no sooner returned than they heard the front door close and then the voices of Lord and Lady Kilforfun.

"That's done it, we are trapped; Angela. They are back a quarter of an hour sooner than usual."

As he said this Frank drew Angela into the room, and softly closed the door.

"We daren't lock it this time, Angela. Too dangerous. They would smell a rat. Quick! Back into the secret chamber. They will be here in a few seconds."

Back they rushed and in less time than it takes to tell the pillar had again been swung open. Angela entered the passage first, and Frank was in the act of closing the pillar when he heard the handle of the Gothic room door turn. He heard no more as with a click the pillar closed with Frank and Angela again prisoners in the Secret Chamber of Huntingham.

"That was a close shave, Frank."

"We shall never have a closer one, Angela. Now let us think things out. One thing is certain and that is that they will never find us in here, but we must whisper or we may be heard. You sit down on the deed box and I shall go round the walls and explore the place. I wonder where the light up there comes from."

"From the way the roof tapers upwards it seems to me," said Angela, "that it comes from a dummy chimney and that circle of light up there is caused by the top of the chimney pot."

"Smart lass," exclaimed Frank. "I bet you are right. One of these many chimneys on the roof never smokes and never has smoked. Whoever built this house in the fifteenth century planned this cute little cubby hole very thoroughly. He knew ventilation and light were necessary. A window was impossible as that, sooner or later, would be spotted. A dummy chimney was less likely to be and time has shown him to have been right. Hello! what's this?"

As he talked, Frank was groping round the wall when suddenly he bumped into an iron bar sticking out from the wall.

"Where is the torch, Angela? Bring it here. Yes, direct it on the wall just where I am."

Frank had reached the part of the wall, the other side of which in the Gothic room was between the entrance pillar and the window.

"Why, Frank, it is a ladder made up of iron bars. Where does it lead to?"

"That's what I am going to find out. Keep directing the torch always on the next bar as I climb up. That's right. Now I can see where to place my feet as I find the bars above to grip with my hands."

Frank was about six feet up when he exclaimed : "Here's a ledge of some kind. Whatever are these two points of light? Pass up the torch, please."

By means of the torch, he found an iron bar about five feet above the ledge, running its entire length, and just above the bar, about its centre, gleamed these two points of light, about two inches apart.

"Why, they are two holes in the wall. Hush, don't speak above a whisper. Well, I'm blessed! I can see right into the Gothic room and dear old Kilforfun is sitting in the armchair reading a book.

Just a minute and I shall come down. You can then come up and see for yourself.''

'' Well, that is clever,'' said. Angela. '' Of course, anyone in here would want to know that the road was clear before attempting to get out.''

'' Yes, and also hear what was being said by those in the room. In those old days everyone was a potential enemy. Few could be trusted, and if the owner suspected anyone he would slip in here and listen to the conversation of both guests and servants. Now climb up and have a look.''

When Angela reached the ledge she bent down and whispered : '' Lady Kilforfun has just come in and I can hear all she says. Come up ; the ledge will hold us both.''

'' I've got it, Angela. Have you ever noticed the portrait of the man in Tudor dress between the mantel-piece and the window? The pupils of his eyes have been cut out and it is through the place where these were that we can see into the room. Who would ever have imagined this to be possible when looking at that portrait embedded in the panelling?''

'' Yes, Frank, and if you put out your hand you will feel that it is canvas in front of us. That is why we can hear so easily. If we spoke above a whisper they could hear us. Are you all right? We can both stand here and hear all they say and see as well. Not a soul knows that we are here. Listen, that is Lady Kilforfun speaking now.''

'' Come along out, Jack,'' they heard her say. '' Come and see the horses. What are you reading?''

"My Bible, my dear; just running over next Sunday's Old Testament lesson. It is safer. Some of these big words make me go all hot and cold when I come to them. I had to take several rather stiff jumps this morning. Did I take them well?"

"You always read the lessons well, dear. The vicar was saying what a relief it is to him that you are such a regular church-goer. He doesn't know who could be found to read the lessons if you were not there."

"It would not kill the vicar," replied Kilforfun, "if he read the lessons himself. Only two services on one day a week when he reads through the morning and evening services and preaches for about fifteen minutes each time. Five hundred pounds a year for life, and a free house, for doing this and carrying through an occasional burial, baptism or marriage is a great attraction for a lazy man. Even if the vicar visited every family in the parish once a year—a thing no vicar I know ever thinks of doing—it would mean less than a visit a day, so he really has six days a week to potter about his garden and generally enjoy himself. A really comfortable job, I say."

"It is not like you, Jack, to criticise the parsons," replied his wife. "It is the first time I have heard you speak like this."

"Anyone with a blind eye," he replied, "can see that the clergy are having less and less to do every year. As the people become more educated they don't want their ministrations and they don't want their sermons. As you know I have always been a strong supporter of the Church and am so still. It has always kept the people in their right place.

All the same I am beginning to wonder if its teachings will grip the people much longer. I am beginning to ask myself what good it can do anybody listening Sunday after Sunday to old stories about an ignorant barbaric tribe. No decent-minded man should be expected to read about God instructing the murder of the enemies of Israel and the butchering and out-raging of women and children. I sometimes wonder what the parsons mean by Christian civilisation and Christian ideals and ethics when they prescribe the reading of those savage and obscene passages.''

''Were you never told, Jack, when you were young and asked awkward questions, that God's ways are not our ways. Ours not to reason why. Ours but to believe and accept. The less we think the less we doubt. That's my philosophy.''

''Well, perhaps you are right, my dear. Didn't the vicar give the Bishop of Alfortruth a dressing down? 'A disgrace to Christianity,' he said he was, 'a backslider.' 'One who harboured a servant of the Devil.' He didn't mince his language. Alfor-truth, the Dean, Trueman and the Devil seem to be one and the same.''

''Well, perhaps he was right, Jack. I don't feel that a Christian Cathedral is a place for a Spirit-ualist. Anyway, Spiritualism leads to the asylum and that is near enough the Devil for my liking.''

Lady Kilforfun, who had been standing looking out of the window, sat down as her husband did not seem to be yet ready to go out.

''Yes, that is what the vicar said to-day, but I happened to notice not so long ago that a census had been taken and that parsons headed the list of those in our asylums, their mental breakdown being caused by religious mania. The article went on to say that though it was often stated that Spiritualism drove people into the asylum yet no case of insanity had ever been known as the result of Spiritualism."

"Then why did the vicar make such a statement?" enquired Lady Kilforfun.

"I'm sure I don't know, my dear; you had better ask him. When a man can always be sure of never being replied to he is apt to make wild statements. As parsons know that their congregations always accept what they say they are not careful to verify their facts. They get off with it every time and it leads to loose thinking on their part. I happened to read Trueman's remarks at Alfortruth Cathedral and in spite of what the vicar said to-day I came to the conclusion that there was a good deal of sound sense in what Trueman said. Much of it I could not understand, but I have been somewhat bewildered at the attitude of the Christian Church towards the Italian-Abyssinian war. Why, the head of the Christian Church actually blessed the soldiers of Italy and encouraged them in their conquest of Abyssinia! When they were victorious he blessed what he called ' the good people of Italy ' and ordered the *Te Deum* to be sung in every church, sermons to be preached extolling Italian valour, and prayers of thanksgiving to be offered up to the same God as the Abyssinians worship."

"Well, it has always been the same," replied Lady Kilforfun. "We did just the same after the Boer war. Our churches resounded with thanksgiving and prayers to the same God as the Boers worshipped. After the Great War we thanked the same God with whom the Kaiser was on such friendly terms."

"Well," replied Kilforfun, "I suppose that the Pope will now crown and bless the King of Italy as Emperor of Abyssinia, just as the Pope crowned and blessed Charlemagne after he had slaughtered all the German tribes who had not become Christians. Cortez for four years carried the cross and the sword through Mexico, exterminating all who would not become Christians. He then received the thanks and blessing of the Pope. The Italian conquest of Abyssinia, backed as it was by the Church, is only history repeating itself. What we have witnessed to-day has gone on throughout the entire Christian era. I am sorry to have to say so, but I am afraid that it is true that the Church, war and slaughter have gone hand in hand down the centuries. Perhaps Trueman is not far wrong in saying that only by the mental level rising will war be stopped."

"Mr. Trueman's remarks seem to have made an impression on you, Jack. I have never heard you speak like this before."

"Oh, don't think that what I am saying is my own production," he replied, "I am only repeating something I once read in a book and am connecting it up with the vicar's sermon this morning. Throughout his sermon, when he was trying to impress us with the evil of Spiritualism and the blessings of Christianity, these historical facts came back to my mind, and it occurred to me that for parsons to stand up and criticise anyone these days is just asking for trouble. When the most Christian nation in the world, the home of the headquarters of the oldest branch of the Church, breaks all its covenants with other nations, wages the most brutal form of war that is possible, uses poison gas and deliberately bombs hospitals, with no word of censure, but only praise from its priesthood, we Christians should surely not have the impudence to continue putting forward the claim that Christianity, and it only, has raised Europe out of savagery, or to use the name Christian as if it stood for something respectable.''

'' These thoughts pass through my mind also from time to time, Jack, but I try to force them back. If one begins to doubt where is the doubting to end? Our Lord has not been faithfully served by those who claim to be his followers, and as for the mental level being raised what would Mr. Trueman say to fox hunting and similar sports? Do you think he would approve of you and me living just for these and these only? I have heard that Spiritualists are against all blood sports and would have them abolished if they had their way.''

'' God forbid, my dear ! Let us be thankful that our religion has always approved of such natural pleasures. I think your philosophy of putting aside these ideas Trueman has expressed is the best. The Christian faith, to the believer, makes life so easy and comfortable. It is a great comfort to feel that Christ has gone before and taken our sins so that there is nothing for us to worry about. That seems to be God's plan and as you know I have always taken the Bible as my guide through life and tried to live as God would have me live. Come, let us go and see the gee-gees, *they* don't raise uncomfortable thoughts. I am sorry now I read Trueman's address at Alfortruth. I wish these reformers———.''

What more Kilforfun had to say was lost to Frank and Angela who throughout this conversation had stood absolutely still, amazed at what they heard. Only after Lord and Lady Kilforfun had left the room did they feel that they could again breathe freely.

'' Well, I'm blessed ! '' said Frank. '' Pleasure and enjoyment comes first with them both. The suffering of the poor fox, the otter, the hare and the stag is never considered. They are selfish to the core and think only of their own miserable souls. They feel that their own souls are safe and they stifle any thoughts that would interfere with their pleasure and enjoyment. They don't want to be worried by having to think. How typical of people in general ! ''

'' I suppose, Frank, that the sermon their vicar gave to-day will be typical of what has been preached throughout the country since Mr. Trueman's address at Alfortruth Cathedral. Mr. Trueman and the Bishop of Alfortruth have given parsons something to wax eloquent about.''

'' No doubt,'' he replied, '' but we must be off. If we go out by the front door they won't see us as the stables are on the other side.''

Frank had by now reached the floor and helped Angela to get down.

'' Slip along, darling,'' he said, '' and open the panel, gently, while I just run up again to see that the room is still empty. Take the light and twist this handkerchief round the end of the bar, otherwise you cannot get a grip to pull on.''

'' All is clear,'' he called.

In about twenty seconds he heard her reply.

"It's open now, Frank. Come along."

Within a few seconds they were both again the only occupants of the Gothic room, rather dusty, but otherwise none the worse of their adventure.

"Look up there," said Angela, pointing to the picture. "Can you see the holes in the eyes? I can, but only by close concentration."

"Yes," said Frank, "I can see them also but they could only be spotted by someone who knows. Come along, we must be off. We are still in the danger zone, and till we are on the other side of the front door we can be trapped and expected to explain what we have been up to. I have my taxi waiting at the entrance gate."

They both walked quickly along the drive and soon they were spinning along in the taxi to Frank's hotel in Bishop's Stortford.

"Frank, look at the will and see what it says."

He took it out and after reading through the long, opening paragraphs, which hedge round the kernel of fact everyone really wants to find, he exclaimed :

"Yes, the old boy was right. Here it is : 'and to Gertrude Eva Edith Wiseman (née Cuningham) I leave the sum of fifty thousand pounds, free of legacy duty.'"

"Didn't you tell me, Frank, that your mother promised you half? That will be twenty-five thousand. We shall be able to start married life quite comfortably. What income will that give us, dear?"

"Twelve hundred and fifty a year at five per

cent," replied Frank, " but we are entitled to interest for ten years, since the date of his death, so that means twelve thousand five hundred more to us, and the same for mother, which will mean an additional sum of over six hundred to each of us, or nearly two thousand a year for us and the same for mother. Well worth the trouble, wasn't it? I hope Kilforfun can pay up."

On arrival at the hotel three telephone calls were put through, one to Angela's home, one to the Wisemans in London, and the other to the Truemans, when all were told of the complete success of the great enterprise.

" You know," said Angela, " that we owe the finding of this will to the Truemans. But for them it would have remained peacefully in the secret room, and the Kilforfuns would have gone on spending money belonging to your mother."

" Yes, we must thank them and also Alfred William Charles. If he ever gives me the chance I shall let him know how grateful we all are."

Lord and Lady Kilforfun had just returned from a day's hunting, the cubbing season having begun.

" He did give us a run," she remarked, as they approached the door of Huntingham.

" But we got him in the end. He was a sly one. I thought we had lost him in the wood, but the hounds did their work well. Why ! there is someone's taxi ; who is it, I wonder ? "

In the entrance hall they were met by Glen, who informed Lord Kilforfun that a gentleman was waiting on urgent business and would like to see his lordship immediately he came in.

"Has he been waiting long?"

"Just about half-an-hour, my lord. Here is his card."

"Mr. Henry Law," remarked Kilforfun. "Don't know him, though I know his firm well. Some legal matter."

"I hope it is not about the two missing servants," broke in Lady Kilforfun. "Better see him at once."

Mr. Law was in the library, and as Lord Kilforfun entered he rose. When shaking hands he remarked: "I have come to see you on very important business. Can you give me an hour at once as I would like to get back to London by the first train?"

"Certainly," came the reply. "Sit down. Have a cigarette, and I shall ring for tea. If it has to do with two missing servants I shall ask my wife to come in."

"Not quite that," came the cautious reply, "but I know Lady Kilforfun will be interested and will have to know about the matter sooner or later."

Lady Kilforfun entered just then and enquired: "Have they been found?"

"No, my dear, it is not about the missing servants, but something else. Let me introduce to you, Mr. Law. Mr. Law, my dear, has some important matter to tell me, about which he says you will have to know. Nothing about a lady, I hope, Mr. Law?"

"Well, it is. Not a rival lady, if I may put it

so, but it has certainly to do with a lady. Mrs. Wiseman, who previous to her marriage was Miss Gertrude Cuningham——.''

'' Oh, Gertrude Wiseman. She is not dead, I hope?'' Lady Kilforfun enquired.

''Oh no ; not even ill. Very well indeed, in fact ; but I shall get to the point at once.

Your brother's will was never found, Lord Kilforfun, and you inherited the entire estate.''

'' Yes, that is true,'' came the reply.

'' Did you know that he made a will?'' Mr. Law enquired.

'' Yes, so his lawyers said, but the one who drew it up died some years before my brother and no one knew anything about its contents. It was never registered.''

'' So you never saw the will,'' Mr. Law went on.

'' No—never. Don't believe there was one. Everything he had was ransacked to find it. Not only was the will missing but family jewels and bearer bonds which he had bought. His books showed that he cashed the coupons regularly ; but the bonds were never found. It was all a mystery, and if you have come to find out from me where the missing will is, and all the jewellery and bonds, you have come to the wrong person.''

The conversation was broken at this moment by tea being brought in.

'' Well,'' went on Kilforfun, '' I was saying that I know nothing about the will, so I can give you no help.''

'' I did not come to ask your help,'' replied Mr.

Law, "but to inform you that the will has been found."

"The will, found!" the Kilforfuns exclaimed.

"Yes, found, and it is now deposited at Somerset House, where you can see it for yourselves. Here is a copy of it. You will notice that Mrs. Wiseman was left by your brother fifty thousand pounds, which I am sure you will pay over to her with interest."

"Fifty thousand pounds!" exclaimed Kilforfun. "That is rather staggering. But, tell me, is a will valid ten years after the decease of the benefactor?"

"Well," replied Mr. Law, "that is a point I thought you might raise, so I looked into the question and I find that there is no definite ruling on the question. If it had been land which was being conveyed to Mrs. Wiseman the lapse of time would probably have given you a good title to what you inherited, though even that is doubtful, and I would not like to be definite on the subject in the absence of a definite ruling."

"But this is a gift of money," broke in Lady Kilforfun.

"Exactly; and I am now coming to that point. Here, again, there is no specific case that I can find as the only one in any way resembling this case was settled out of court. When I discovered this I rang up our Conveyancing Counsel and put this case before him. Though he could give no definite opinion, yet his view was that the lapse of time was not sufficient to have invalidated the will and that the law would support Mrs. Wiseman's claim."

"Well, I don't think I shall invoke the aid of the law," remarked Kilforfun. "What you have said answers my question so far as the legal aspect of the case is concerned. The moral aspect is another matter, and from that angle there seems no doubt that the money, which I have been using, rightly belongs to Mrs. Wiseman."

"Quite so," replied Mr. Law. "I was sure that you, as an honourable man, would not press the legal side but look at the question purely as to what is just in the circumstances. I shall now leave you this copy of the will, and I might also mention some-thing which will somewhat soften the blow. I think that the missing bonds and jewels have also been found."

"Why do you say, you think. Don't you know?" enquired Lady Kilforfun.

So Mr. Law started to tell them the whole story from the day Frank met Mr. Trueman at Turnberry till he handed over the will to Mr. Law the day previous to the conversation.

"Well, I'm blowed! I always looked on Spiritualists as daft people," exclaimed Lord Kilfor-fun. "Though I have never met you before, Mr. Law, the standing of your firm makes me take seriously all you say. I can't imagine that you have come to tell me a cock and bull story."

"I know Mr. Trueman by reputation," Mr. Law replied, "and I took the liberty of calling on him this morning before coming here. He confirmed all Frank Wiseman told me, so I think you will find that it is all true."

"But you have not told us whereabout in this

house is that secret chamber," remarked Lady Kil-forfun.

"That must remain a secret, meantime," replied Mr. Law. "Mr. Frank Wiseman wants to show you it himself and go through the deed box with you. Your brother also left his mother some jewellery so I would suggest that you invite them both here and go through its contents together."

"Quite a good idea, Mr. Law, and please tell Mrs. Wiseman that she will get every penny and interest to date, and that I am more than sorry that she has been deprived of her rights all these years. I have been using money which did not belong to me. Matters will be put right without delay. Don't you agree, dear?"

"Quite," replied Lady Kilforfun. "I would never think of contesting the will. If the will had been produced when Alfred died Mrs. Wiseman would have obtained what was left to her. It was no one's fault that the will was not found, if we except Alfred, who seems to have been very stupid in not leaving it where it could easily be found. However, we must face facts as they are and I shall write to her at once and ask her, Colonel Wiseman and Frank to come here and visit us."

"Well, if you ask Angela also, you will have your two missing servants back," remarked Mr. Law.

"Now, that's awkward," said Kilforfun. "We don't want this all spread abroad. We dare not ask Frank as everyone in the house will recognise him."

"Just what I was thinking," remarked Mr.

Law, " and I would like to make this suggestion. Ask Mrs. Wiseman and her husband to stay the night here. Include me in the invitation and I am sure Frank will not mind being left out. Both his father and mother know the secret and we can get the box out and go over its contents. I am accustomed to checking up deeds and bonds and it would be better to have it all done correctly."

To this the Kilforfuns willingly agreed, and Mr. Law left well satisfied with his visit.

CHAPTER XI.

THE BISHOPS IN CONFERENCE.

The great day had at last arrived, the day when the Bishop of Alfortruth was called on to make his defence before his brother bishops.

"At last the time has come when I shall tell them just what I believe," he said to his wife on his way to Churchisall where the convocation was sitting. "They will censure me, remind me of my vows, and I shall be asked to resign. This I shall do, but not before I have spoken out in a way I have never done before."

"Then you will be happy, dear," replied Mrs. Leader. "You have not been so for years past. Even before you accepted the claims of Spiritualism you knew that the Church was built on a foundation of sand and only kept itself in being because it has managed so artfully to make the people think that its doctrines came from God."

"Well, I have my defence prepared ; but this is the last day Edward Leader will be a bishop."

Their car had now arrived at Churchisall and half-an-hour later the bishop was sitting with his brother bishops awaiting the time when his case would come up for discussion.

When the time came for the President, the Archbishop of Churchisall, to rise and open the proceedings there was present a full bench of bishops.

The Archbishop was evidently intent on conciliation and that nothing should be said or done which might some day be regretted. After reading over the Bishop of Alfortruth's pastoral letter, which was the cause of the present hearing, he continued :

'' This pastoral letter is so unorthodox in its tone and contents that it has made inevitable these proceedings. No one regrets more than I do the necessity of this enquiry. No good to the Church can come from it, as the opinions we express will be ridiculed in some quarters, applauded in others, but to the majority of Christian people they will cause unrest and increase the prevalent feeling of distrust towards the teaching of the Church.

This being so, I wish my friend the Bishop of Alfortruth—and whatever happens I hope he will always remain my friend—to understand that he is not being tried for heresy. The time has gone past for such a thing to happen in England to-day. The Church of Scotland, I am sorry to say, has done the cause of true religion no good in recent years by its various trials and punishments for heresy, which as the years have passed are now looked back upon in sorrow by all professing Christians, while those who are always ready to scoff at us make use of them as examples of our intolerance.

I am sorry to have to admit it, but it is true that the history of our Church, throughout the Christian era, reveals a state of mind which I am glad to say is passing and I hope will soon be passed without recall.

In these days of increasing knowledge, there naturally ensues increasing toleration. Having said this I have said perhaps more than my Lord Bishops will think wise, so I hasten to remind the Bishop of Alfortruth that, though I have dwelt on the wisdom of toleration in these days, he has made solemn vows to be loyal to his Church, to uphold its doctrines and conform to all that is laid down for the guidance of one holding his high office.

We can admit latitude in views and opinions, but only up to a point. When opinions are expressed which cut right through the doctrines of our religion we feel bound to invite the bishop responsible to appear before us at this convocation and explain his meaning. Perhaps he has said more than he meant to say. Perhaps he now regrets his action. I hope he does, and if he expresses his regret and gives an undertaking that it will not be repeated I am sure you will all rejoice with me at such an ending to this unfortunate occurrence.

You will, however, realise that not only has the bishop advocated Spiritualism but actually, with the consent of the Dean, has broken one of the cardinal rules of the Church in inviting a man who does not profess our religion to speak in a consecrated Cathedral, upon the subject of the life after death, which was presented to the congregation from an entirely different aspect to that which we consider true and proper. Our Church has held very definite opinions about the after-life and these are to be found in the Prayer Book.

I have no doubt that Mr. Trueman is a man of the highest integrity and honestly believes all he said that day, but, as it is apparent from the shorthand notes taken at the time, the views he expressed were not those of a Christian. His definition of God was quite unchristian and he discards entirely the doctrines of the atonement, the resurrection on the last day, and the judgment.

Besides this he rejects what all Christians accept, that Christianity is the only true religion and that its founder spoke as never man spoke, suffered and died for our salvation, and to-day sits at the right hand of God making intercession for all believers.

Mr. Trueman, moreover, accepts and preached what the Church at all times has condemned, namely, communication with the dead. In my opinion it is unscriptural and contrary to the teachings of the Church.

So much for the preacher at the service to which exception is taken ; but if we turn to the bishop's Diocesan letter we find admissions which are quite contrary to the bishop's oath to uphold the teachings of the Church which are contained in its creeds and doctrines. He expresses the view that the creeds and dogmas are contrary to the teaching of our Lord.

Such an assertion is a very grave matter and one on which I am sure you will wish to express very decided opinions. What the teachings of our Lord were I prefer not to consider. It is wiser not to dwell on such a debatable matter. In this age of scholarship and Biblical criticism who dares to say what these teachings were?

But this we know. We know what the Church Fathers said they were and on this the Church is founded. Once we depart from the doctrines laid down by the founders of the Christian Church in the fourth century we are like a ship at sea without a compass. To them we must be loyal. In them we must believe.

Though I admit that they were men who blundered, that they showed at times great ignorance, were one-sided and often foolish in their opinions, yet on these opinions rest the creeds, dogmas and doctrines of our Church and to them we must adhere as loyal churchmen. I quite admit that not only great scholars but leading divines have written and spoken of these Fathers of the Church in a most contemptuous manner. Doubtless they felt in honour bound to make their opinions known, but it is unfortunate that they did so because it makes it all the more difficult to establish the unity of thought which is so necessary if the Christian Church is to withstand the onslaught of Rationalism and the insidious undermining influence of Spiritualism.

Once admit that the Church Fathers were mistaken, once admit that they erred in their judgment, and we open the floodgates to revolt, to doubt, and to disbelief in the teachings of the Christian Church.

The publication of Rationalist literature has made our position difficult enough, but this insidious cult, which goes under the name of Spiritualism, attracts many who have not the intelligence nor the education to understand the scholarly works published by the great Rationalist thinkers. Consequently the Christian fold is being thinned and those who were once our prominent supporters having, as they believe, received proof that life continues after death, find no comfort and little help from the teachings of the Church.

This is the real danger we have to face. The thinking, intellectual people we have already lost beyond recovery, but now that the rank and file are finding comfort and help from facts and have now no need of faith, on which the Church rests, the need of a united front by the clergy to this menace is more essential than ever. In the days of old, when the Church was powerful, we were able to prevent this communing with the dead from taking place ; in fact we nearly stamped it out, but not quite, and I doubt the wisdom of this method, as mediumship seems to be a natural gift, which cannot be destroyed.

Our only weapon then is our past prestige. On this and this only we must rely. We must continually be warning the people about the dangers of being entangled in this spider's web, in which, if they are caught, they will gradually lose hold of the teachings of the Church of their fathers, to the everlasting detriment of their souls.

I have now said enough, too much, perhaps. I have made admissions which some of you may think unwise, and I have dwelt on matters we clergy find it much wiser always to avoid. I, however, wished to be fair, to face the facts as they are and not minimise the danger with which we are faced.

These dangers I trust I have made clear to you all. You must realise them just as much as I do, and my emphasising these dangers will make you realise, and I trust also the Bishop of Alfortruth, how important it is that at this crisis in our Church's history a bold and united front should be maintained by the bishops and clergy to meet a common danger."

The President then resumed his seat and the Bishop of Diehardham rose.

" My Lord President, Your Grace, My Lords, I have listened with growing consternation to my Lord President's remarks, but, as it is not our duty here to-day to criticise these but to censure, and censure severely, our brother bishop, who has erred so grievously and diverged so far from the way of truth, I shall confine my remarks to his behaviour and his alone.

We have heard read to us the pastoral letter. The typewritten copy of Mr. Trueman's remarks has been circulated so that we know, without it being necessary for me to state them all over again, the heterodox views expressed by the bishop and those he, with the consent of the Dean, allowed to be expressed to the congregation in Alfortruth Cathedral.

Either we must hold to the fundamental truths of our religion or perish.   *Semper Idem* is the only barricade against the present-day onrush of unbelief. Our sister Church, the Church of Rome, is right. The Church is either right in all or it is wrong in all. The faith of our forefathers must be our faith.   The creeds of the Church must be our creeds, its dogmas and doctrines our dogmas and doctrines, the Holy Scriptures our only guide, and the gospels our only means of knowing the way of salvation.

We must hold to the Christian faith in its entirety ; otherwise we have no means of knowing God's will to man, which we believe has been revealed to those, and those only, accepting the Christian faith, and that we bishops and clergy are the human means appointed by God to interpret God's will to mankind.

If we do not maintain a united front our preaching will be in vain.   So I repeat that the Faith of our fathers must be our Faith, their Bible our Bible, their Creeds our Creeds, their Church our Church. On this I take my stand. On this I base my preaching. By this standard, and this standard only, I define a Christian. Otherwise the name is a misnomer.

Spiritualism, in my opinion, is mostly fraud. Its teachings are atheistic, its God is not our God, and its Heaven is not our Heaven. That communication can take place between the dead and the living is impossible and has never been proved. What the Spiritualists claim to be communications from the dead are the vapourings of hysterical women. These communications reveal that the dead are as ignorant as they were on earth. Their mental level, judged by the messages, is such that matters of a trivial nature seem to interest them, such as moving a table or that Johnny sends his love to Susan.

Whether the dead are conscious after death till the great resurrection day is a debatabe question. Admitting, for argument's sake, that they regain consciousness after death, then those who have died in the Christian faith are certainly not interested in earthly affairs. I prefer to believe that they are continually praising God, day and night. This being so they have no time, thought, or wish, to return to earth.

That, however, is only one side of the question. God's Holy Word condemns all intercourse with the dead, and on that I take my stand. If the people commune with the dead there will be no place for the Christian Church, as, according to the teachings of Spiritualism, all find their happiness in the next world irrespective of creeds or beliefs, and the unbeliever is as happy as the believer. Such teachings are so contrary to our faith that we as a Church must fight them till we conquer.

It is quite contrary to all that our Church has taught and believed that those who do not profess the Christian faith reach the same place after death as do believers. To say, as Spiritualists do, that it is not what doctrines you believe that matters but what you do, how you live, and what your thoughts are, that determines your place in the hereafter is contrary to all our Church has taught and believed. To quote from the Gospel of St. Mark, ' He that believeth and is baptised shall be saved, he that disbelieveth shall be damned.' If you give up belief in Hell you must give up belief in a Saviour. He came to save us from Hell, so both must either be believed or rejected.

Holding thus firmly to the Christian faith, I condemn the words and actions of the Bishop of Alfortruth. If we did not utterly condemn then we should be lacking in our duty to our Church and to the people over whom we are placed by God. The bishop has so fallen from grace, so departed from the true faith, that I implore him to resign and thus save the Church from further contamination, from having to suffer the views and opinions of one who has broken his vows and brought discredit on our faith.''

The Bishop of Creedalbury then rose and briefly supported the views expressed by the Bishop of Diehardham. The view he emphasised was that Christ was the Head of the Church, which was his body, through which he was working, and that it was the sole avenue of divine truth.

He was then followed by the Bishop of Dogmaham who emphasised that the dogmas and doctrines of the Church must be retained, as without them the people, not knowing what they must believe to be saved, would have nothing to direct them. Consequently they would wander through life without a guide and ultimately perish. He emphasised the cardinal Church doctrine of the Atonement, how by the fall of Adam all mankind came under the wrath of God, who, in the person of the Eternal Son, the second person of the Trinity, came down from Heaven and became man. He suffered as a sacrifice so that all believers might be saved while all unbelievers would suffer eternal damnation in Hell.

Then the Bishop of Latitudeham addressed the convocation.

" We have now heard various expressions of opinion on the attitude of my friend the Bishop of Alfortruth. May I just say these few words before he rises to make his defence. We are now living in a new age, an age of increasing knowledge, of great discoveries, which of necessity means an age of greater toleration, of more latitudinarian views. This we must admit.

We must also accept the fact that with greater education has come a great mental expansion, a new outlook on life, which more and more inclines the people towards a mode of thought contrary to the Church's teaching. The majority have no use for these teachings and seldom if ever enter a Church. This I am bound to admit would have come about much sooner but for the opposition of the Church to education, so that throughout the Christian era illiteracy and ignorance prevailed everywhere, in

great contrast to the Greek and Roman world before
the Christian era.

The people now think for themselves, express
freely their thoughts, and I regret to say, to an increasing degree, these expressions of opinion are
critical of us, the upholders of what we claim is the
true religion.

Before coming to any decision to-day we must
remember the changed times in which we live, the
greater knowledge, the higher mental level of the
people who wish to a greater and greater degree to
think their own thoughts, live their own lives, than
ever before.   The authority of the Church has gone
except amongst the ignorant, amongst those who fear
to think for themselves, and who never read except
upon one line of thought, what we might term
orthodox literature.

Now I come to my second point which is that
in my opinion Spiritualism has come to stay whether
we like it or not.   The Bishop of Diehardham I
think can only have taken his opinion on the subject
from the religious press, whose interest it is to condemn the subject, as, if the people accept the teachings
of Spiritualism, they will not read these publications.
Let him read, as I have done, the works of the leaders
of Spiritualism, and he will, if he is mentally honest,
come to the conclusion that Spiritualists are not the
people he makes them out to be, that a tilting table
may lead to our knowledge of unknown forces in the
Universe, just as the twitching of a frog's leg led to
important discoveries in electricity.

It was Faraday, I think, who, when telling some
silly society woman about his discoveries, answered

her futile question, ' And what, Mr. Faraday, is the use of all your experiments?' with these words, ' Madam, what is the use of a baby?—it grows to be a man or woman.' The baby of Spiritualism, born some ninety years ago, is now growing into manhood in spite of the jeers, contempt and warnings of the Christian priesthood. Our attitude to Spiritualism is just as wrong as was our attitude to evolution and all the other discoveries and reforms of the past.

The time has now come for us to change our attitude before it is too late and use this great new revelation to further the spiritual development of mankind. Let us cease being priests and become the guardians of this new knowledge. With our organisation let us protect it from all harm.

To me Christianity is not a religion of creeds and dogmas, but a life to be lived. I contend that the Christian life is not the only good life but that others bearing different labels can also have their share in this life. All humanity is reaching out after God, each following his own path according to his capacity, and it is not for us to say who is wrong and who is right. The revelation of the past which we worship should not blind us to the revelation of the present.

Let the Church go hand in hand with the Spiritualists, learn from them that survival and happiness after death is a fact and is no longer dependent on faith. Let us learn also from them the new philosophy which they teach, and remember that trivial messages can prove the survival of the personality. Much of our daily conversation is trivial and when the communicator is unseen his only way of demonstrating his presence is to remind the person on earth of some

event and something or other about which these two
only knew.

Spiritualism, if adopted by the Church, would
fill our empty pews and bring back to the Church the
millions who now attend Spiritualist services or none
at all.

Until, however, the Church gives me authority
to preach Spiritualism, I feel that I can do more good
in the Church than out of it, leavening it with my
opinions, until it ultimately gives me authority to
teach this new philosophy.   I shall never go against
the authority of the Church, nor express from the
pulpit views contrary to its teaching, but here in this
place it is different.   I feel that I am on this occasion
privileged to express my honest thoughts untrammelled by past tradition.

I would, therefore, ask you to condone the
Bishop of Alfortruth's opinions and action and give
him sufficient latitude to enable him to remain as a
pillar of progress within the walls of the Church,
which for a century has come to be looked on as the
broadest and most tolerant of all the sects of Christendom.''

Murmurs of disapproval were heard coming from
most of the bishops present, but as the president
announced an adjournment for lunch and ruled that
the Bishop of Alfortruth should make his defence at
two o'clock the Bench of bishops rose and the convocation adjourned.

'' You and I are the only two here to-day who

see the danger signal,'' Alfortruth remarked to Latitudeham during the interval. '' The others cannot
see where the Church is heading. . It has always
been the same. It is always contended that the creeds
and dogmas must stand, and that the opinions of sixteen hundred years ago should guide us to-day.''

'' One would think,'' replied Latitudeham,
'' that the world had stood still and that we knew no
more about the Universe to-day than they did when
everyone thought the world was flat, that the sun
circled the earth every twenty-four hours and thus
gave us day and night. Sixteen hundred years ago
America was unknown to Europeans, China, Africa,
and Asia were known only to a slight extent, only the
fringes and only in parts. Next to nothing was
known about medicine or the make-up of the human
body. Science, as we understand the word to-day,
did not then exist. Life was crude and cruel. Travel
was difficult and dangerous. Most of Europe was in
a state of barbarism which continued till within the
last few hundred years, and thoughts were passed by
writing from one to another only to a very limited
extent.

Little wonder that the early Church Fathers
were ' credulous, blundering, passionate and one-
sided,' to use the words of our great Church authority
Dr. Davidson.''

'' From those ignorant men,'' said Alfortruth,
'' our creeds, doctrines and dogmas came. I shall
deal with their vain imaginings in my remarks, but
may I tender you my grateful thanks for your support.
We are the only two who face facts and seek truth
for truth's sake.''

Then he went on to tell Latitudeham of the séance at which he had been present at Sureway Court and his various experiences with mediums over the past ten years.

" Oh yes," he remarked in reply to his friend, " I am sure Trueman would invite you to be present at one of his séances. It would be a revelation to you. Nothing you can read in books can compare with the actual experience. Yes, I must try to arrange a séance for you some day soon. You will then see more clearly than ever that the line I am following is the only possible one for me, who have had such overwhelming evidence that our Church doctrines are based on error and ignorance."

The Bishop of Latitudeham and the Bishop of Alfortruth were somewhat apart from the others so that their conversation could not be overheard. As the conversation proceeded, Latitudeham became more communicative and confidential. Stretching out his hand he put it on the shoulder of his brother bishop and in an impressive undertone he remarked :

" My dear Edward, if I had your money I would take up a much more independent attitude than I now do, dependent as I am on my stipend. I am now nearly seventy. I cannot turn to another way of earning my livelihood.

The minds of our brother bishops have been twisted out of the straight during their theological training and they have entirely lost the reasoning faculty. Can you imagine any other institution making the claims and statements which the Christian Church does in its published documents, and through its priests, without any foundation whatever to support them? When statements are made which affect the public, evidence must be available to support them ; if they are false, those who make these statements, and gain money in consequence, go to prison.

If anyone in the city of London tried to obtain money for an enterprise, on the flimsy basis on which rest our creeds and dogmas, they would be imprisoned for obtaining money on false pretences, and yet our Church is raising millions every year, and has done so throughout the Christian era, by giving false information to the public. It sickens me, Edward, and you are about the only one to whom I dare mention it. It is a melancholy fact that to a conscientious man like myself the more knowledge I gain the more miserable I become. I cannot leave the Church, and yet I cannot reconcile its teaching with what I know to be true. I wish I had known, when I was a young man, what I know now about the origin of Christianity. If I had I certainly would never have taken the vows I did."

"Your state of mind," replied Alfortruth, "is similar to my own. It is a very uncomfortable position for any intelligent individual who has a conscience."

The Bishop of Latitudeham drew his chair closer up to that of his brother bishop and whispered in his ear :

"Have you ever thought, Edward, what consternation it would cause to Christians if they really knew the truth about their religion and how it originated, if they were as acquainted with the facts as you and I are, and all scholars are? I hesitate even in a whisper to say what I am now going to say.

I am so accustomed to the atmosphere of hypocrisy. It is blunt and candid but it is as true as that you and I are sitting together here just now. Christ, and all that this word stands for, is a mythological creation. The entire gospel story is therefore untrue and the events recorded therein never happened. Our Church is consequently founded on lies, lives on lies, has grown and developed on lies, and can only remain in being by progagating lies and by bluffing and hum-bugging the people into believing that what is false is true.''

Latitudeham, after he had got this heretical pro-nouncement off his mind seemed relieved. He drew his chair back to its original place and the conversation continued in an undertone which could not be heard by anyone near by.

'' Only too true, my friend,'' replied Alfortruth, '' and the people need not rely on secular history to find this out. They have only to read *The History of the Christian Church*, by Robertson, who was Canon of Canterbury and Professor of Ecclesiastical History in King's College, London. The history he gives of how Constantine and Eusebius manufac-tured the Nicene Creed, and how it was carried at the Council of Nicæa, is enough to open the eyes of the blindest Christian to see how the beliefs of his Church came into being through the Christian priests, with the help of Constantine, adopting old beliefs and giving them new names.''

'' The strange thing,'' remarked Latitudeham, '' is that the people think that Constantine was a Christian ; but this is very doubtful. He worshipped Apollo to the last, retaining throughout his life the office of Pontifex Maximus, the highest in the pagan hierarchy, and took part to the last in pagan ceremonies. He certainly gave the Christians equal liberty with those professing other faiths and but for him Christianity would never have become an organised religion. He and Eusebius, the Bishop of Cæsarea, who was his trusted henchman, and lived constantly at his profligate court, had more to do with the establishing of Christianity than anyone else. They were both thoroughly unscrupulous men. Constantine was a murderer and a sadist, and Eusebius, though he is called the Father of Church History, was really the Father of Liars, as his writings have been found out to be impregnated with lies. He and Constantine between them manufactured the Nicene creed from surrounding pagan material and Constantine forced it through the Council of Nicæa. That we both know to be true.''

Alfortruth sat pensive for a time, drumming his fingers on the table before him, and his eyes took on a far-away look. The ordeal he was about to experience was evidently constantly before him. Latitudeham now sat silent, realising as he did what a weight was on his friend's mind. For a minute or two they sat thus and then Alfortruth rallied to the realisation of his present situation.

'' Excuse me,'' he said. '' You are a great strength to me at this time. Our conversation is giving me added strength and encouragement. To continue what we were discussing, just cast your mind back to the conditions prevailing in the fourth century in Rome, and as you have read Gibbon's great work, *The Decline and Fall of the Roman Empire*, you can easily picture to yourself what things were like. The Emperor Constantine was the autocratic Ruler of that great Empire. His word was law ; no Senate questioned his authority. Continually annoyed by the disturbances caused by the numerous sects which held divergent opinions about Jesus and Christ he determined to bring this quarrelling and squabbling once and for all to an end. How best could it be done? By bribes, threats and force. He thus welded these insignificant communities, with divergent views, into one powerful organisation and this took place at Nicæa in 325. By the force of his Imperial will, by appealing to the priests' lust for power, he consolidated a group of communities into what was to become the most powerful institution the world has ever known.

He was wise enough to see that all the divergent views could only be converged by insisting on a creed which all had to sign, or be considered outcasts. This creed he and Eusebius produced between them and Eusebius, after he had signed it, described it in a letter to his flock as more creditable to his ingenuity than his honesty. Constantine, you see, looked on Christ and Apollo as one and the same, as names that were interchangeable, and that the mother of Christ was the same as the Goddess Lotana, the mother of Apollo. The priests, to keep Constantine's friendship, accepted all the paganism that he desired and so produced at Nicæa just new names for old ideas and beliefs.

I apologise for telling you what you already know, but it helps to give me confidence for my forthcoming speech, so just let me talk on, as talking helps to lubricate my mind.

In exchange for submission to his Imperial will, Constantine promised the bishops and prelates assembled at Nicæa that if they passed his pagan creed he would recognise their religion as the State religion of Rome and give them his Imperial benediction.   For this bribe the priests sold the pass and accepted in return the pagan doctrines.   The gospels and epistles and other Church literature were altered to suit the added beliefs, and all who would not conform to the teachings of the now established Christian Church were cast out and murdered.

Thus the various sects, which adopted the god Christ, with all its pagan attributes, were welded into one organised body under the name of Christian. The old pagan beliefs remained, only the names given to the three gods in the pagan trinity, which was taken over, were changed.''

Here Latitudeham remarked : ` `` All true, Edward, all true. If you keep on in this style you will give them all nightmare. On this great fraud, perpetrated by Constantine, the Christian Church rests its foundations. Constantine, in my opinion, is the author of the biggest hoax in history, the most colossal, the most impudent and the most successful fraud that has ever been planted on humanity.''

`` I am honest enough to admit that what you say is only too true,'' replied Alfortruth, `` and the sad part about it all is that when our Church became supreme it exterminated all the philosophers and substituted for philosophy creeds and dogmas.   It thus kept back progress for at least fourteen hundred years because, with both philosophy and education stamped out, ignorance and barbarism became rampant.

This greatest of all crimes, the annihilation of philosophy and education, gave an entirely new meaning to religion, which came to be looked on as solely the belief in creeds and dogmas, whereas before Nicæa many religious people were reaching out to the Infinite in their attempt to solve the riddle of the Universe, and the mystery of existence. This free expression of opinion on life's mysteries was gradually stifled, libraries and books everywhere were burned, until hardly a book remained in Europe. Thus the Church became supreme and its history from the fourth century onwards proves that it does not stand for righteousness, and never has stood for righteousness but only to protect its creeds, dogmas and ceremonies which, the more earnestly the people believed, added to its wealth and power. Heresy hunts, torture, burnings, imprisonment, curses and anathemas then became general, so much so that in the reign of Theodora no less than one hundred thousand inoffensive and religiously-minded people, who could not accept the Nicene creed, were slaughtered.

That was just the beginning of the slaughter and torture which went on throughout the centuries of the Christian era, during which time countless millions became the victims of the Christian Church. After the Reformation the Protestants were as cruel as the Catholics when they had the power. In Germany alone, according to the *Encyclopædia Britannica*, during thirty years, no less than fourteen million innocent and religiously-inclined people, out of a population of twenty millions, were slaughtered and destroyed by the Christian Church, and yet it is our business to make people think that it is a divine institution, holy and sacred.   What humbugs we priests are !   Why the name Christian does not stink in the nostrils of all right-minded people can only be accounted for by their complete ignorance of history. This ignorance is directly due to the influence of the Church on education.   Just as it is strong enough to prevent the B.B.C. from broadcasting a Spiritualist service so it is strong enough to influence what is taught in our schools.

No schoolmaster or schoolmistress would dare to tell their pupils the truth about the origin of the Bible, or the origin of the Christian Church, or about our Church's bloody record.   This influence on education extends right up to our Universities, and if this ban on the truth is so effective in our more enlightened age think what it must have been in the past.   Now at least books are permitted to be published telling the truth but this has only been possible since the middle of last century.

Need we therefore be surprised that the people are so ignorant about the origin of the Christian religion?   Because they are ignorant they are prejudiced, and sentimental books sell like wildfire, as the people will mostly read books which they think must be true, appealing as they do to their religious feelings.   The books which keep strictly to historical facts, and are therefore unorthodox, are consequently rare because they have a limited sale, and that amongst thinking people only.   Authors must live like other people and they naturally write the books which will sell the best.   Only now and again an author appears who writes candidly and truthfully on the subject, but you will find that he is not writing for

profit, only from a sense of duty. Such an author,
it will be found, is absolutely independent of public
opinion and is quite indifferent whether he offends or
not. No man who has to earn his livelihood, pro-
fessionally or otherwise, can afford to take this risk.
Besides this independence of and indifference to public
opinion our author must have made a deep study of
the subject and been able to throw off, at an early
age, all the religious falsehoods he was taught in
youth. Unless he has been able to do so all his
study and research will be in vain, because to get at
the truth one must start with an absolutely unpre-
judiced mind.

Now we can realise why so few books appear
which you can thoroughly rely on to relate only what
is true, and which keep only to historical facts. When
you realise this you will understand why we clergy
have managed to get over so successfully all the humbug that goes under the name of Christianity.''

The bishop had become so absorbed in his subject that he was speaking much louder than his friend
thought wise, so Latitudeham held up a warning
finger.

"Quiet, Edward, not so loud! Don't waken
them yet! You will upset their digestions quite
enough within the next hour. Leave them in peace
to talk their usual platitudes which, so far as their
Christianity is concerned, always keep clear of anything fundamental and never get down to history
and facts.''

Alfortruth then continued in a lower voice :

'' Constantine gave the Church the key to autocratic power and with this it opened the flood-gates to

every brutality that it is possible for the mind of man to imagine. Truth and honesty have meant nothing to this monster of iniquity. At Nicæa it buried Truth so deep that we are only now getting down to it, but thank God truth has never yet been buried so deep that it has not ultimately been discovered. Now that it is being discovered the price of deception will have to be paid, and those who have been responsible for propagating and sustaining the delusion that Christianity was a God-given revelation, fresh and free to a heathen world nineteen hundred years ago, will some day have to take the consequences, and the consequences will be decidedly bitter.''

'' And yet,'' said Latitudeham, '' you are here to-day to be censured for telling the truth, and you have a bench of bishops going all out against the facts of history and condemning you for keeping to historical facts and discarding what is not true. Could anything be more absurd ! Human folly is enough to make the gods weep, and here at Churchisall human folly in concentrated into its very essence. Bluff and fraud, set in motion by Constantine, and approved by the priests at Nicæa, have continued throughout the Christian era, and been sponsored and supported by every priest and parson in Christendom up to the present day.

However, we cannot go on talking like this any longer, as it is nearly two o'clock. I am sure you will give a good account of yourself, Edward, so good luck to you, and remember that you will have at least one in your audience who admires your stand for truth and honest thinking. Though you are the honest man who is being pilloried to-day—when it should be the other way about—remember that ' The Mills of God grind slowly but they grind exceeding sure.' You, and your stand for truth, will go down to history. On the other hand, your accusers will be remembered with contempt, or be entirely forgotten.

Carry on, my friend, fortified with the armour of truth. Courage and confidence will carry you through to-day with flying colours.''

The two men shook hands and then rose from their seats, the Bishop of Alfortruth proceeding to the seat reserved for him beside the President, while the Bishop of Latitudeham resumed his seat in the front row of seats facing the platform.

CHAPTER XII.

THE BISHOP'S DEFENCE.

At two o'clock the Bishop of Alfortruth was called on by the President to make his reply.

" My Lord President, your Grace, my Lords, I rise to defend my words and actions. My guide in life is not what the Church teaches but what my reason, my intelligence and my knowledge show me to be true. The Church of Truth is my Church, and if the Church of Christ does not come up to the standard of my Church then I prefer to withdraw from it, if I am to be prohibited from expressing my honest opinions.

I took certain vows at my ordination which I now regret because I see that these vows limit my opinions to those held by my brother bishops. I must either think as they think or be deemed as having broken my vows, and as having been disloyal to the teaching of the Church and the Christian faith.

The line where orthodoxy ends and where heterodoxy begins has always been hard to define, and I object to being subject to a definition of heterodoxy by a body of men who put the Church first and truth, as I see it, last. I must abide by the dictates of my conscience. If I am allowed to do so, if I am allowed to speak and act as I think right, then I remain a Bishop of the Church. Otherwise I resign.

Let me now put before you my point of view. We have heard various expressions of opinion to-day ranging from those of the Bishop of Diehardham to those of the Bishop of Latitudeham. Such a diversity of opinions surely shows how divided is the Christian Church.   Even its Bishops cannot reach agreement as to what is Christianity.   One holds that only belief in the creeds and dogmas constitutes a Christian ; the other that it is the life we lead that constitutes a Christian.

If you all were in agreement with the views expressed by the Bishop of Latitudeham, then my position would be in no doubt.   I would not be called upon to resign, because to me it is the life that matters, not the theological beliefs we hold.

Let me, however, briefly take you back to the early days of the Christian religion and then on to the present day.   I take it for granted that you all keep yourselves informed as to present-day thought, the writings on comparative religion and the conclusions reached by scholars on the origin of the various world religions, including Christianity.   I take this for granted and this being so I need not give references for all I say.   My remarks can or should convey nothing new to you.   What I am about to say should be known to you all.   With the rank and file of the clergy it is different.   Few of them read outside their own subject.   If they obtain some fresh material for their Sunday's sermons from perhaps some other sermons, or from current orthodox literature, that suffices.   What is said and written by men of scholarship and wide learning is seldom known to them, but with you, my Lords, I presume it is different ; that you are widely read in all branches of thought, including the best works on Spiritualism, though, judging from the remarks made by the Bishop of Diehardham, if he has ever read such books, he has forgotten all he has read.

Now Christianity, like everything else, had a beginning, but like everything else on earth it was not new, only something dressed up in a new garb and given a different name.

I cannot find in Christianity one new thought, one new idea, one word of wisdom and instruction which was not contained in the religions and philosophies which preceded it, and I challenge you to prove me wrong. Like all ancient religions, produced in the days of ignorance, it inverted the order of nature and preached the fall instead of the progression of humanity.

That being so, what goes under the name of Christianity was not new. Christianity was but a new name for very old ideas. Its immediate ancestor was Gnosticism, whose followers worshipped the Son of God, as Saviour and Redeemer, under the name of 'Christos.' I would recommend a study of the writings of Philo and the Wisdom literature for confirmation that Christ was worshipped prior to the Christian era.

The Gospels teach us many things about Jesus. My Lord President wisely refrained from dwelling on this subject, and confined his remarks to the opinions of the early Church Fathers about Jesus and his teaching. How contradictory these are I shall have occasion to mention later on in my remarks.

Christianity has now been discovered by scholars to be the greatest fraud ever practised on humanity, and the people will some day make the same discovery. Though I admit that the Church just produced, at its inception, what its supporters desired, this does not do away with the fact that what it did produce had no basis in truth but was a theological speculation, based on pagan mythology, from first to last, which was given to the people as actual historical fact.

Children in the nursery are told fairy tales to keep them happy. The human race in its infancy required similar legends to satisfy its craving about the hereafter, but when the race evolves it cannot do otherwise than look back on the organisation responsible for these stories with contempt unless it makes the effort to rise mentally along with the community. Instead of so doing, it continues to preach these stories as the Word of God, under the cloak of being God's representative on earth, when every intelligent person now knows that they are merely legends and myths, and that the clergy have no basis whatever for their divine claims.

Though all intelligent people know that what I am now saying is true, yet it is the first time a bishop has been courageous enough to stand before his brother bishops and tell them the truth, which they secretly know or they would defend bravely and courageously their faith against all attacks and challenges of modern scholarship.

Which one of you, I ask, is brave enough to accept the many challenges to debate which have been hurled at us by those who have no interest in keeping the truth from the people? Why do we not reply to the attacks made in recent books? What is the Christian Evidence Society doing with its shabby two-roomed office in a garret, up a long flight of stairs, with only a girl to attend to callers? When I called there the last time I found no literature worth taking away, even if it had been given to me as a gift.

When I asked for a book to answer the challenge of those critics who make out a case that Jesus never lived, I was referred to the Rationalist Press Association, as this Association produced all the best literature on the subject.

Why do we not reply to all the attacks made on our claims and assertions? The answer is clear to everyone. We cannot; and when in the presence of one who knows the truth we keep dumb and shelter ourselves under the umbrella of convention. Thus our impossible assertions, our out-of-date dogmas and doctrines are never open to criticism either in public or private, it being considered bad taste to discuss openly the most vital subject on earth. In the pulpit, however, we hold forth freely because there we are in a sheltered corner, in our own building, with our own followers who accept all we tell them without reply or criticism. There we keep clear of origins, of history, and of anything basic or fundamental. Let me, however, on this occasion get down to fundamentals.

Jesus, or, to give him his correct Hebrew name, Jehoshua, for the last two hundred years has been the subject of intense research, and the thoughts of the greatest minds of the most erudite scholars have been centred on him for the purpose of discovering who he was, when he lived, and what he taught.

I need not remind you of the worthless nature of the Gospels and Epistles as historical documents. This must be known to you all, though you may not admit it. As histories they are valueless, and most scholars are in agreement that only some scattered words can be taken as the foundation on which were built up over the centuries what are now called the Gospels. The gospels are an attempt to tell as history what is mythology, they are a réchauffé of the Egyptian and other sacred writings, and the teachings of the Gnostics ; but I shall make this clearer before I sit down.

Paul hardly mentions Jesus. His gaze is concentrated on the heavenly being called Christ. To the man Jesus he gives scant attention, and it is generally accepted that the basis of what has become known as his writings preceded the gospels in date. Much, as you are aware, was added to the epistles, as well as to the gospels throughout the first four centuries of the Christian era.

Jesus is a misty, a very misty, figure in history, and some great scholars and thinkers believe that such a man never lived, that he was but another Odysseus who, though not having a Homer to conjure up his legendary greatness, had others equally capable of producing a hero to fit in with their theological speculations.

Let us, however, treat those documents relating to him as we would other documents which have come down to us from the past. Let us reject that for which there is no evidence, always remembering that the same supernatural legends, which have been woven round Jesus, were woven round most of the other saviour-gods of the past, with all of whom, I presume, you are well acquainted.

Before I finish I shall attempt to give you some of the opinions scholars have arrived at about the man

Jesus. The god Christ I shall deal with later as that is quite another matter.

Let me, however, refer you to a book by a great student on the subject, and one which was published within the last few months in this country. I refer to the book entitled *Jesus*, by C. Guignebert, Professor of the History of Christianity in the Sorbonne, Paris, a man whose opinions, owing to his scholastic attainments and learning, are worthy of the greatest respect. It is a sober but devastating exposure of the false claims made by Christianity, and its weight lies in the fact that its author considers every side of the question and quotes or gives references to every authority on the subject. The book thus embraces a wide range of thought and contains the most recent conclusions on this subject.

I shall now give you the professor's main conclusions, which he has reached after years of thought and research. They are as follows :—

' Ever since investigators, unbiased by religious motives, first applied themselves to the study of the problem of Christianity, not one has failed to reach the fundamental conclusions that the traditional explanation, the orthodox account of Christian origins, will not bear critical examination, because the gospels and the apologetic literature do not introduce us into the historical plane.' He refers to ' the desert of our knowledge ' and ' the dark gaps in our information,' remarking that ' the editors have sought to make up for their lack of knowledge by moving but fictitious narratives founded either upon supposedly prophetic writings or upon popularised myths or folk tales.'

'Christianity,' the professor declares, 'by no means appears to be, as was so long believed, a break in the ancient religious pattern.   On the contrary, it quite naturally assumes its place in that pattern,' the reason being that 'it was on Greek soil, in the atmosphere of the salvation mystery cults that this great mythification of Jesus and the gospel was effected.'   In consequence, ' Jesus the Nazarene disappeared and gave place to the glorified Christ. Paul has deliberately sacrificed Jesus to Christ.'

' All the work of early Christian thought on the oral and written tradition regarding Jesus may be summed up in one sentence.   It tends progressively to discard historical reality and substitute for it edifying legend.

' It was not the essence of Jesus that interested the authors of our gospels, it was the essence of Christ as their faith pictured.   They are exclusively interested, not in reporting what they know, but in proving what they believed.

' We may concede that the breath of life is still discernible in our gospels and that the outline of a man and the traces of an individual activity are still to be distinguished, but that falls far short of what we need to see and know in order to form any clear and certain conception of the person of Jesus.

' The more we are convinced that there is no confidence to be placed in the evangelist arrangement of their source material, the more we are forced to the conclusion that a reconstruction of the life of Jesus is impossible.

' Jesus was arrested, tried, condemned and executed.   That is all of which we are certain,' but

' he was not the founder of Christianity because Christianity issued from Christ.'

Such, then, are the conclusions of one who has devoted his life dispassionately to the history of the Christian religion and confirms the opinion I have already expressed that the Christian Church has been teaching as history what was nothing more than Pagan mythology.

It is possible to have Christianity without Jesus, but you cannot have Christianity without Christ. That, I say, is unchallengeable, because the world had Christianity before Jesus was born. It flourished under many names, but is now spoken of as Paganism, which covers the religions of Rome, Greece, Persia, Egypt and Babylon, the countries surrounding Palestine.

I say that there were Christians before the time of Jesus in this sense, that the followers of these religions, in these countries, worshipped a virgin-born Saviour-god, who suffered death for the sins of mankind, rose from the dead and ascended into Heaven. Similar legends surrounded these gods to those that surround the Christian Christ, and similar convulsions of nature are reported as having occurred at their deaths to those we are told accompanied the death of the Christian Christ.

In other words, Christ, which is the Greek for the anointed one, is a theological name, which stands for a god who never lived on earth, who was one of a trinity of gods and had no relation whatever to a man, a human being.

No Christ ever lived on earth, but only in the imagination of those who worshipped him.''

Cries of protest and dissent came from all parts of the hall, but after the noise had ceased the bishop continued, quite unperturbed.

" I have sufficient facts to enable me to support this statement, and all your protests will not alter facts.   If I state anything that is untrue I shall withdraw it if you raise the matter after I sit down ; but wait till I have finished, when I shall gladly hear your criticism.   Please, therefore, do not try to silence me. I am here making my defence.   A prisoner is always allowed a hearing, so whether you like what I have to say or not I shall say it, and must request you to listen to me quietly and decently.

I repeat that I have sufficient facts to support my statement that Christ never lived on earth, that he was a heavenly being conjured up by the theologians of the past.   Mythology was turned into history by the founders of the Christian Church and it is in thus turning mythology into history that the fraud of Christianity lies.   Seas of blood have been shed and incalculable agony and suffering have been caused by the Christian Church trying to maintain its beliefs as history.   The earth has been honeycombed with the graves of the martyrs who saw its error and suffered in consequence.   In the past the Church was strong enough to keep down this heresy, but now it is not, and as every year passes the truth is becoming clearer to the people and the fraud of Christianity is becoming more fully realised.

I, for one, as an honest man, prefer to admit this

fraud. I ask you to do likewise and thus readjust the course of the Protestant Church from the way of error into the way of honest thinking and honest preaching, leaving for ever the path of dishonesty and humbug.

It seems extraordinary that I should have to stand here and emphasise the necessity for honest thinking, honest acting and honest speaking. You cannot plead ignorance as to the facts I have related and am about to relate to you. They must be known to you as well as they are known to me. If they are not, you are culpably ignorant. If the facts I am about to relate to you supported the claims you make, you would preach them regularly. As they do not, you put them to the back of your minds and try to forget them ; but this will not absolve you in the eyes of the public. You are wilfully ignorant of the basis of your religion, and laymen are far more honest about what they believe than you, my Lords, who set yourselves up as the spiritual leaders of the people.

The study of comparative religion proves that all religions are related in some way or another. Some are distant relations, some are cousins, but others are brothers. Christianity is related to those which were its brothers as they had a common parent, namely, Sun and Verdure worship. These developed into those religions which worshipped Osiris, Horus, Mithra, Prometheus, Christos and other Saviour god-men long before the Christian era. To-day they are grouped under the name of Mythology, which stands for myths and legends of the gods in the heavens, and their relations to the people on earth. This mythology embraces the fall of man and his redemption by one of the gods coming to earth to take the punishment for the sins of humanity.

The theme throughout is the same ; the only difference is in the names of the gods, each nation having a different name for the saviour-god just as each nation had different names for Adam and Eve, the transgressors.   This interchange of the names of the gods was quite common in mythology.   After the Romans adopted the Greek myths in their religion, the Greek god Zeus became the Roman god Jupiter, but they were identified with each other, and when a Roman citizen spoke to a Greek about Jupiter the Greek associated Jupiter with Zeus and vice versa. Other instances could be given, the Greek god Apollo being the Roman god Appellon, and so on.

From this you will see that the gods Osiris, Horus, Mithra, Prometheus and Christos, all of whom were worshipped prior to the Christian era, stood for the same ideas.   One could therefore travel from Egypt to Persia, from Persia to Babylon, from Babylon to Greece, and worship the same god, the only difference being that the gods of Egypt were Osiris and Horus, the god of Persia was Mithra, the god of Babylon was Bel, and the god of the Gnostics was Christos.

I have not the time to go over the ground detailing to you the beliefs held by the worshippers of all these gods.   I shall confine my remarks to the Egyptian religion, as what I say of it can be taken as referring also to those other religions.

Christianity was produced in Alexandria, which at the beginning of our era had the most influential theological school the world had ever known.   Alexandria was dominated by Gnostic and Greek thought, and this is best represented by the writings of Philo. Into Alexandria flowed the stream of beliefs comprising the Egyptian, Persian, Babylonian and Greek religions. Under the name of Christ or Christos, the Gnostics worshipped the god of Egypt, the god of Persia, the god of Babylon and the god of Greece. Just as Jupiter meant to a Roman the same as Zeus meant to a Greek, so Christ meant to a Gnostic what Bel meant to a Babylonian, Osiris and Horus meant to an Egyptian, Mithra to a Persian, and Prometheus to a Greek. Each of those names stood for a Divine Being who, according to current myths and legends, was believed to have come to earth and suffered as the redeemer for the sins of mankind, which had incited the wrath of the Supreme Deity owing to the disobedience of the first man and woman.

It is therefore not surprising to find that this religion believed in by the Egyptians, Persians, Babylonians, Greeks and Gnostics spread westward in pre-christian days along the shores of the Mediterranean and ultimately, as Christianity, dominated Europe. There was nothing new about it so far as those eastern countries were concerned ; all that was new was that the religion spread over Europe. As the theological centre was Alexandria, the centre of Gnosticism, it was natural that when the religion spread west and north it would adopt their name Christ for the god the people worshipped and that those worshippers should be called Christians. The Christians, therefore, were just the western and northern offshoot of the religions of Egypt, Persia, Babylon and Greece, worshipping the same god as they worshipped but under the name of Christ.

As Prometheus was the Christ of the Greeks, Bel the Christ of the Babylonians, Mithra the Christ of the Persians, what therefore applies to one applies to the others, and what I now tell you of the religion of Egypt applies equally to the religions of Greece, Babylon and Persia. Thus you will see that the Christianity of Europe was believed in by these Eastern people just as the Christianity of America is believed in by Europeans. Christianity flowed westward to America as it flowed westward from Alexandria into Europe.

What I am about to relate is taken from papyri, from coffins, from inscriptions, ritual texts and scenes on the walls of temples in Egypt, which are at least fifteen hundred years older than the commencement of the Christian era. From them we have learned the religious beliefs held by many along the shores of the Mediterranean till within as recent a date as the fifth century of the Christian era.

From these well-preserved relics we can read and appreciate the religious faith of the Egyptian people, who gave as much thought to the after-life as they did to this one and whose mythology was fashioned by two great natural objects, the Sun and the Nile, both of which had such an effect on the annual death and resurrection of vegetation.

' That which thou thyself sowest is not quickened except it die ' are words we attribute to Paul, but they are only an echo of what was ever in the thoughts of the dwellers by the Nile. The Greeks, Romans and the entire Mediterranean world were likewise influenced by the annual cycle of dying and reviving vegetation, and on it they based their mythology.

Imagine Egypt, with its clear atmosphere, the sun day after day giving evidence of its power, its all-enveloping glory, and the mighty Nile swelling and overflowing its banks in spring, then receding to repeat this same fertilising process when spring returns the following year. This has gone on as long as man has lived on earth. What a profound impression it made on the religious feelings of those dwellers on its banks ! As the Nile brought salvation to Egypt, so in their mythology it became their principal god, the saviour of the people.

The sun was likewise deified, and these two gods became the basis of their religious beliefs.

Round the sun the story grew, of how the sun-god fought for the people against the god of darkness, how by this god he was conquered at night and then went to the underworld to rise again the next day triumphant and ascend to the heavens.

The annual increase and decrease in the power of the sun and the yearly rise and fall of the Nile made the Egyptians, dependent on them both for their food and sustenance, realise that life and death came by their waxing and waning. Consequently they were worshipped as gods and became the saviours of the race, who died to rise again so that by their resurrection man might live.

The Nile was personified by Osiris, the saviour-god, and the Sun by the saviour-god Horus, who were looked on as Father and Son because of their close relationship to the life of Egypt. Against them both Set, the god of darkness, was for ever at war.

The Egyptian religion is thus composed of Sun worship and Vegetation worship, and these two forms of belief at a later date in Egyptian history merged into one.

As vegetation died and came to life again, as the sun died to rise again, so man likewise died to rise again. What was obvious in nature, it was argued, must occur to man himself. Vegetation died and returned to life by the help of the Sun and the Nile. So man died to return to life by the help of Horus, the prototype of the Sun, and of Osiris, the prototype of the Nile.

Mother earth was likewise deified as Isis, the creator of vegetation, and round this trinity circled the religious beliefs of the Egyptians, from which came the beliefs of Christians at a later date, as you will see as I proceed.

From this short introduction you will understand better what I am now going to tell you of the beliefs which became centred round these three gods. Round them was woven a story of their deeds for the salvation of mankind. These legends are known as mythology, and as this story is the same one as is told in the New Testament regarding Christ you will have no difficulty in perceiving where Christianity originated and that it is just mythology. I need not quote to you the parallel incidents in the Christian legend, so I shall go straight on and tell you what the Egyptians believed regarding Osiris, Horus and Isis, the father god, his son and life-giving mother.

The Egyptians worshipped Osiris and Horus as father and son, and Horus at his birth, as the result of the overshadowing by Osiris of his virgin mother

Isis, was hailed by angels, who proclaimed him ' Lord of All.'

All the incidents in the Christian story of the Annunciation, as did those of the Adoration, came from Egypt, the god-child Horus being depicted as receiving gifts and being visited by three Magi.

Osiris was worshipped as the Father God, the Lord of Eternity, the Judge and Saviour of mankind.

Osiris was termed the Resurrection and the Life.

Osiris was the God of Truth, the God of Righteousness, the God of Justice and the Judge of all the earth.

Osiris was represented as a scourge-bearing god. He was looked on as the Shepherd of the flock.   He was the most beloved of all the gods of Egypt, and known as The Good Being.   Believers in Osiris were born again and saved from their sins.   He was the giver of Immortality and the Judge of the Dead.

Osiris is represented as a King with Sceptre. He, like Horus, was hailed as ' Lord of All.'

Osiris was the First Fruits.

Osiris was lifted to the sky and drew all men unto him.

He was the Lord and Saviour, the Justifier and Redeemer, the substitute, and suffered vicariously for the sins of mankind.

Osiris was the Water of Life and gave freely to them who thirsted.   He was also The Tree of Life and the Vine.

Osiris gave his body to be broken.   He died so that his followers might live.

When listening to me you must have realised how all these terms and beliefs could be applied to the Nile, and the growth and decay of vegetation.

Horus, the prototype of the sun, received similar affectionate and appropriate terms.

Horus was termed The Good Shepherd.   He was likened to the Morning Star.

Horus was called the Lamb of God, the Beloved Son, and Our Lord.

He was the Redeemer and by the Gnostics termed The Cross.

Horus was the Bread of Life, the Way, the Truth and the Life.

He was the Path of Life and the Door of Life.

He was the only begotten Son of God.

Horus, like Christ, was the Prince of Peace, and also like Christ, the Sword bringer, just as the Sun brings sunshine and storm.

Horus was born at Christmas, he descended into Hades and rose again at Easter, the two principal periods of the year held sacred by Sun worshippers.

Horus came to earth to suffer for the sins of mankind.   He was at constant enmity with Set, the Egyptian Satan, just as the Sun is at constant war with darkness.

Horus is pictured as a child in the arms of Isis, which is the origin of the Madonna and Child.

Such, then, were the terms of adoration and reverence showered on both Osiris and Horus. Now I shall briefly relate some of the things believed about them during their sojourn on earth when they entered matter so as to bring salvation to mankind.

Isis, the virgin mother of Horus, takes the child Horus on a journey.   Horus is heard of again at the age of twelve and is slain in his twenty-eighth year.

The Herod of the Gospel story of the slaughter of the infants was the Egyptian Heru, a mythological character, known as the terrifier, who shed the blood of the innocent.

Horus when a child was lost and his mother searched for him.

Horus was baptised, the Spirit of God as a dove descending on him.

The story of the transfiguration came from Egypt, as did the story of Christ at the well talking to a woman with five husbands.

The Egyptian Pool of Peace, in which the infirm were healed when an angel descended, became the Pool of Siloam in the Christian gospels.

Osiris was termed the Lord of the Harvest, and had twelve reapers.

Likewise the Christian religion copied from Egypt the stories of the loaves and fishes, of Horus offering up thanks to Heaven, which is the origin of our grace before meals, and of the devils entering the swine.

The Egyptian god brought back the dead to life, saying to the mummy on one occasion ' Come Forth,' as Christ is reported as saying to Lazarus. He wept over Rem-Rem as Christ did over Jerusalem, and had his feet washed by Meri as the feet of Christ were washed by Mary.

When the Egyptians prayed, they did so in the name of Osiris.

Osiris is represented as a god-man. He gave laws as to how to live and guidance as to worship. He wrought miracles, exorcised evil spirits, cured the halt and the maimed, raised the dead and made the blind to see and the deaf to hear.

Osiris had a triumphant procession to the temple.

After Christ had dipped the sop of bread we are told that Satan entered into Judas.   So likewise was Osiris betrayed by the eating of bread.

The story of Osiris in his agony and bloody sweat in Semen was the source of the story of Christ in Gethsemane.

Osiris was tried in the Judgment Hall, arrayed as a King and, like Christ, found innocent.   He is depicted as the silent one.

Osiris also had a seamless robe.

In the seventh hour the mortal struggle took place between Osiris and the deadly Apophis, Osiris emerging the Conqueror of the Grave.

Thus, as Osiris overcame Satan, in the likeness of the serpent called Apophis, exclaiming as he did so 'I have bruised the serpent, I have passed,' so Christ is represented as the conqueror of the serpent.

Osiris was slain and his body broken.   In one temple on the Island of Philae he is represented as crucified.

The cross to the Egyptians was the symbol of immortality, and every believer considered that after death he lived in a celestial realm with Osiris, who had conquered death.   On the other hand, the destiny of the unbelievers was a sea of flame which they entered through two fiery gates.

After death Osiris goes to the underworld, helping those in darkness.   He became the God of the Underworld and the Judge of the Dead, as did Christ.

Two women, who were sisters, mourned over

the corpse of Osiris, as did two sisters over the body of Christ.

The body of Osiris was swathed in linen bandages which were thrown aside when life returned.

As Osiris rose from the tomb the two protecting angels held before his face the cross. A similar story is told about the risen Christ in the non-canonical gospel of Simon Peter.''

Here the bishop paused and pointed to the cross worn by the Bishop of Diehardham, who was seated in front of him.

'' Do you realise, my Lords, that the cross, which some of you wear, has been the symbol of love and sacrifice for thousands of years before the Christian era? How many of you realise that historians know of at least sixteen Saviour Gods who were believed by their worshippers, in the centuries preceding the Christian era, to have been crucified for the sins of the world? Do any of you think that the Saviour God Thor, of our Nordic ancestors, to whom we have dedicated Thursday, carried with him a hammer in the form of a cross, with which his followers believed he destroyed the serpent of evil and raised them to life eternal? Your Pastoral staffs originated in Egypt, in fact all the emblems and symbols of Christianity came either from Mithraism or Osirianism. If our pagan ancestors had known the words of our hymn *Rock of Ages* they would have sung it with the same fervour, and received from it the same comfort, as do Christians to-day.

This, however, is a diversion and I am wandering into the similarities between the Christian and other religions, instead of keeping to my subject, namely, the Egyptian religion. I had got to the point where the cross was held before Osiris as he rose from the tomb. Now let us consider what follows.

The body of Osiris could not be found. While it was lost the people fasted and mourned and when it was found they rejoiced saying 'We have found him, Rejoice!'

Two angels guarded the tomb of Osiris and after his resurrection he is seen again, just as happened in the story we have about the resurrection of Christ. The supposed tomb of Osiris became to the Egyptians what the supposed tomb of Christ became to the Christians.

Osiris after his resurrection is seen and recognised but he must not be touched, just as Christ is reported as saying 'Touch me not.'

Osiris showed himself after his resurrection exclaiming 'Give me your arm, I am made as ye are,' just as Christ before his ascension appeared to his disciples and drew their attention to his pierced hands and feet, and asked to be touched so that they might see that he was flesh and blood as they were.

Osiris was the risen and glorified Lord, who ascended into his Kingdom.

A ritual sacrament was observed to commemorate the death of Osiris, the partakers of which believed that they thus shared the god's immortality, which view is also held by Christians.

At Egyptian funeral services the priests committed the departed to the keeping of Osiris, who could raise their bodies to life eternal just as Christian priests commit the dead to the keeping of Christ.

Similar words to those quoted at every Christian funeral service, taken from Paul, were used by the Egyptian priests because Paul, or someone else, just copied them from the Egyptian Ritual.

My Lords, I could go on giving you one parallel after another, taken from the religions of Egypt, Babylon, Persia and Greece, until I had pieced together the entire Gospel story of the Christ, from birth to his ascension into heaven. What I have said, however, must suffice. I have confined the parallels to the Egyptian religion, to the gods Osiris and Horus, from which you will realise the significance and truth of the words in Matthew's Gospel ' Out of Egypt have I called my Son.'

I apologise for acting as your teacher, because all I have told you I must presume you know already. It is part of your profession to know these things just as it is part of your profession never to tell the public about them."

At this point in the bishop's speech the Bishop of Faithford rose and in a loud voice addressed the President :

" My Lord President, I protest. I vehemently protest. All these statements will appear in to-morrow's newspapers. What will the people think? How ever are we going to explain them to our flocks who have never before had their faith shaken by thinking along these lines? "

But he got no further, as the President rose from his seat and requested him to sit down.

" I must request you, my Lord, to be seated. We must listen to what the Bishop of Alfortruth has to say. Had we known that his defence would include a review of the origin of our religion we would certainly have excluded all newspaper reporters. We cannot, however, do so now, and we cannot refuse a hearing to one on trial. This day's proceedings must have unfortunate and disturbing results. It is indeed a most unfortunate affair from beginning to end, and no one regrets more than I do what is taking place to-day."

The President then looked across to the Bishop of Alfortruth and remarked : " I suppose nothing I can say will keep you from expressing your opinions, so please proceed."

" What I have told you about Osiris," continued the Bishop of Alfortruth, " came from Nature worship. He was a vegetation god. Horus was the prototype of the Sun, the giver of life and light to mankind, which died at night and rose again in the morning, the conqueror of darkness to bring light and life to the earth. The Sun was the Saviour of mankind who was at perpetual war against the darkness of evil, and at its death each night went to the underworld, to rise again the victor. The ancients transformed the doings of the sun into the doings of god-men, and in myth and legend told the story of these mythical heroes taken from the different phases of the sun in relation to the earth throughout the year. A visit to the Catacombs at Rome and a study of the imagery on the walls will establish the fact that the symbolism, allegories, figures and types of ancient mythology were passed on and accepted by the early Christians. The Christian Christ is a mixture of a vegetation-god and a sun-god, having the attributes of both types of god.

Thus all the sun god-men were depicted with the sun as a halo behind their heads and in their worship their followers turned to the east, to the rising sun, which brought life and light to earth. Likewise these heroes were born, died, and rose again on the same dates, and the Holy Days which were observed were the same for the worshippers of all these god-men, the Christian Christ included, as each Holy Day marked a phase of the sun in the annual journey of the earth round its Protector, Saviour and Life-giver.

The Crucifixion, determined by the full moon at Easter, is doubtless astronomical in origin, and the darkness which followed refers to an eclipse of the sun, when the Sun God was angry and withdrew its face from the earth.

The Sun God, or the reflection of the sun, walked on the waters as did his prototypes, and just as the sun waxed and waned so also did his prototypes, to rise again in strength, the conquerors of death and the grave, in which the sun had been hidden throughout the night.

Our religion is the mythology of the ancients, and this mythology originated in sun worship. Till the hieroglyphic texts were translated by Champollion, who discovered the clue to them from the Rossetta stone in Egypt, the story they had to tell remained buried throughout the Christian era. In

like manner, Rawlinson discovered the clue to the
Babylonian language on the Behistun rock in Assyria,
which revealed to us the Babylonian religion and its
similarity to Christianity.   Thus, what was just
mythology is believed by Christians to be a divine
revelation by God through Christ to man as recorded
in his Holy Word.

Christ never lived on earth.   I do not deny his
divinity.   I emphatically assert and emphasise it.
He was a heavenly mythological being, nothing more,
and nothing less.   As such he was worshipped under
various names by the pagans for thousands of years
before our era.

The Christian scheme of redemption is founded
on a fable which has been mis-represented and mis-
interpreted.   This fable has been given to the world
by the Christian Church as an historical fact.   In its
essence it is of both vegetation and astronomical origin
and the belief in the end of the world and the coming
of Christ refers to the sun in its relation to the earth.

The ancients mapped out an imaginary zone in
the heavens within which lie the paths of the sun,
moon and principal planets.   It was divided into
twelve signs and marked by twelve constellations
called the Zodiac.   As the sun passed each sign the
Messiah or Christ was expected on earth.

For thousands of years, prior to the Christian
era, this idea was believed in by the pagans.   In the
form of myths and legends the Christian gospel story,
from beginning to end, is the story of the sun and
vegetation, the Christian Christ being the prototype
of both.   The Gnostic Christ, the Egyptian Horus,
the Persian Mithra, the Babylonian Bel and the Greek

Prometheus were sun-gods who were written about as legendary heroes by the ancients and turned by the Christian Church from fiction into fact, from mythology into history.

From first to last the Christian gospels contain the drama of the sun-gods Horus, Prometheus, Bel and Mithra, believed in by the Christians as history, believed in by the Christians as true, believed in by the Christians as having happened on earth, whereas it all happened in the heavens, the sun being the Christ.

The Gnostics of the second century of our era asserted, and these assertions have been proved to be true, that the Christians had transferred celestial persons, celestial scenes and celestial ideas to earth, and that what had been taught in the past as mythology was being taught by the Christians as history.

From the descent of the Holy Ghost to overshadow Mary, to the ascension of the risen Christ, the events, the occurrences and the characters embodied in the story, together with the sayings and acts reported of the hero, came from Pagan mythology which dates back at least six thousand years. These events are not history. These events constitute mythology. Paganism is this mythology, and Christianity is Paganism, nothing more and nothing less. Every trait and feature assembled to make up the Christ, and the entire story which surrounds his supposed life on earth, were pre-existent to the Christian era, in Egypt and the surrounding countries.

We have therefore the extraordinary spectacle of witnessing about one-third of the world's population believing and worshipping as did the pagans, but calling themselves Christians, and brought up from childhood to look upon paganism with contempt. Surely this is as great a delusion as the delusion that the sun circled the earth. The discovery that the Christian religion, which propagated this delusion, is paganism, and not a new revealed religion to humanity nineteen hundred years ago, is as important as was the discovery of the true relationship of the sun to the earth. My Lords, your flocks will some day demand an explanation of this fraud, and you will have to face the disgust, indignation and contempt which is always aroused in those who have been defrauded when they discover the truth."

Here the bishop paused for a few seconds to adjust his notes. Then he continued :

" The Christian God is impossible to contemplate, a Trinity in unity and yet a person with human attributes and feelings. To me God represents the over-ruling Mind of the Universe, the cause of all we experience, but the Christian God, according to what is taught by the Church, sacrificed part of himself in the person of his Son to satisfy his wrath against humanity. This is one of the most illogical and savage doctrines ever conceived. Little wonder that the social record of Christianity is the history of a ghastly failure, when the religion itself is based on the belief in a wrathful, revengeful and unjust God, who must satisfy his blood lust in this way, enabling only a minority of believers to be saved ! On the other hand the great majority must be damned in spite of the fact that the sacrifice was made. The Church which adopted this doctrine from Paganism thus kept Christendom in its grip just so long as it could keep the people ignorant and a prey to superstition. This it managed to do from the fifth century, when it became all powerful, up till the end of last century, when the people conquered by obtaining general education.

My Lords, we cannot keep the people ignorant any longer ; they are learning the facts for themselves, and the sooner we realise this, and trim our sails accordingly, the better it will be for our future and for the world at large. We must admit the truth. We must admit that we have mis-interpreted mythology and turned it into history. We must, if we have any pretence to honesty, admit our mistakes and our numerous past errors and shortcomings, otherwise the sword of truth will be for ever hanging over our heads, liable at any time to fall on us when the cord of ignorance is broken by education.

Now, to continue my theme. Though we have discovered the theological and mythological Christ, it still remains for us to discover the historical Jesus. Did such a one ever live ? On that question I reserve a definite opinion, but as I have already said, you can have Christianity without Jesus, though you cannot have Christianity without Christ. The belief that a man Jesus ever lived is a pure assumption. We have nothing historical whatever to guide us. He was never mentioned by any contemporary historian, and later historians referred to him as a god. The claim that the Christian Jesus ever lived on earth was denied from early times by those who were not Christians.

Here we come to the region of assumption, not to the region of history.

What I have so far related to you, however, are facts which cannot be contradicted and which prove that the Christian Christ was the same mythological being as was the Egyptian Saviour and Redeemer, who, under different names, was revered and worshipped prior to our era in the countries surrounding Palestine.

How all these beliefs took root and, over the centuries, spread throughout Europe and along the shores of the Mediterranean is another question. The books which have been written on this subject are highly technical and the opinions vary considerably. These opinions range from the belief that the real Jesus lived one hundred years prior to the Christian era to the belief that the Jesus of the gospels was no more than a teacher, a healer, a reformer, and either believed himself to be the Messiah or was believed to be such by his followers.

The opinions of those who believe that the Jesus, as portrayed in the gospels, never lived are based on the belief that a Jesus cult had been in existence in Palestine for hundreds of years prior to the Christian era. This cult, it is claimed, worshipped a divine being called Jesus, or in Hebrew, Jehoshua, and had been suppressed by the Jewish priesthood. Owing, however, to the fall of Jerusalem, which brought about a break-up of the Jewish Hierarchy, it was released from its suppression to take firm root and spread. It then came to be believed by the followers of this cult that their Jesus god had actually lived on earth, under the name of Jehoshua ben

Pandira (Ben meaning ' the son of '), and was hung on a tree on the eve of the Passover by the Jews about one hundred years earlier than the time ascribed to the Gospel Jesus. From this the story grew by incorporating from Alexandria all the mythological stories told about the Gnostic Christ.

So there was a fusion of two forms of belief, that of the Jesus cult and that of the Christ mythology, but there was no difficulty about this fusion because the beliefs of the Jesus cult were similar to the beliefs of those who accepted the Gnostic Christ.

This view satisfies this school of thought as to how Christ came to be associated with Jesus, both being gods, and why everything about the Gospel Jesus is so indefinite and misty, it being impossible to trace him as an historical character. His worshippers did not even know the date of his birth, but years after his supposed death they assumed the date to be during the reign of Herod. Herod is now known to have died in 4 B.C. Jesus, according to gospel chronology was born four years later, so that the Gospel Jesus was not born in the reign of Herod, as the gospels state.

The Gospel records then began to make their appearance in a very simple form. To begin with they were founded on the doings of Jesus ben Pandira, just as a story was told of what Osiris did on earth as a man. This was added to and added to from surrounding pagan material until Jesus was portrayed as a god, just as happened to Osiris, possessing all the attributes of the other pagan Christs.

Our information about Jesus is so vague as to be practically negligible. We do not know when or

where he was born.   We do not know when or where
he lived.   We do not know when or where he died.
The date given for his birthday is years out in relation
to the historical events which, it is stated, ran con-
currently with his birth.   Tradition is so vague on this
subject that the early Christian writers varied from
4 B.C. to 9 A.D. as to the date of his birth, and between
21 A.D. and 58 A.D. as to the date of his death.   So
much for the historical Jesus !   It is very doubtful if
his supposed birthplace existed at the date of his birth.
We do not know who were his parents, or his ancestors.   We know nothing about his appearance.   We
do not know how he lived ; in fact we know nothing
whatever about him.

And yet most scholars, men who have devoted
their lives to the quest of the historical Jesus, accept
the fact that he lived somewhere in Palestine and met
a martyr's death, about the time recorded, as otherwise they cannot explain the origin of the Christian
religion.   They have to postulate someone who had
the power to attract followers, who had a local reputation, had a message to deliver and a deep and sincere
faith in what he preached.   In other words, they
picture Jesus teaching the virtues, namely, purity,
humility, compassion, gentleness, charity, simplicity
and forgiveness, as one who takes the religion of the
prophets and moulds it into the religion of humanity.

Such is the impression they get after lifting layer
after layer of interpolation from the story of one who
set himself the task of calling the people in his neighbourhood to repentance, because of his belief in the
near approach of the Kingdom of God, which meant
the end of the existing order.   Quite possibly he had

strong psychic power and because of this his followers during his life and after his death looked on him as one who did and said things quite above the ordinary. Jesus, however, had no idea of founding a new religion, and he lived and died a Jew. His preaching, teaching and healing attracted followers and his criticism of the ruling classes stirred up their enmity, which brought about his martyrdom, after only a few months of missionary effort.

But for Paul the death of Jesus would have been the end. As events worked out, Jesus became the foundation stone of an immense world-wide theological structure, which he would have been the last to support or countenance. As to how this happened I shall consider in a few minutes.

Lastly, there remains the orthodox view that Jesus was God incarnate ; that all which the gospels record of his life on earth is true and that the Christian revelation is the only true faith, by the acceptance of which we are saved.

If I tried to analyse all these diverse opinions I should keep you here listening to me for a week.

Owing to the fact that the early Christians destroyed all the writings of those who denied this orthodox way of thinking, it is doubtful if we shall ever know the facts relating to the origin of Christianity as a separate religion. We know where its myths, legends and doctrines originated, and this I have briefly related to you. As to how and why these doctrines took root in Europe, these questions may forever remain an enigma.

After studying carefully all these different opinions I should like to put forward a theory which may be right or may be wrong.   At least it is a possible theory and contains as many threads of probability as any other.

How was it that Jesus became the basis of this great theological scheme?

Paul starts the idea that Jesus was the Christ because he saw an apparition of what he believed was Jesus.   He evidently believed it intensely and is reported as believing that other followers of Jesus had had a similar experience.   Those stories of Jesus appearing after his death may be true or they may not—who can say?   Who can pick out the true from the false, when every line is suspect, when we know that forgery was rampant, interpolations were numerous, and theological speculations took the place of facts and of history?   At least it is a possible explanation of how a human being came to be incorporated with a god, related to mythology, because in Paul's day an apparition was looked upon as a god. In his day the Christ was expected to return to earth, and Virgil and other gentile writers anticipated the coming of Christ, just as the Jews anticipated the coming of the Messiah, the Jewish name for the Christ.

Osiris, Bel, Prometheus, Mithra and the Gnostic Christ had satisfied the religious aspirations of Egypt, Babylon, Greece and Persia.   The ground was ready for other races to adopt the same religion, and Paul fanned this experience of his from a spark into a flame which gathered strength till in time all Europe was ablaze, not with a new religion worshipping new gods, but with one of the world's oldest religions in a new guise, the Father, the Son and the

Holy Ghost taking the place of the Trinities of the religions surrounding Alexandria.

Paul, let us assume, started the idea that Jesus was the Christ, and, drawing from Philo and other contemporary writers, affixed to Jesus all the mystical speculations of the age. Jesus, the man, so far as Paul was concerned, then went into oblivion. Christ was all and in all.

Then came centuries of wranglings as to the meaning of Christ and his relationship to the other members of the Trinity. From the fourth century onwards it was not how you lived that constituted a good Christian but whether you interpreted Christ according to the rulings of the many Church Councils, which were forever being convened to decide this futile question.

This, then, may be the explanation as to how Christianity originated. Its doctrines were not new. The only thing new about it was that all those doctrines came to be centred round this hitherto un-known Jesus, who ceased to be a man in the minds of the ignorant and superstitious, who made up the early Church, and became a virgin-born Saviour, who had died for the sins of the world, the second God of a Trinity of Gods, at whose name every knee should bow. Thus, that which was planted in the soil of ignorance grew and flourished as the years went on, because the soil was only capable of producing such a product.

A simple meal of farewell was turned by Paul into the Eucharist, a Pagan rite, celebrated by the Pagans who drank the wine as representing the blood of their slain god, and ate the bread as representing the body of the slain god, and this at a later date became incorporated in the gospels. Earlier in history, and in other contemporary religions of the time, the actual blood of the victim was drunk and the body eaten. If we go further back all these rites and ceremonies can also be traced to Sun and Nature worship.

Christianity has no relation whatever to Jesus, except that he was the human being used by the Church authorities of the second, third, and fourth centuries for the purpose of exemplifying theological doctrines, which had for their purpose the attainment by the worshippers of at-one-ment with their god. These doctrines are symbolic of man himself, his death and resurrection to a higher life ; but this is a subject by itself and I just mention it in passing.

Christianity is mythology, nothing more and nothing less. Christians are pagans now and always have been, and for bishops to say, as many have done of recent years, that this country is reverting to Paganism is untrue and just another example of the want of truthfulness which is so evident to all thinking people in the utterances of the clergy. The Church always comes first and the truth last, so do not complain, my Lords, as some of you have done, at the amount of perjury in divorce cases. When you think of the fact that the marriage service commences with what is untrue and continues throughout making untrue statements, it is illogical to complain of perjury in divorce proceedings till you clear the marriage service of its present obvious falsities.''

The Bishop of Alfortruth here paused for a few seconds. Then he continued :

" I have now told you what you all should know about the origin of Christianity, which explains why the Church, its priests and parsons, have never resembled the lowly Jew, who, if he returned to earth, would not recognise the teachings uttered in his name. Can anyone imagine the man Jesus worshipping in St. Paul's, Westminster Abbey, or St. Peter's? What an incongruous idea—too fantastic, in fact, to contemplate !

He who is reported to have said that there is but one God, and that he was the son of man, listening to a priest or parson coupling his name with this God and the Holy Ghost, and making him the second person of a Trinity of Gods—such a conception is surely the height of absurdity.

Again, can we imagine one who is reported as going about doing good, raising the fallen, healing the sick and denouncing the priests of his day, because of their false teachings, one who we may assume was a reformer and a teacher, a rebel in his day, countenancing the doctrines, dogmas, rites and ceremonies of the Christian Church, with its vast wealth, its bishops living in palaces and drawing large incomes from the earnings of the workers? Can we imagine such a one countenancing the Athanasian creed, the Nicene creed, or the Apostles' creed, the insistence on specific beliefs, and on the damnation of all unbelievers? Quite impossible. So again I say that Christ and Jesus are as different as night is from day.

I can easily see why our President refrained from giving consideration to the gospel narratives. In them there is so much that is at variance with the creeds of the Christian Church that I commend him for his wisdom.   Again, I can understand why he laid emphasis on the teachings of the Church Fathers, those who manufactured Christianity out of available material.   If they are thrown over and we return to the man Jesus, there would be no Christianity left. We should be compelled to fall back on simple teachings and admonitions, such as were uttered by many other teachers before the time of Jesus.

The Christian Church would collapse, as it is founded on creeds, rites and ceremonies, and not, I say again, on the teachings of Jesus.

So much for this brief outline of the origin of Christianity, which doubtless is all known to you; but before I deal with the subject of Spiritualism I wish to make one observation.   Up till the beginning of the nineteenth century we priests could honestly accept all that we were required to with a clear conscience, believing that Christianity was the only revealed religion and that its teachings, as handed down to us from generation to generation, were true and God-given truths; but we can do so no longer. Before then we knew next to nothing about the religions of Babylon, Persia and Egypt, and naturally thought that Christianity was a new revelation, whereas we now know that it is the continuance of the oldest religion in the world.   The age of science, ushered in by the great Copernicus, was then beginning to have its effect on thinking minds.   The result was a great awakening of thought, culminating in the French Revolution.   It was a time of great mental awakening, political and religious, when men like Voltaire, Rousseau and Paine gave their thoughts to the world on the subject of the Christian Religion.

These men were the forerunners of our present leaders of modern thought, the representatives of awakened intellect, which had been asleep since the sixth century, when the Christian Church closed all the schools in Europe, Asia Minor and Egypt and burned all the books and libraries.

Where would we not have been to-day if the Christian Church had never been? I assert that there is every reason to believe that we should have been at least fourteen hundred years in advance of our present-day knowledge and civilisation.

However, so it is. Nothing comes of bemoaning past mistakes!

Let us repair this damage done by the Church we represent as quickly as possible, because not only did it keep the people ignorant but, in its own interests, it burned hundreds of thousands of mediums called witches, who are the instruments nature has provided to enable communication to be conducted between this world and the next.

Our President has stated that he doubted the wisdom of destroying what seemed to be a natural gift. It is unfortunate that our predecessors did not realise this sooner, as, apart from the appalling cruelty the Church inflicted on those harmless people, we prevented, so as to keep ourselves in power, a gift from developing which would have opened up the other world to humanity and given infinite comfort to millions upon millions, besides greatly increasing our knowledge of the Universe. But for this cruel folly of the Church, the age of materialism, in which we are now living, would never have been known.

It may be new to you, but it is true nevertheless,

that part of the early Christian Church employed mediums and encouraged mediumship, just as did the priests of the religions from which Christianity came. These, however, were the days before creeds and dogmas which, when they took hold, brought about the abandonment of this practice.

In the fourth century St. Ambrose, Bishop of Milan, persuaded the Emperor Theodosius to issue an edict against churches employing mediums. Thus began, from Lyons in the west to Angora in the east, the massacre of Motanist Congregations which continued till the sixth century. After some centuries of respite, the massacre of mediums broke out again and continued till the eighteenth century.

We now know that mediumship cannot be destroyed. We now know that the discoveries of the last one hundred and fifty years have destroyed the entire foundation upon which rest the claims of the Christian Church, and now I put it to you—What are you going to do about it?

Is the Christian Church intending to fight to the last ditch and then go down still preaching the false doctrines of the Church Fathers? If so, its oblivion is as certain as the fact that night follows day. The Moderator of the Church of Scotland recently said that the forces of Christ were in retreat all along the line, and he spoke the truth because the people are learning the truth, and more and more turning away from our teaching.''

Here the bishop paused and looked round the assembly, but he was met by a stony silence. Strong disapproval was pictured on every face except that of the Bishop of Latitudeham.

'' Let me now consider the question of Spiritualism. That its claims are true there is not the least doubt. I have tested them myself over the past ten years. My experiences reveal the fact that communication with the departed is as true as that communication takes place between man and man on earth. From these conversations I know that we survive death, as those who have spoken to me have proved to me that they retain their memories, characteristics and affection which they had on earth.

Can you, my Lords, say that you know that we survive death? No, you cannot do so unless you have experienced the return of those called ' dead,' and to this experience you refuse to submit yourselves. Consequently you can only say that you hope that we survive death.

You do not know where we go, or in what form we survive. The burial service in the prayer book is so illogical, contradictory, and contrary to present-day knowledge that it is the subject of criticism on all sides. We bishops are, or should be, aware of the reason for this contradictory nature of the Christian belief about what follows death. The belief in our entering into glory at death came from Gnosticism and the belief in the resurrection of the body on the resurrection day came from Hebrew and Egyptian theology.

I was reading a recent article in a newspaper written by one of my Lords present to-day. His conclusion is that, because he believed in God, he survived death. He, however, was not sure, his words being that ' I think that man's personality survives the death of his body.' This is all a bishop knows about the after-life after nineteen hundred years of Christianity.   He did not quote from any Christian source, because he can find nothing therein which has any weight with thinking people to-day.

So this great revealed religion, the only true religion, the only revelation from God to man, according to my Lords and the teachings of the Church, has told us nothing.   We know no more, according to my Lord just quoted, on this vital subject, than was known before Christianity came into being, as such vague beliefs of an after-life are as old as man himself.   What then has this great revelation revealed that was not known before? Nothing, absolutely nothing.

I shall now tell you what I know, not what I think.   Those who have died tell us that it is the life we lead on earth which determines our place after death.   There our characters are known.   We cannot hide our thoughts or disguise our character there as we can here.   Consequently the upright, the true and the good keep company, and those who are not dwell apart.

Mental regrets of missed opportunities and misdeeds cause unhappiness there in a way that they do not do here, as our past misdeeds are more apparent to each, with the result that those who are happiest are those who have led good, upright and unselfish lives on earth.

This is what the Church should teach the people, that as we sow we reap.   It should discard once and for ever its creeds, dogmas, rites and ceremonies, which have had their day.   It should concentrate on the life lived.   It should stand for all that is good for the uplifting of the people, their greater education, for better homes, and last but by no means least it should set its face against war, lust of conquest and all cruelty to man and beast.

Has the Church ever stood out for these attainments? Never in the whole course of its history. The Prayer Book actually countenances war in its Thirty Nine Articles! During the age of Christendom most of the wars were religious wars, the people were treated like serfs, their homes were hovels, and cruelty to man, woman, child and beast prevailed everywhere.

You will say that all this has passed. No, it has not passed; but it is passing owing to that education which the Church did its utmost to prevent. Let me, however, ask you one question.

Has the Church ever raised its voice against cruelty to animals, blood sports, hunting the fox, stag or otter hunting, for instance? That will pass some day, and doubtless when it does the Church will take credit for it just as it claims that all we are to-day is due to Christianity, one of the most absurd claims, one of the most arrogant lies, the Church has ever told, and it has told many. The deeds and preaching of the Church have always represented the mentality of the time. It is not a Divine Institution, instituted by God, as we falsely claim, but only a man-made organisation.

Slums are being cleared to-day not as the result of the Church's influence, but by a free and educated people. The Church has been and still is the largest owner of slum property. The Church has spent its money on magnificent buildings, and allowed the people to live in hovels.   War now shocks the moral conscience, not because of the Church's influence but owing to the higher mental level of the people.

Cruelty to and the torturing of prisoners came to an end, not because of the influence of the Church, but because the people, by education, became less cruel.   There are, however, many still as cruel as ever in their sports and enjoyments.   I fail, however, to find the Church to-day denouncing this form of pleasure at the expense of the suffering of the lower creatures which have feelings like ourselves.   Instead of discountenancing this form of pleasure the clergy have approved it and have partaken in its brutality. Some have kept their own packs of hounds, with no word of censure from the Church authorities.   In fact one of you present to-day, who made a violent attack recently on Spiritualism, has followed this up by defending fox hunting and stag hunting, and, when animal lovers protested, sneered at them, calling them ' old women.'

This is an example of the Church's attitude throughout its centuries of power.   It ruled Europe for fifteen hundred years and only when the people came into their own, by the mental level rising as the result of the discoveries of science, were its cruel laws repealed, the Church laws being the most cruel and unjust of any the world has known.

If you are not convinced by the claims made by Spiritualism your duty is to examine them.   You may say that you have done so, and have turned them down.   The Church authorities did turn them down, not because they were untrue, but because it was not in the interest of the Church to accept them.   You call Spiritualism the work of the devil, you call it fraud. Who are the frauds? Who are the real infidels? You, my Lords, and your brother clergy, because you preach lies and are unfaithful to the light of Truth.

It is not in the interests of the priests and parsons to have the medium making contact with the other world, because the Church has always claimed that through its teachings, and by this means only, can we reach what it terms Heaven. Yet the Christian belief in survival after death is so nebulous that one of you, my Lords, present to-day, stated in a daily newspaper recently that he believed in it only because God created the Universe ; as if that is a logical answer. The claims made by the Christian Church as to the elect who survive death are amongst the most arrogant and absurd of any religion in the world. They are false, and if you do not know that they are false, the more shame on you for your ignorance and conceit.

What the people want to know is how to live and what awaits them after death. They want facts and not theories composed by ignorant men sixteen hundred years ago. Spiritualism can give them these facts. It can supply the reason for living up to our best, and demonstrate what is our destiny. The Church cannot do this, and for that reason the Church, as it is presently constituted, is doomed.

Sooner or later, owing to empty pews, the Church will come into line with modern thought, but then, as always, it will be led into the way of truth, never lead. It has ever been so and, so long as it is based on false teaching, ever will be so.

May I then plead with you to change your teachings, your ideas and your policy, to scrap your creeds, discard your rites and ceremonials and look facts in the face. Get away from Mythology based on Sun worship. Cease teaching the celestial myths and legends of the pagans, and teach the facts and knowledge of to-day. Leave aside the speculations of pagan priests about salvation and damnation and learn from those who have died and now return to tell us what life after death really is like. Examine the claims and teachings of Spiritualism and cease mis-representing it and denouncing it. Though I am a voice crying in the wilderness, and though my pleadings will not be heard to-day, what I plead for will some day be accomplished. Not in my day, perhaps. I do not expect to live on earth long enough to see it, but come it will some day.

How I should have liked to tell you some of the teachings I have received from the great minds in the other world, how these have raised my thoughts to a greater at-one-ment with the Divine Mind of the Universe! How I should have liked to tell you what true religion really is, as it has been revealed to me by the great minds in the beyond, and would be revealed to you also were you willing to listen! Before, however, you can hear you will have to come out of the shell of complacency in which you live. Your ignorance of the vital facts of life and death is as colossal as is your self-complacency.

The truly religious man is the one who, besides following the laws of nature, seeks behind appearances to find the cause, to reach out to the source of his being, who tries more and more to reach at-one-ment

with the Divine ; in other words, to grow in knowledge and wisdom.   Just the opposite is the policy of
the Church to-day and always has been throughout
the age of Christendom.

I am, however, here to defend my actions, not
to teach you the philosophy of Spiritualism.

Now I have made my defence.   I have spoken
my honest thoughts.   I have besought you to throw
over the tradition of the past and accept the knowledge of the present.   I have advised you to take
mediumship into partnership with you and both work
hand-in-hand for the comfort and the upliftment of
the people.   Finally, I have charged you to denounce
all that is cruel, all that is wrong in the world to-day
and not to allow the reforms which must come, to come
only from the people.   I beseech you, as the leaders
of the people, to show them the way in which they
should go, whether it is popular to do so or not.   What
is popularity where right and wrong are concerned ?
The duty of the Church is to raise the mental level of
the nation, encourage education, and bring about a
better world, freed from the cruelties and the wrongs
of the present time.

It is ours to become real truth seekers and truth
teachers.   The words and opinions we utter are given
prominence in the public press, not because of our
wisdom, but because of the fact that we have reached
a high office in the Church, carrying with it the power
in the House of Lords to legislate for a free people,
without their having a voice as to whether they wish
us to do so or not.

Although we hold the title of Archbishop or
Bishop, our knowledge and wisdom are no greater,

and often much less, than those of men who get no
public recognition or publicity.   A public, as ignorant
as ourselves about the vital things of life, accepts
without thinking the words we utter, reads our
opinions and studies our lives, which some of us publish in book form, while they ignore men of the past
and the present, of far greater attainments, who have
really done something to educate and elevate the race.
Truly, it is a case of the blind leading the blind, while
those who can see look on in amazement at a deluded
population, ignoring the true leaders, and being led
by those whose interests it is to lead them, not in
the way of truth, but in the way of prejudice and past
tradition because therein lie their interests, their
comforts and their position.   Our titles carry such
weight with the people that they accept as true the
words we utter, which are often very stupid and quite
unworthy of the position given us in the State.

Let me give you an example, one which occurred
the day after the Commission, which had been sitting
for five years to consider the subject, reported against
women being admitted to the Priesthood.   This
decision was arrived at, to use its own words, ' On
a revelation of God's will for the Church as manifested
in the New Testament.'   One of you, my Lords—
and I shall out of good feeling refrain from mentioning you by name—took this opportunity to have
your opinion broadcast far and wide that Christianity,
and it only, had been responsible for raising women.
No greater lie was ever uttered ; but it is only one of
the many trillions of lies which priests and parsons
have uttered throughout the Christian era.

John Knox, the founder of Presbyterianism, the

cruelist collection of beliefs on earth, which wrung from the believer every ounce of happiness in life, described women as the ' Port and the Gate of the Devil ' and ' Like the gulf of Hell.'' He stated further that this opinion was supported by the Bible and that men would be less than beasts to think differently from God.

I quote this as an example of what one of the greatest and one of the most earnest of Christians felt towards women. It aptly typifies the attitude of Christianity towards women, and yet one of my Lords has had the temerity to say that Christianity, and it only, has been responsible for raising women.

No class of men has fooled the people, lied to the people and spoken more humbug to the people than Christian priests and parsons, and some day the people will realise it, to the lasting shame of the Christian Church. As to this lie by my Lord present to-day—Have you ever read Roman history? Of course you must have done so, and also the high status that women occupied in the Roman community. You must also know that whenever Christianity obtained power it commenced to degrade women, looking on them as impure, the cause of sin, and that they were in every way inferior to men, due to the degrading teaching of the Old Testament, with which Christianity is so bound up. A woman was not allowed to touch the Eucharist with bare hands because she would defile it.

Study the history of the attitude of Christendom towards women and you will be studying the history of the Christian Church. The emancipation of women in Christian countries has kept pace with the decline in the belief in Christian doctrines. The Church's treatment of women throughout the centuries of its power has been one of the greatest crimes in history, and yet it is on women that the Church rests. If they abandoned us, where should we be? They are our principal supporters, and always have been, and yet we have treated them as if they were our inferiors and told them that they are as much beneath men as men are beneath Christ.

This wall of ignorance, called the Christian Church, I shall make it my business to break, either from the inside or from the outside. If you censure me to-day it will mean that you wish the wall to remain intact ; if, on the other hand, you give me liberty of thought and action, then I remain. Your decision then means progress and reform or this stagnation of the *status quo*. To-day you make your choice. By adopting the policy I advocate, present-day knowledge and true religion can be united. If you oppose it, then they will remain apart, officially at least, because nothing the Church can now do can keep them indefinitely apart.''

The bishop now paused, glanced down his notes, and then commenced his peroration.

'' The message of Spiritualism is that we get away from ancient mythology, that we break down creedalism and narrow nationalism, teach friendship amongst nations and so stop war, destroy squalour, set our face against all forms of cruelty, raise the standard of living and increase education.

Kingship in this country has moved with the times and we never hear about the Divine Right of Kings. Let the same happen to the clergy, and let us hear no more of the Divine Right of Priests and Parsons, that they have been appointed by God, and all such nonsense. Let us get down to our right level and cease imagining ourselves beings superior to the rest of humanity, with a mission in life which we only can accomplish.

Let us get away from the mis-interpretations of the past and remember that in Egypt six thousand years ago, and not in Palestine, we have the earliest record of man's realisation of moral values and that he is a spiritual being. Our Old Testament is but a late echo of the moralising of this ancient race which lived by the banks of the Nile.

Putting aside its history of the Jewish people, the contents of the Old Testament came from either Babylon or Egypt, both countries in which the Hebrews were captives and from which they brought the myths and legends current in the days of their captivity. The entire Book of Proverbs was lifted *en bloc* from Egypt, where such ideas and exalted precepts were current for thousands of years before the Hebrews existed and where lived a race with a code of morals far superior to that of Moses, dating back thousands of years before the books attributed to him were written. Civilisation in the countries surrounding Palestine existed for thousands of years before it reached the Hebrews, whom we erroneously claim to be the first recipients of the only revelation from Heaven. It was in Egypt that the virtues were first practised and character and righteousness elevated above force and might. The moral ideals of early man we now know to be the result of his own social experience and not the effect of a special revelation.

Out of prehistoric savagery, because he is a spiritual being, man emerged. At first might and might only was right. That continued for perhaps a million years. Six thousand years ago in Egypt we find the first trace of the insistence on righteousness. This developed and from an acorn grew slowly the tree, the fruits of which nourished Babylon and at a much later date Palestine. The gods, from being gods of force like Ra and Jehovah, became gods of love like Bel, Prometheus, Osiris, Horus, and Christ, who taking pity on the sins of humanity came to earth to save and cleanse us erring beings, conquer evil and give eternal life to all believers.

From force, hitherto the master of the Universe, developed the idea of love triumphant, told to the ancients in myth and legend. The legends we can put aside as we did the fairy stories of our nursery days. What is important is the discovery that man came to realise the difference between right and wrong, selfishness and unselfishness, force and justice. The more he has recognised the importance of considering his brother man the greater has been the moral and social advance of the human race. This great discovery we find is but six thousand years old and man has been on this earth at least a million years! While this knowledge gives us great hope for the future it also explains how our actions fall so far short of the ideals we have but so often fail to practise. The race in its attainment of the virtues has covered only a few milestones compared with the long road man has travelled on earth. The fight to conquer the material world goes far back into pre-history. The attempt to conquer himself and the discovery of his social responsibilities are, in comparison, recent history.

Spiritualism teaches first and foremost that it is character and what we are that counts, that the development of character, of the moral sense and the increase of knowledge and wisdom are the all-important things of life. Material wealth, important as it is, is but a passing possession, the virtues, knowledge and wisdom are eternal as they are always ours here and hereafter. Such has been the theme of the great teachers of the past and had the Christian Church preached and practised that, and that only, down through the Christian era, how much greater would its prestige be to-day !

We are the heirs of this heritage which first took root in Egypt, a heritage which emphasised the importance of righteousness and the fact of survival. In both cases our wisdom and knowledge in the intervening centuries have increased. The Egyptians laid the seed, to-day we are reaping the harvest. Isaiah, David, Solomon, Socrates and Cicero were even in their time just echoes of men of as great wisdom and knowledge, such as Pharaoh Khufu, who had lived some three thousand years earlier.

What a great vista we can now look back upon ! This has now been revealed to us by the excavations in Egypt and Babylon. What a great vista we as etheric beings can now look forward to ! This mediumship has revealed to us. Not only can we envisage this earth transformed by the discoveries of science, but also by the development of man's moral sense. Not only can we contemplate increasing happiness for the human race on earth but increasing happiness and content throughout our eternal existence just as we develop in knowledge, wisdom and righteousness.

Development is but another word for the history of the race. We look back and see, as a spiral, steady, continuous progress in man, animal and plant. We look forward and realise that this must continue as otherwise we have stagnation, which means decay. In spite of nature's warning, the Christian Church never makes any advance and holds to the creeds and dogmas of an ignorant past. I want to free myself of these. I want to free the Church of these ancient crutches and shackles. I want you to boldly tell the people the truth. I want you to strike out on a new path and lead the people with you to greater heights and to nobler thoughts. Your decision to-day will show me if my desire will be realised or not.

I will say no more. Much more I would like to say, but time does not permit. My future so far as the Church is concerned is in your hands. If you censure me then I resign, when I shall obtain that freedom of thought and action which I so ardently desire.''

The bishop then resumed his seat, and the President called for someone present to move a resolution either of censure or approval of the Bishop of Alfortruth's opinions and his action in inviting a Spiritualist to preach in his Cathedral.

The Bishop of Diehardham then rose, and moved :

" That in the opinion of this Convocation the views expressed by the Bishop of Alfortruth are heretical in the extreme and quite contrary to the teachings of the Christian Church ; that by the inviting of one who did not profess the Christian faith to preach in his Cathedral he has violated a cardinal law of the Church, as such action is expressly forbidden by the Church of England and that any bishop who refuses to conform to this ruling be asked to resign his office as he is now unable to keep to the vows he made when he took office."

The Bishop of Creedalbury seconded the resolution and it was carried with only one dissentient, the Bishop of Latitudeham voting against it. The Bishop of Alfortruth did not vote.

The Bishop of Alfortruth then rose and intimated his resignation in the following words :

" My Lord President, your Grace, my Lords, I accept your motion of censure as indicating your wish that I resign my bishopric. This I now do without delay, but in doing so I affirm that this day you have made a fatal decision. It is one that I expected you to make. You and your organisation are endeavouring to keep back, with all your power and influence, the light which nature wishes to reveal to man. Your action is but a repetition of what has gone on before in the Church's history through the ages of Christendom. Always reactionary, always against education and reform, always against the light of knowledge, you now show yourselves determined to oppose the truth of survival coming to the knowledge of the people as nature intends it to come.

I, while I live, will devote my life to breaking the ecclesiastical system which stands between the people and the truth.   Besides this I shall devote my life to spreading this truth amongst the people who will slowly but surely detect the errors in your teaching and turn to that which is true.   Thus and thus only will your reactionary influence be broken and you will be left to deplore your lost power, your departed glory and your empty churches.   To-day you have lived up to the reputation your predecessors have made throughout the Christian era, which can be summed up in two words, *Semper Idem.*''

When the bishop resumed his seat the President intimated that the Bishop of Alfortruth's resignation had been accepted and that the proceedings were now closed.

CHAPTER XIII.

PROFESSOR STOREY VISITS SUREWAY COURT.

The following day the newspapers gave great publicity to the proceedings at the Convocation of Churchisall and many and varied were the placards. The five leading London dailies brought the previous day's events before the public in the following headlines :—

BISHOP DENOUNCES CHRISTIANITY.
RESIGNATION OF BISHOP OF ALFORTRUTH.
CHRISTIANITY IN DANGER!
HERETICAL BISHOP RESIGNS.
ARE CHRISTIANS PAGANS?

Every newspaper devoted several columns to the speeches and some gave nearly verbatim the Bishop of Alfortruth's remarks. The leading articles varied greatly, but most were very guarded in their opinions, being evidently anxious to be non-committal about such a controversial subject, and one about which so many of their readers were profoundly ignorant.

The *Daily Post's* leader, however, revealed a grasp of the position new to British journalism and read as follows :—

" The proceedings yesterday at the Convocation of Creedalbury undoubtedly represent another crisis in the Church of England, and not only for our National Church but for all denominations of Christendom. Its repercussions will be world-wide.

Present-day scholarship is so far removed from

Church teaching that we cannot now look to the past for any guidance. Those who say that the Christian Church has withstood such onslaughts, from both within and without, over its chequered career since its foundation at the Council of Nicæa in 325 forget the changed times in which we now live.

Its troubles in the past have been caused by different interpretations of doctrine. It is difficult to remember the number of different councils which were called to discuss and decide on such points as the nature of Jesus, the man, and Christ, the God, the relationship of Jesus to God, and Christ to God and the respective positions God, Christ and The Holy Ghost occupied in the Holy Trinity, ending up as they did in the eleventh century by the expulsion from the Holy Catholic Church of what is now the Greek Church.

Then came the Reformation, but this did not bring controversies to an end. They still continued in the Church of Rome but to a far greater degree amongst the Protestants, who based their beliefs less on the teachings of the Church Fathers and more on the Holy Bible.

As every Protestant considered he was free to interpret the sayings in the Bible as he thought right we have witnessed over the last four hundred years, hundreds of sects all claiming to possess the true interpretation of God's will to man.

During the last hundred years the authenticity and accuracy of the Bible has become more and more questioned, as our knowledge increased, with the result that one section of our national Church is again becoming anchored on the opinions of the early

Church Fathers, who decided what Christianity was to be and took little heed of what is now called The New Testament, as in their day it was not considered inspired, or the 'Word of God,' as it came, later on, to be believed.

The Church of Rome and what is termed the High Anglican section of the Church of England have thus a foundation for their beliefs, whereas every day the ground is being taken away from under the feet of those who hold to the Bible as the inspired Word of God. They are becoming as a ship without a compass.

Such, in brief, is the history of the past and present-day position of the Christian Church. No longer do we hear of wranglings as to the nature of the Trinity. That has ceased to interest intelligent men and women of to-day. The scene has shifted to quite another point of view. In the past the controversy was never as to whether Christianity was true, but as to how it should be interpreted. To-day the subject of controversy is reversed, and is centred on the question, is Christianity true?

To that question history is to-day giving an answer. This is, however, only one problem before the Church. If its doctrines were built on a sound foundation it need fear no rival. Not only, however, are its doctrines questioned, but it now has to face the onslaught of a very serious rival.

The claims made by Spiritualism over the last eighty years are becoming more and more accepted by thoughtful people. Spiritualism stands for a rational religion, freed from all the theological speculations of the past and thus attracts those given to rational thinking, but who at the same time cannot accept the negative teachings of materialism. This new religion therefore throws over what thinking people have now come to realise is quite unnecessary, while, at the same time, it teaches that from facts which have accumulated it can now be accepted that life does not end with the grave but continues in another world surrounding us, and that as we live here we shall live there.

If this claim becomes accepted—and everything points to this happening over the next twenty or thirty years—the creeds of Christendom will cease to be believed and the Christian Church, therefore, will have either to change its teaching or cease to be. Its only assets to-day are its wealth and past tradition. What will its leaders do with the vast sums obtained from the people in the years gone by when it frightened the faithful with the fear of Hell, and obtained its wealth and its present favoured position in consequence of the fear it raised in the minds of the people?

That is a question which we do not propose to answer here, but one thing is evident, and that is that the stand the Bishop of Alfortruth took yesterday will be looked back on by future generations in much the same light as the stand taken by Luther, Wycliffe, Ridley, Latimer and others. Fortunately, our heretical bishop will not suffer death at the stake as did most of those ancient lights. Instead he has been compelled to resign his bishopric.

All thinking people will watch with interest the events of the next few years, as everything points to religion changing from a form of belief in theological doctrines to a rational religion based on the fact that we survive death.''

'' What a wonderful change knowledge brings into our lives ! ''

The speaker was George Trueman. He was sitting in the library of Sureway Court with his wife and his old friend Horace Storey, Professor of History at Knowledgehall University.

Dinner was just over, and Mr. and Mrs. Trueman and their guest had settled down to an evening's talk.

The Professor, when he visited Sureway Court, much preferred to be the only visitor, as then he had the opportunity of talking things over, as he expressed it, with his friend, whose advanced opinions, combined with great knowledge and wisdom, were as a mental tonic to him, which he always found most stimulating.

'' To what do you refer, dear ? '' asked Mrs. Trueman, in reply to her husband's remark.

'' I refer to the leading article in this morning's *Daily Post.* Let me read it to you both and then you will understand what I mean.''

After he had finished the Professor remarked :

'' Well, George, that is as revolutionary in journalism as is the Bishop of Alfortruth's stand against creeds and dogmas.''

'' It is, indeed,'' said Mrs. Trueman. '' Do you know who wrote it, George ? ''

'' Do you remember one evening, a year ago,

I brought home with me Mr. Scribewell? He then occupied a prominent position in Fleet Street on one of our leading dailies."

" Yes, I remember him quite well. He seemed a very able man, one who took a very all-round view of things. He told me how foolish editors were to ignore Spiritualism as they did, because, from a journalistic point of view, it was the best selling story he knew, and that whenever a newspaper gave it a fair deal its circulation increased."

" 'Tis certainly so," replied Trueman. " I know that one of our leading Sunday papers doubled its circulation some years ago when its editor gave Spiritualism fair play, and then lost all it gained some years later under a new editor, who made out that a famous medium had cheated, when it was afterwards discovered that for a stunt the newspaper had itself faked the deception. But that is by the way. It was Scribewell who wrote this article or got someone to write it. He is now the editor of the *Daily Post* and told me recently that he has been giving Spiritualism and the history of Christianity his special study of late. The séance he had with us when he stayed here a year ago started him on the serious study of the subject and not, just as journalists do with most things, in a tabloid way. Most journalists carry about with them so many tabloids of information. They know a little about everything and nothing much about anything. Scribewell had a tabloid knowledge of Spiritualism before he came to visit us and with his journalistic genius saw that it was a good story, which is what every journalist wants."

" Now," said Mrs. Trueman, "he sees it is

more than a story, that truth is much more interesting than fiction.''

'' He does, indeed. He told me the other day that after the wonderful evidence he obtained here that night, which proved to him that his wife was still alive and knew all about his doings, since she passed on, he felt he was up against the biggest problem he ever had to tackle. I gave him some books to read on Spiritualism and when returning them to me he said I had put him on the right path at last, as he had been wandering down bye-lanes which had led him nowhere.''

'' Well, he has been brave enough to tell his readers what he has learned,'' remarked the Professor, '' but I would like to know what are the bishop's plans. I suppose he will now be known as Edward Leader, no more ' my Lord this ' or ' my Lord that '. How terrible it is for a body of men, the chief representatives of an organisation which has been responsible for fastening on the people the greatest delusion ever imposed on mankind, to set themselves up above the rest of the people as Prince Bishops or Lord Bishops, divide one hundred and eighty thousand pounds a year among themselves, live rent free in palaces, and be addressed as if they were superior to you or me, George.''

'' Quite so, Horace, but it is all part of the fraud, and the people just get what they are mentally fitted for. ' A man of independent mind, he looks and laughs at a' that,' to quote my old friend Burns, and he wonders how long they will continue paying thirty-three million pounds a year to be taught pagan mythology which a child could learn in a day.

Millions of pounds a year are taken as tithes from the land from hundreds of thousands who are not in sympathy with the propagation of this superstition and everyone suffers because this burden on the land adds to the cost of our foodstuffs, which thus places the home producer at a disadvantage with the foreigner. Besides these tithes our National Church has a capital of thirty-two million pounds, and it and the Roman Catholic Church are the two richest organisations in the world, though their founder is believed to have lived in poverty and preached the virtue of poverty, exhorting his followers not to lay up treasure on earth but to devote their lives to the attainment of character which would pass with them to the life beyond.''

" It is a public scandal of the first magnitude,'' remarked the Professor. " The people subscribed their money and mortgaged their lands through the fear of Hell, which was the Church's chief stock-in-trade. By preaching Hell the Church blackmailed the people into mortgaging their lands and parting with their money. Its wealth has accumulated by this most despicable form of robbery. I for one would not like to touch this tainted money, but anything can be expected from men who can pocket their conscience so deeply as to subscribe to the Thirty-Nine Articles. No one out of a lunatic asylum could believe the arrant and cruel humbug these contain, and yet every parson, before he is ordained to the Church of England, has to swear solemnly before God Almighty that he believes them and will consistently uphold them.

What confidence would you put in your stockbroker if you knew that before he became a member of the Stock Exchange he had sworn to something he knew was not true? Would you have any confidence in a Lloyds Insurance Policy, backed by the members of that famous Institution, if you knew that before a man could become a member of it he had to swear solemnly before God that he believed something which no sane individual can believe? Of course, you would not, and yet every parson bears this stigma of swearing to something he does not and cannot believe. The people are so ignorant of this fraud that they look up to and respect these men, calling them ' Reverend ' and those who are their leaders ' my Lord ' or ' your Grace ' and allot to each of these leaders a seat in the House of Lords so that they may legislate for them.

Dr. Leader, as I suppose he now is, will miss all the subservience accorded to him by the faithful, but he has the sense to realise how much better it is to be an ordinary fish in an intellectual ocean than a big fish in a sea of ignorance. The pronouncements of the bishops and clergy get far more publicity than they deserve when one considers how few attend Church. For instance, in Greater London not more than five per cent of the people do so.''

'' If those who strive after titles only knew,'' said Trueman, '' that carrying a grand label does not make them grand men and women, and that they are just like children in the nursery pretending to be kings and queens, all of which nonsense ceases to appeal when the nursery stage of life on earth has passed and they enter the real life at death ! Earth titles, like all earthly things, are left behind. There, no titles nor honours are awarded and only character, and what each one is, matters.   I have spoken to those in Etheria who on earth were kings, queens, dukes, lords and sirs, and they have asked me to just address them by the names they received at birth, as they are now known by these only.''

   '' That is what Spiritualism has taught Dr. Leader,'' remarked Mrs. Trueman.   '' What are his plans for the future, George ? ''

   '' He intends to write a book to encompass as much as possible the history of the world's different religions, from sun worship right on through the more primitive to the more complex religions, and show, as Max Müller showed, how they are all related, how one grew out of another.   He will have this great advantage over Müller, Robertson, Drews, Smith, and many others who preceded him, in that he now knows what is the cause of mankind's religious instinct, namely, his survival after death.   He will start with the primitive instinct, trace it through the centuries of religious history, show how every religion is based on a greater or lesser knowledge of the hereafter, and thus make past beliefs understandable in the light of the facts which we have to-day.   These show that our ancestors' crude ideas had a basis of fact, but that in ignorance and fear of the unknown they wound round this basis draping after draping of theological speculation in the form of doctrines and dogmas, which throughout the history of ecclesiastical religions has hidden the truth from the people.

   Those of us who have the power of reaching down to fundamentals cannot but be impressed by the thought that all the religious ceremonials and beliefs throughout Christendom can now be traced to the rise and fall of a great river and the rise and setting of the sun, the waxing and waning of both of which constituted the material basis on which a deeply religious race erected a spiritual edifice which sustained them through life and comforted them at death.   These religious speculations they handed down to posterity and they have influenced a third of the inhabited globe for the past six thousand years, giving comfort to believers who, considering them divine and unalterable truths, obstructed progress and murdered and persecuted all who would not think as they did.

You have never found that in any of your history books, Horace ! "

" Indeed we don't.   And besides that the priests turned man's religious instinct into a trading commodity to benefit themselves.   Just as the tradesman caters for his customers so they catered for theirs. Something like the old Trade Guilds which were so powerful and wealthy that they had the say as to who could enter them, what they were to trade in, and how they were to trade.   By persecuting, destroying and ostracising all outside the Christian Guild they retained a monoply.   On every occasion from birth to death a priest had to be employed, and after death the dead body could only be buried in consecrated ground belonging to the Church.   Fancy the dead body requiring consecrated ground !

It seems very absurd till we remember that it is because of the old belief that our bodies would rise from their graves on the Judgment Day—a belief still held by many.   Consequently they had to lie in consecrated ground to show the Lord when he came that this reserved area contained his elect. Naturally, everyone wanted to be buried in consecrated ground, owned by the Church. The people got their desires satisfied, which had been fostered by the priests, and the Church got the people's money for the graves, and it was often much more than the poor dupes could afford.

If the priests could they would have leased out land in Heaven at so much an acre, just as they took payment for getting people out of Hell. Religion has been one of the best paying professions in history ; the more dupes the priests had the richer they became. When their dupes became more intelligent and ceased being fools, the priests became fewer, and some day, when the people are really educated, the profession will cease to exist. Education will in time kill the trade of middleman between God and Man. Don't you agree, George?"

"Undoubtedly this must come about. The Non-conformists are feeling the effect of the greater intelligence amongst the people, its consequence being less money for propagating superstition ; but the State Church in both Scotland and England has great wealth in its tithes or the capitalisation of them. They have a first mortgage over all the land of this country, and only a revolution, such as occurred in Russia, will ever take it from them. What they will do with this vast wealth in the years to come is the question, but one thing is certain, and that is, if they do not use it for the good of the people, it will be taken from them. The people in the years to come, when they have ceased to accept the Church's teaching, will never stand by and see their wealth—and it is theirs—

being devoted to supporting a body of ignorant men whose work in life will be to preach to empty pews."

"Well," said Mrs. Trueman, "we may not know what will eventually happen to the Church's wealth but one thing is certain, Dr. Leader will have a busy time. He is evidently throwing himself wholeheartedly into his new mission. He will have no lack of opportunities as he will be asked to address Spiritualist propaganda meetings all over the country. To-day the largest halls are just sufficiently large to accommodate all the people. In another ten years no hall will be large enough. The Albert Hall, which a few years ago was always refused for Spiritualist meetings, is now being taken several times a year by different Spiritualist Societies. George thinks that before long it will be possible to fill it every Sunday evening. Isn't that so, George?"

"Not only that, but every other large hall in London, as well, just as the Queen's Hall and others are now filled every Sunday evening. We are getting more and better speakers each year and more and better clairaudient mediums. This year, at least three new clairaudients are appearing in public who can give consistently evidential messages from the platforms of our largest halls. If this goes on at the present rate we shall soon have a small army of first-class clairaudients, a mobile band capable of covering the entire country. They draw the people, who in greater and greater numbers are hearing our message. In almost every town of any importance at least one propaganda meeting takes place in the year and in most several such meetings. The leaven is slowly but surely working in every part of the land."

" When does your painstaking husband intend to start putting all the evidence he and you have received into book form?" enquired the Professor. "You could give the public a most remarkable accumulation of facts proving survival."

" If he could only get clear of business affairs he would have the book published in a few months. We have some of the best evidence typewritten but if that were all it would not be so much of a labour. When it is finally ready for the public it must, however, contain more than just the evidence."

"Any book I am responsible for," broke in Trueman, " must consider the whole question scientifically and philosophically. As you know, I am gradually relinquishing my many duties in the city, and in a few years I hope to be free to devote more of my life to the spreading of the new knowledge, just as Edward Leader and many others are now doing. I shall then have ten years, I hope, in which I can tell the people what my wife's wonderful mediumship has revealed to me and many others. After that I may not have the strength to go about the country teaching, but I could always devote the rest of my life to writing, and that is probably even more effective, as my writings would outlast my day. I believe our standard works on Spiritualism will become classics to future generations, and I would like to add at least one of my own to that great collection. That is my aim, Horace, and I hope you will live to see it realised."

" I do hope so. Yours will be one of the greatest contributions to a great and growing science, George, of that I have no doubt. Few people of the present day realise what you and other Psychical Researchers are doing for the future good and happiness of humanity, and yet you are giving them the knowledge of the very thing about which they most desire to know. As a student of history I can give you this assurance that you will be appreciated here on earth after you have reached what you call Etheria. The people in the past have always either ignored or persecuted their great thinkers and then worshipped at their graves. It is so to-day. Your work is not appreciated. Doubtless the majority, if they knew what you are doing, collecting and tabulating evidence received in the supernormal way you have obtained it, would think you were just wasting your time. But wait till you are dead and then you will know how much posterity values your work. Rather an Irish way of putting it, but you have this advantage over previous pioneers. You can always think now that you will know, when you reach your abode in Etheria, that you have not worked in vain. Other pioneers did not know when on earth, fighting the battle of progress, that after their death they would find that they had fought a good fight and helped to raise humanity to a higher level."

While the Professor was speaking Trueman rose and paced up and down the room and finally anchored himself in front of the fireplace, leaning on the mantelpiece with his right arm, his left hand being in his trouser pocket. Standing thus he looked down on his friend, with a smile, remarking :

" Quite an encouraging outlook, my friend, for all pioneers, but in spite of this future attractive state of mind, which you envisage for me and others, I cannot feel that it quite compensates for what is suffered. I have had a great admiration all my life for all pioneers of progress. If I had my way with the education of our young I would see that one of the subjects taught was the fight for human progress made by the heroes of the past. Unfortunately this side of education is neglected and our young people are not taught to reverence, as they should, the heroes of the past. I am sure you agree, Horace.''

" Indeed I do. The last four hundred years has produced more heroes than any other age. In all branches of knowledge and human progress heroes have appeared to fight the Church and State which had Christendom in its clutches. That is why people are so ignorant of these battles for progress. The Church made certain that history was taught in such a way that its past terrible record would not be realised by the people.

From the time of Justinian in 529 when the Church closed all the schools and libraries, and burned all the books, the Dark Ages set in. It was a terrible blow to civilisation and put the clock of progress back a thousand years. When the time came last century that the Church could not keep the people ignorant any longer then it set about influencing what was to be taught. We are only now emerging from this state of affairs.''

" What a fight there was before education came to the people,'' remarked Mrs. Trueman. " I think I am right, Professor, in saying that it was only in 1870 that this came about.''

" Yes, after eighteen hundred years of Christianity the great majority of the people in Christendom

could neither read nor write.   That, of course, suited
the Church best.   But when it saw that education was
inevitable it started Church schools so that the children
would be taught in the way it wanted them to be
taught.   When you tell a Christian how his religion
was responsible for stopping all education in the
civilised world of the sixth century he replies, ' Oh,
but Christianity was not responsible, it was the
Church.''

" Ah ! but what is Christianity ? '' enquired
Trueman.   '' Christianity is just the teaching of the
Church.   Jesus the man never originated Christianity.
All that is termed Christianity came from Gnosticism
and the old pagan religions.   Jesus never said anything against education, and for that matter he never
said anything to justify the creeds and dogmas of the
Church, which falsely claims him as the authority for
all its erroneous teaching.   It was the Church Fathers
who put into his mouth words to suit the creeds and
dogmas they wound round his simple teaching.   It
was these ecclesiastics who said that philosophy and
learning were at variance with their doctrines and that
in consequence the schools had to go.''

" Only too true,'' replied the Professor.   " How
many schoolmasters were turned adrift we shall never
know, but they were a large company.   By the sixth
century the Church made it impossible for them to
live in Europe.   We know that some wandered as
far as Persia and were there welcomed by the then
reigning ruler.

Compare the condition of barbarism which prevailed wherever Christianity took root and the state
of the countries surrounding the Mediterranean sea

between the years 600 B.C. and 500 A.D.   Instead of Christianity coming into a world of intellectual and spiritual darkness and giving light it was quite the other way about.   It extinguished the enlightenment of the times and only brought darkness.

Between 600 B.C. and 500 A.D. the then civilised world had made great steps forward in commerce, art, literature and morals ; in fact civilisation was steadily rising to a higher level.   Ships of five thousand tons were trading between Mediterranean ports, public baths could be found everywhere, libraries existed in all the towns, which latter were laid out with taste and culture.   Education and philosophy were encouraged, science was making headway and knowledge was increasing.

This era of eleven hundred years was one of the greatest periods of the world and there seems no reason why it would not have continued if Christianity had not taken root.   Christianity pronounced all this progressive development as evil, that wealth, art, knowledge, relief from pain, comforts and enjoyment were contrary to God's will and must be avoided as deadly sins.   In the sixth century came the destruction of all that was good, pure and noble for the human race.   The Dark Ages set in and this continued for over a thousand years, the Church torturing and murdering everyone who tried to raise the level of intelligence and comfort, but taking good care to feather its own nest well from the labours of the people.   During the Dark Ages poverty and filth took the place of wealth and cleanliness.   The mind of man became a stagnant pool.

Then came the great fight between Christianity

and the Scientists and Humanists, which lasted from the fourteenth to the nineteenth century. Science and humane principles won and since their victory Christianity has been a dying superstition, but what havoc this malignant religion wrought everywhere before the thinkers, humanists and teachers came into their own !

When anyone studies Christian history as I have done it is easily realised what a blight this religion has been, how it has kept back progress and opposed every discovery and addition to human knowledge. Every educated person should know that as well as you and I do, George.''

''Yes, that is so. All who could not think obtained comfort from the Church's fables and myths, whereas those who thought remained outside the fold and were imprisoned, tortured or burned. I have just been reading Joseph McCabe's new book, *The Social Record of Christianity*. The facts he gives, from the time the Christian priests obtained control of affairs in Rome in the sixth century up to the present day, will be a revelation to all who have been satisfied with school history books, which the Church authorities made sure were written so as to omit everything which would disclose the cruelty, tyranny and obstruction of the Church to all progress and reform.''

'' I have not read that book,'' replied the Professor, '' though I look on McCabe as one of our greatest authorities on the subject. He has made it a life study. We need not go far back to realise what the obstructionist policy of the Church has meant to the people of this country in their endeavour to raise themselves to higher things. Read *The Bishops as*

Legislators, by Joseph Clayton, a Churchman, with a preface by the Rev. Stewart Headlam, who calls it a record of the crimes and follies of the bishops. When you have read it you will agree with me that it is.   The pages of *Hansard* show that scores of measures for the improvement of the conditions of the poor and the working-class have been opposed by the bishops.

No bishop supported the Bill for the Prevention of Cruelty to Animals in 1809.   Only three attended the House of Lords when, in 1815, a Bill was introduced to Prevent the Use of British Capital in the Slave Trade.   The bishops took no part in the discussion of the Prevention of Cruelty to Cattle Bill in 1824, and opposed Martin in his life-long attempt to bring in his Bill for legislation to punish all guilty of cruelty to animals.   In 1832 fifteen of them were still in opposition, though even the King was intimidated, to the Parliamentary Reform Bill to extend the franchise to the middle-class.   Only two voted for the Bill for the Total Suppression of the Slave Trade, and only one or two ever supported the various temperance measures that were introduced from 1839 to 1844.

Lord Brougham bluntly said that ' only two out of six-and-twenty Right Reverend Prelates will sacrifice their dinner and their regard for their belly . . . to attend and vote.'   They opposed every measure to relieve the workers.   Lord Shaftesbury was so angry when they opposed his measure for improving the lot of the people that he described them as ' timid, time-serving, and great worshippers of wealth and power,' and said ' I can scarcely remember an instance in which a clergyman has been found to maintain the cause of the labourers in the face of the pewholders.'

The bishops opposed non-conformists having University degrees and the removal of disabilities on all outside their Church. They opposed women becoming members of London Borough Councils and the providing of seats for tired shop assistants. Not one bishop gave support to the Bill to abolish the flogging of women in public or the flogging of women in prison. Such are only a few of their crimes and follies, but their greatest opposition was always exerted against education for the people. Education has always been the greatest danger to the Church.

Christian priests and parsons owned slaves and justified this by quoting from the Bible. The slave owners were devout believers in Christianity, the author of *Jesus, lover of my soul*, for instance. Charles Wesley, the brother of John Wesley, for years after he wrote this hymn and others like it, was the owner of a slave frigate which transported captured slaves from Africa to the Cotton Plantations of America. Pope Gregory the Great owned thousands of slaves. Slowly the facts McCabe and others have given to the world are becoming accepted. He and they have up till now been ignored, ridiculed and abused by the ignorant majority led by the Church, but these are the men who have helped to educate humanity. Yet so far they are unknown except to educated people.

When, however, archbishops or bishops now say something about social reform or clearing the slums the newspapers give their opinions large headlines and long columns. How few know that the Established

Church of England is and has been the largest owner of slum property in this country.   How few realise that practically every bishop in the House of Lords over the past two hundred years has consistently voted against every reform and everything introduced into the House of Lords for the upliftment of the people."

"I was amused," remarked Mrs. Trueman, "to see in to-day's *Times* the prominence given to the remarks made in the Albert Hall by one of our leading ecclesiastics on the need for action in social problems on the part of the Church.   Instead of leading the people in the past on social questions the Church has not only lagged behind but opposed and abused all social reformers, and now you will see, a few years hence, that it will claim the credit for slum clearance and its followers will say that all we are and have to-day is due to Christianity.   If it had not been for the Infidels, the Rationalists, the Free-thinkers and the Humanists of the past we would never have emerged from the Dark Ages, but these men and women are forgotten and never referred to by our newspapers.   The Rip Van Winkle priests are now awakening to the fact that the people have advanced socially, mentally and morally, with no help from them, and some now wish to be in the running and take the credit for what the priesthood did its utmost to oppose."

"Yes, and with its great wealth the Church will work the Press in its favour in every possible way," remarked Trueman, "and the stupid will accept everything they read in the newspapers, about the wonderful civilising influence of Christianity, just as they believe that their pet political party has brought in every reform measure, whereas it has been the radicals, under whatever party they stood, who have slowly overcome the opposition of those who never wanted reform or change. Radicals such as you, Horace!''

"You flatter me, George! One does not criticise political parties because they are human, and know that they are so, and have never claimed to be anything else, whereas the Church claims to be a Divine Institution, guided by God, affirming that the Almighty guides and directs all its decisions. If the history of the Church in any way reveals God he must be a most reactionary and cruel potentate. As everything new and for the good of the people has always been attributed by the Church to the Devil, this gentleman must be a much more enlightened being than the one that the Church claims to represent, and whose will it claims to interpret to mankind. This false claim doubtless kept up the Church's prestige when the people were ignorant, but now that people are better educated they are realising how ridiculous it is. The Church is now suffering from the reaction which all false claims, when they are found out, bring in their train on those who make them. Only as the masses came to believe less and less in Church doctrines did education increase and the happiness and the welfare of the people improve.''

"It is a tragic story, the story of the Christian Church," remarked Trueman, "and it is unfortunate that so few know the facts, but they will some day become acquainted with them to their lasting good. Think where we might have been to-day had education been allowed to develop and not been looked on as a sin. Think of the psychic knowledge we have lost through witches being burned instead of protected and developed.''

'' A thousand years of progress lost,'' added the Professor. '' Contrast the civilisation of Europe during the reign of the Christian Church and the civilisation of Spain in the twelfth and thirteenth centuries, under the Moors, who were the first to light the lamp of knowledge in Europe. Yet the people are so ignorant that they still think civilisation came through Christianity. You must be continually coming across them, George.''

'' Everywhere. Their name is legion. They implicitly believe in the greatest fallacy that was ever implanted in the mind of man. The very opposite is the truth. Not only by persecuting all the thinkers did the Church keep back the progress of the human race so that China for instance, was ahead of Europe up till the eighteenth century, but the pain and suffering humanity had needlessly to bear by the Church abolishing all anæsthetics in the early days of its power is incalculable.''

'' I am glad you mentioned that matter, George, because I have been looking into that very subject of late. I wonder whether you know, Mrs. Trueman, but because the Christian religion taught that God had cursed the human race because of Adam's dis-obedience, all anæsthetics, which were in common use in pre-Christian days, were abolished by the Church and then forgotten about. When chloroform was discovered last century once again the Church re-newed its opposition.''

'' I am glad to have your confirmation of this,

Horace, because this is a very little known fact. For the reason you have just given women were deprived of relief from pain at childbirth, though this was afforded in Roman times by means of a drug which was given to women in their maternity hospitals. Think of the pain and suffering Christendom would have been saved but for the belief in this cardinal Christian doctrine.

When I was a boy I remember listening to a sermon preached by our vicar, when it was the common practice for parsons to denounce chloroform and all forms of relieving pain. I have never forgotten his words, they stuck to me like glue. He described chloroform as

' A decoy of Satan, robbing God of the deep, earnest cries of pain that should rise to him in time of trouble.'

I have never forgotten these words and I never shall. That was the mentality into which we were born. The God of our fathers and mothers was a monster who seemed to delight in the suffering of humanity. That was the effect of the worship of Jehovah and the Holy Bible, and accepting the Christian Scheme for Salvation, the object of which was to satisfy a revengeful God.

That is the kind of stuff parsons preached, and we as children had to listen to twice a Sunday. The wonder is that we did not all become insane. The wonder is that we had enough strength of character to think our way out of this ghastly fogbound mental sphere, into which we were born, to the serene philosophy which we three hold to-day.''

Trueman now went across the room to one of the

bookshelves which covered the walls of the library. He took down a book entitled *American Slavery justified by the Law of Nature*, written by the Reverend Samuel Seabury, D.D., published in 1861.

"This book, from cover to cover, embracing three hundred and sixteen pages, tries to show that slavery is morally and socially right, justified by the Holy Bible, and the author concludes with invoking the benediction of Almighty God on all true Christian believers."

"That book," said the Professor, "is just typical of the attitude of the clergy in the early part of last century towards slavery, but it is only one of their many crimes. From quite another aspect their teaching was harmful and pernicious.

How few people realise that throughout sixteen hundred years of the Christian era the belief held by most people that the world was coming to an end, and that Christ was coming to gather his elect, stifled enterprise and made people quite indifferent about improving their conditions on earth. The belief, moreover, that their sins had been atoned for led to the utter abandonment of self restraint. License was rampant throughout Christendom from the time this doctrine was promulgated by the Church at the Council of Nicæa in 325, because the Church taught that everything would be forgiven to all believers, no matter how they lived or what they did."

"The worship of the Holy Bible as a God-given book," said Mrs. Trueman, "meant that the people naturally took all it said as a guide to life and so they thought they were right in moulding their lives to conform to all its injunctions about slavery, the treatment of enemies in war, in believing that war was approved by God, that all mediums should be burned and that all who took a different outlook on religion should be tortured and burned. The Christian idea of Hell has been the cause of immense suffering. Only the faithful obtained comfort by their belief in its fantastic heaven ; those who had sufficient brains to be unable to accept the Christian doctrines were given Hell on earth and consigned to Hell after their death.

George, hand me that book of Spurgeon's sermons which you will see there on the second shelf. Thanks ! now just listen to this."

Mrs. Trueman turned over the pages quickly, remarking : " Spurgeon preached and wrote that the majority of human beings were destined to eternal torture in full view of the Christian God. This is what he says :—

' In fire, exactly like that which we have on earth to-day, will they lie, asbestos-like, forever unconsumed, every nerve a string on which the Devil shall forever play his diabolical tune of hell's unutterable lament.

Look up there on the throne of God, and it shall be written " For Ever ! " When the damned jingle the burning irons of their torment they shall say, " For Ever." When they howl, echo cries, " For Ever."

Think of that being preached in our life-time. That was the kind of stuff we had to listen to twice a Sunday. Remember these were not the words of a certified lunatic or criminal but of a man who was universally respected, looked up to and admired by every Christian and whose writings were diligently read and given to us as children to read as our Sunday reading.   Such is the Christian mentality !   Such is the work of the Christian God ! "

"The belief," exclaimed Trueman, "in a personal God, made in the image of man, and that he wrote a book, which was produced by a tribe little better than savages, has been the cause of infinite misery and suffering.   The people made God in their own image and believed that all they did and said had his approval, and that all the evil injunctions in his book came from Heaven for the guidance of mankind.

I was listening-in on the wireless last night to one of our Deans broadcasting on ' The Hope of Immortality,' during which he gave utterance to the silliest statement I think I have ever heard.   It was that ' the dignity of man demands that he should be capable of being damned.'   This reflects the present-day mentality of the priests and parsons of the Christian Church, and also the mentality of the people who, as a whole, are on a similar low mental level.   Otherwise the B.B.C. would be forced to stop their futile religious services and the clergy would be made to occupy the place for which they are mentally fitted."

"Their mental level," said the Professor, "fits them best to be in the company of the Hottentots or similar tribes, and if Europe were really intelligent that is where they would all be sent."

Amid the laughter this remark caused, Mrs. Trueman said : "Orthodox religion seems to bring about paralysis of the brain."

" Quite so," both men remarked.

From this topic the two friends wandered on into other branches of thought and their conversation covered a wide range of subjects.

Mrs. Trueman now took no part in the conversation, but sat listening to what was said, busily occupied with some knitting she was anxious to finish. When she had completed her work she looked up at the clock and exclaimed : " My dear George, do you see what the time is—nearly twelve o'clock. You two have been sitting so busily chattering and I have been so keen to finish my work that we have never realised how the time was flying. If Hope had been at home we would soon have been told."

" Well," he replied, " we won't have her with us much longer now. Ralph Leader and she seem set on an early marriage and as there is no reason why this should not come about we must be prepared for the next few years to have the house to ourselves, at least when the boys are at school. Come, let us get to bed ! "

CHAPTER XIV.

LOOKING FORWARD.

ONE YEAR ON.

George Trueman and Edward Leader were seated on the balcony of the Iglerhof Hotel at Igls in the Austrian Tyrol, looking over a wide expanse of plain and valley to the massive Alps rising to heights of ten thousand feet.

Igls, known as the " Pearl of the Tyrol," is a small village three thousand feet above Innsbruck, the chief town of the Tyrol, which lies in the valley beneath. Its situation is unique. Imagine this long, deep valley running east and west, into which runs a deep ravine from the south, which in past ages was just as deep and just as wide as is the valley. Nature's artillery of rain, frost and snow, and her infantry of wind have, however, been at constant war with the surrounding mountains and beaten from them the rocks, which have been hurled down and pounded into soil, with the result that instead of a valley there is now this deep ravine running from the south into the valley running east and west. On either side of this ravine are fertile plains, on one of which is situated Igls.

From the hotel the view extends over this plain to the distant mountains across the valley. Looking down from Igls, high above the valley, produces the effect of making the mountains on the other side stand out like massive walls.

" Can anything on earth look more beautiful than this scene?" asked Trueman. " In the evening glow, with the sun reflected from these snow-covered peaks the Alps look their best.''

'' Just like giant rugged marble statues,'' replied Leader, '' making a wall thousands of feet high. That rugged white line against the pale blue sky gives these mountains a setting in the evening which one cannot appreciate in the daytime.''

'' Don't those trees, which have climbed just so far up the mountain side and no further, look like silver wreaths round their base?'' remarked Trueman.

'' Yes, and the ravines with their black depths are such a contrast to the surrounding white. Several glaciers ploughed their way through that valley during the ice age.''

As they were speaking the setting sun changed the colouring of the snow-white landscape so that the mountain-tops, from being glistening white, slowly turned, first to a light pink, then to a deeper hue, and finally to a deep, soft, rose colour.

'' What a wonderful sight,'' remarked Trueman, '' and now look behind you at the contrast, the black mountains which receive no rays from the sun. One could draw from this a parable of nature and a great moral lesson of those who perceive the light of the new knowledge and those who still live their lives in the darkness of ignorance. To the former the hill-tops are illumined, to the latter all is in darkness.''

'' True enough, but just like those who do not perceive these rays they do not know what they are missing.

Look at those picturesque houses in front of us, and this fertile plain. The lights are now beginning to twinkle everywhere. Up there on the mountain side you can see them. That house must be six thousand feet up. What a climb!"

"We can now just see the distant mountains, and no more," remarked Trueman. "What a study for an artist! I often think that an artist—one who can make nature live again on canvas—can never be dull or lonely. They tell me from the other side that artists and flower-lovers are always occupied because there, nature, in flower and shrub, in landscape of varied scenes and colours, is so beautiful that one never comes to the end of the ever-changing scenes. Let us go in. In the sun it was so warm, but after sunset the atmosphere chills immediately."

The two men then sat down at the window of the hotel lounge, and while talking gazed out at the gathering darkness.

"Tell me now about your recent doings," asked Trueman. "You must welcome this change from your self-imposed task of enlightening darkest England."

"Indeed I do, I have had a very strenuous year since I left the Church. I have travelled over the length and breadth of England, Scotland, and Northern Ireland, and spoken to large and enthusiastic audiences. I shall tell you more another time. I want to hear about your journey here."

"Oh, we arrived a week ago, coming by Harwich, Hook of Holland, Cologne, Frankfurt and Munich. There was only snow on the heights when we arrived, and my wife and I had some splendid walks in the pine woods behind the hotel, right up the slope of the mountain. A car was waiting for us at Innsbruck when we arrived and we tore up that winding road. It was fortunate we met nothing coming down.

I was very struck in coming through Germany to see how all the arrogance, so noticeable before the war, has disappeared. The railway employees are so courteous and attentive. None of the pre-war aggressiveness. The people have learned a great lesson through suffering.''

"Indeed they have,'' replied Leader. "I remember being in Berlin in 1912. What a contrast to to-day. Then the restaurants were full of proud, swaggering officers, and in the streets everyone had to make way for them. Militarism was then rampant.

We stopped on our way here at Nuremberg and Munich, staying a night at each place. Nuremberg, surrounded by a ring of old walls, is a veritable museum. Its ancient buildings, some going back to the eleventh century, its wonderful churches and public buildings, not to speak of the old market place and the marvellous clock of the Church of My Lady, with its seven figures moving round the figure of the Emperor Charles IV, are all worth a day's visit.

Nuremberg is very proud of its museum with its rich collection of art, which tells the story of Germany from Roman times to the present day.''

"And I am sure Munich is hardly less interesting,'' remarked Trueman.

"Just as interesting. Just another museum in stone and lime, splendid squares and streets, beautiful old gates, churches, and well laid-out gardens. After Berlin and Dresden it has the richest and most valuable art collection in Germany.''

" By the way, your mention of Frankfurt reminds me of that message Ernest Keen got from that German boy who was killed on his motor bicycle. Did he ever follow it up and find out if it was true? "

" Oh yes, he did ; it was quite true. Ernest was very tactful in the way he went about it. He wrote to Karl's parents, at the address given, to say that he heard that Karl had been killed on his motor bicycle, and that he hoped it was not true, but that they might let him know. They replied telling him about their great loss and sorrow, to which he sent a very sympathetic reply."

" Did he know their address before Karl spoke to him? "

" No, he did not know where Karl lived in Germany. It was some years since he had heard from him and that was from some other part of Germany. He wrote to the address he received at the séance, which was correct.

Besides that, Ernest told me that everything else his mother told him that night was true, his father confirming all the details."

" Just two more bricks on the cairn of evidence," remarked Leader. " Some day the cairn will rise so high that all will believe in the truth of survival just as naturally as they accept the other things in life."

" Just so ; but here come the ladies. We will continue our talk another time."

Ralph and Hope arrived the next day, Hope now being Mrs. Ralph Leader, they having been

married in the Spring.   They had started married
life in a flat in Chelsea.   They chose this part of
London as Ralph had now become Member of Parliament for Alfortruth, and Chelsea was convenient for
its proximity to the House of Commons.   The high
respect in which his uncle was held and the fact that
he was the grandson of one of Britain's foremost
Prime Ministers undoubtedly did much to help him in
winning the bye-election.

Being keen on ski-ing it was he who suggested
that his father and mother-in-law should also spend
a week or so at Igls.   He could not leave as early
as he intended, so Mr. and Mrs. Trueman had come
out alone a week earlier.   The slopes around Igls
are eminently suitable for this sport and the ski-er has
his pleasure made as easy as possible by being conveyed to the slopes by an aerial railway.

"Isn't this a wonderful view, Ralph?" said
Hope in the aerial car as they were being carried up
the mountain side.   "I wish Frank and Angela were
here."

"Well, they can't have everything.   They
married as soon as Kilforfun handed their money
over, and now that they have a small boy their duty
at present is at home."

"Did you ever hear the exact amount in the
way of bonds and jewellery which was found in the
deed box?" enquired Hope.

"Frank told me a few days ago that the various
coupons, going back over ten years, had now been
cashed, and that jewellery, bonds and coupons had
amounted to a sum which would make Kilforfun feel
that he had got nearly as much as he had to hand over.

As the legacy was free of duty he had to pay the duty as well but even with the additional payment he came out not much the worse off for the discovery."

"I am so glad," said Hope, "because they did take it well. I was rather sorry for them at first. They faced up to it bravely, and now everyone can feel that justice has been done and that no bitterness has resulted."

"Quite the reverse. They are all now on excellent terms. Colonel and Mrs. Wiseman, you will remember, visited Huntingham to show Lord Kilforfun how to enter the secret room. Frank and Angela could not go as the servants would have spotted them. It was the only way to get at the deed box. I am glad Frank has gone on with his career. In a few years he will be setting up for himself as Dr. Wiseman, but he is set on Harley Street, and he can now well afford it. But he must have a good many years of experience before he can attain his ambition. Here we are at the top. Let us go to the café and have some coffee before we start the run home."

Away across the valley, six thousand feet below, the panorama of mountains, rising above the valley of the River Inn was revealed to Ralph and Hope as they sat in the cafe at the window looking over the wide expanse.

"What a marvellous scene," Hope remarked, as they had gazed at it for a minute in silence. "That brown patch, I suppose, is Innsbruck. No houses can be seen in detail, but I can see the bridge from which it gets its name. It seems to me to be just like a short silver thread."

"Look over at that mountain," remarked Ralph, "its top has a cup formation. I wouldn't be surprised if it had once been a volcano—millions of years ago. These mountains over the ages have been gradually reduced in size and much of what was at the top is now filling up the valley. From here you can see quite clearly that flat plain running right through the valley, making it several miles across. That has all come from the mountain tops, carried by the rivers, so that once upon a time the valley was really a deep gorge. The soil has gradually silted up and changed entirely its original character."

"So these mountains must have been higher at one time?" enquired Hope.

"Much higher. Perhaps some as high as fifty thousand feet. Where did the rich plains of Germany, Austria, France, Hungary and Italy come from? The soil which forms them to-day was once rock, and that rock was once part of the Alps."

"Well, Ralph, whatever their past height was they could not have been more beautiful than they are now. I heard daddy tell your uncle that he had been through the Rockies and at Darjeeling, and grand as the scenery is there it is hardly more beautiful than the view from our hotel."

"Talking of your father, Hope, reminds me of John Matterson. You remember what a materialist he was ; well he is up against something he can't explain. His faith in matter has been rather shaken, and he was asking me to tell him of some of the experiences I have had at Sureway Court. Rather a change, isn't it?"

"It is, indeed, but don't you think we should

start off. I can't go as fast as you can and it will be dark by tea time. Don't run off and leave me. I could never find the way back alone."

" Don't be a silly girl, as if I ever would ! "

FIVE YEARS ON.

" Well, John, I am glad you were able to accept my invitation. I got your letter, and I thought that much the best way was to invite you to lunch here at my club in the city, when we could talk things over. You have evidently been a psychic investigator over the past five years."

" Yes, sir, I have and I want you to hear about some of my experiences, because with your great knowledge of the subject you will be able to help me."

" First of all," replied Trueman, "let us wash our hands and then tell me everything at lunch. I have engaged a table."

When the two men were seated at a corner table in a quiet part of the large dining-room of London's leading city club, John Matterson began his story.

" Well, sir, you are perhaps aware that I am making a special study of Biology, and up till a few weeks ago I required no further explanation about the origin and meaning of life than is given in our text books. I have been a follower of Hæckel, for whose great work I have an immense admiration."

" I don't wonder," said Trueman. " A great man ; one for whom I too have the profoundest respect ; but don't let me interrupt you."

" Well, briefly, up to now I and far greater

thinkers than I am have held and do still hold the view that physical matter, or in other words the ninety-two chemical elements, resolved as they are into electrons and protons, with the addition either of a luminiferous ether or photons, is alone responsible for the production of all the phenomena of the Universe, and that nothing outside that is involved."

" I quite understand your train of thought, John. I once thought like that myself ; but go on, please."

" It follows then that all theories which bring in other forces or substances are wrong because the materialistic belief covers everything and that nothing outside of matter can exist.

On the other hand, if forces and substances are discovered which do not come within the scope of these chemical elements it follows that the materialist theory is wrong because something has been discovered which is not physical matter. That is quite logical, sir ? "

" Naturally. Quite logical and very clearly put. If some non-material substance is found and some non-physical force is discovered then the materialist theory has had its day and can be reverently buried, it having served its purpose by having taken man's mind away from attributing natural phenomena to the gods, to the super-natural. I, as you know, hold the opinion firmly that this has been discovered, but I am interested to see how your mind seems to be moving in the direction mine did many years ago."

" Well, it is, sir, and here I come to what I wanted to speak to you about. It was not to tell you, as you can imagine, what the materialist believes.

You are too great a scholar for me to do anything but sit at your feet and glean something from your vast experience of physical and non-physical matter."

Trueman smiled but said nothing.

"You have heard, I suppose, of the International Institute for Psychical Research in South Kensington?"

"I have.   Not only am I a member of the Institute but I copied my séance room at Sureway Court from their séance room, which is the most up-to-date room of its kind in the world.   I am glad you have got into touch with the people there as they conduct their investigations on sound scientific lines, and record everything that is visible or audible by photographic and acoustic instruments."

"Yes, that is the case," went on John Matterson.   "Quite a number of scientific men are now becoming interested in their methods and the results they are obtaining.   These results are such that official science has to explain them because it cannot ignore them any longer.   The facts are too much even for our materialistic scientists just as they were too much for Professor Richet, the great French Scientist who accepted, as you doubtless know, the fact of survival in consequence of the results he and other psychic investigators had accumulated over the past forty years."

"Yes, I know that.   He became convinced some months before his death owing to the evidence his friend Ernesto Bozzano, the great Italian scientist, had accumulated.   Bozzano announced this a few days after Richet had passed on.   Richet spent nearly forty years investigating psychic phenomena before he accepted the fact that survival after death was scientifically proved.''

''Well, sir, let me now tell you what I experienced. I met recently the Research Officer of the International Institute for Psychical Research and he asked me to attend one of the series of séances he was having with a famous materialising medium. I did so and this is what I saw with my own eyes.''

'' Yes, tell me, I shall not be startled because I have seen it over and over again in different parts of the world.''

John then started his story : '' There were no trap-doors because I myself made quite sure of that and there were no secret doors anywhere. The cabinet in the séance room consisted only of a curtain, divided in the centre, hung across one corner of the room. Two of the walls were outside walls a hundred feet above the street, the other two were solid wood. It was quite impossible for anyone to get into the room except by the door which was locked. But to get over to the medium from the door any stranger would have to walk over the bodies of the ten sitters, who were sitting close together in a semi-circle round the medium. I searched the entire room from floor to ceiling.

The room was well lit by a red light, which gave us enough light to see the medium sitting on our side of the curtain ; so he was in full view all the time.

Soon after we were seated, a form emerged from between the divided curtain, where I was told the ectoplasm from the medium was concentrated. This being—I can call it nothing else—spoke to us at the same time as the medium was speaking to us on quite a different subject. The medium also held in his mouth a mouthful of water when the materialised being spoke to us.

Altogether sixteen materialised forms came out of the cabinet, men, women and children, and some were recognised by the sitters. The women spoke with female voices, the men with male voices and the children like children.

The medium, during the séance, asked me to hold his two hands, put my two feet on his, which I did, but still the forms came out of the cabinet, and they walked up and down the floor in front of us. Some gave the sitters present messages which they claimed could only have been given by those the beings claimed to be.

One or two kissed and put their arms round the necks of several people present. One female form opened her mouth and showed a row of beautiful white teeth, even and regular, and then asked the person she claimed as her husband to look into her eyes and examine her eyelashes. This he did and he said that only his wife had such teeth, eyes and eyelashes. After the séance was over the medium's teeth were examined. No false ones were discovered, but instead a broken row of decayed and tusk-like teeth.

After each form had said something and touched some of us, or had been touched, he or she just disappeared from sight. Sometimes this disappearance was gradual and we could see the disintegration slowly going on. On other occasions it was almost instantaneous.

All the earth people present were above reproach, specially picked by the Research Officer, and several were men of high scientific attainment, who were just as much mystified as I was. These forms came quite close to me. I touched them and they appeared solid. I could see the colour of their eyes. Eyes of all colours. One little child actually sat on my knee, looked up in my face and, with the sweetest smile, said ' This is how I used to sit with my daddy.' ''

'' Extremely interesting,'' remarked Trueman, ''but, as we have finished, come upstairs to the smoking-room and have a cup of coffee.''

When the two had seated themselves upstairs, John went on : '' Well, after that séance was over I was shown the photographs taken, so it was no optical illusion. The figures were there. Where did they come from I wanted to know, so I asked the Research Officer if I might return to the next séance, to which request he agreed. Well, I have attended in all six séances and have witnessed each time the materialised forms of from ten to thirty beings, of all ages, of both sexes. Now, sir, what does it all mean ? If it is not trickery or illusion, what is it ? I am convinced it is neither.''

'' Well, my friend, it is much too involved a subject for me to start and tell you what I have been told from the other side as to how they materialise themselves and make it possible for us to see and hear them, but if you will come to Sureway Court for next week-end we can go into the subject more deeply, and I will lend you one or two standard books on the subject so that you may learn what scientific men have discovered over the last twenty years.''

" Thank you, sir, I shall accept with pleasure. You realise that this question is intimately related to my subject Biology. As you know, the germ cell which grows and becomes animal or man is a minute, thin-walled, sac, filled with a sticky liquid somewhat like the white of an egg which contains very complicated chemical substances, the basis of which are the four elements hydrogen, carbon, nitrogen and oxygen. Inside this little bag is another one, containing other chemical compounds, in the form of straight or curved rods which are known as chromosomes, and these play a very important part in the development of the cell. First, this nucleus divides into two, and then again and again, the various cells becoming more and more unlike as they grow in number.

The female germ cell, before it is fertilised, is unique in the female body in possessing a nucleus with only half the normal number of chromosomes. The male cell, when it enters the female germ cell, unites with the female nucleus, and the chromosomes individually unite in pairs and then each cell divides into two again, and so on. That, then, is the beginning of growth which continues from now onwards by the mass absorbing food from the surroundings. Such is the origin of an oak tree, a worm, a monkey or a man.

" Now, how does this cell develop into a plant, animal or man? That is the question the Biologist asks and yet from the materialist view-point there is no answer which satisfies me.''

" And there never will be,'' answered Trueman.

" My explanation, which I can give you, and which has been derived from my experience in the séance room, which most scientists ignore, is that each cell is endowed from its parent with mind, which is an intangible, invisible substance at an extremely high rate of vibration.

This substance images itself into the form the cell grows, just according to the species from which it comes. In other words, scientists to-day are considering only the shell, the physical visible part, and ignoring the rest, which consists of an etheric duplicate, guided, moulded and developed by the third and finest substance of all, namely, mind. Each germ cell is a trinity made up of these three elements, mind, etheric and physical. That is why I cannot believe in re-incarnation, because all we are originated from our parents, who handed down to us a minute fraction of themselves, who likewise are a trinity. Round this we have absorbed physical and etheric nourishment which accounts for growth, while the mind, which in the early stage only directs growth, is absorbing mental nourishment from the mind substance of the Universe.

As our mind is, to begin with, so it attracts the same mental substance, which accounts for heredity and sex, according to which mind takes control at conception, namely, the mind of the father or mother. Our environment accounts for our mental development because, as the environment is, so is the mental growth. A good and pure environment encourages the mind to develop mental images of a like nature, whereas the opposite environment develops the reverse.

But I must be off as I have an important directors' meeting at which I must preside. We shall continue this talk over the week-end.''

Both men rose, and when walking downstairs John remarked : '' You will see, sir, that I am not now so materialistic as I was when we were at Turnberry, over five years ago. I am beginning to learn wisdom.''

'' That's right. We all live and learn. Never close your mind to facts. The wisest man is the one who has accumulated the largest number of facts and assorts them correctly in his mind.''

As they shook hands to say good-bye, John remarked : '' I must congratulate you. I hear that Hope has just had a daughter.''

'' Thank you ! Yes, a daughter this time. Her first was a son, so it is only fair now to have a girl. Turn about and then no one is disappointed. Goodbye till Saturday. Drop my wife a note saying by what train you are coming and the car will meet you at Tunbridge Wells.''

TEN YEARS ON.

'' And now we ask that all that remains of our friend's physical body be removed and restored to the earth whence it came. His mind, which is himself, has left that which belonged to the earth, and now has as its sole habitation the etheric body which is untrammelled by the earthly body. He has, now that he has attained his freedom, the capacity to live in a finer range of vibrations which we term Etheria, to which he has now doubtless risen, as it is above us in space. His interest in us has not lessened ; he is just the same in memory and character as he always was, and doubtless when he has become accustomed to his new environment he will return to earth and report his safe arrival in his new surroundings. We are here to rejoice at this liberation, and while we greatly sympathise with his dear wife in the loss of his bodily presence, she has the knowledge that communication with her husband is always possible under suitable conditions, which are easily made as the love tie between them was strong. This will bring her husband back every time she gives him the opportunity to come through some suitable medium. Moreover, she has the satisfaction of knowing that only a few years on earth stand between her and him, and that when her earth-life ends they will meet again and renew their lives together. Let us not mourn but rejoice at our having the knowledge of this great truth, and may it spread and become accepted in time by all mankind to their great comfort, joy and advancement.''

With these words George Trueman concluded the short address he gave at the service of rejoicing over the liberation of Edward Leader, once Bishop of Alfortruth, from the limitations of the physical body.

Dr. Leader's death had occurred suddenly just after he had returned home from addressing a series of meetings throughout the country. Over the last ten years, by both writing and speaking, he had worn himself out and was in no physical state to throw off a chill he had contracted.

At the funeral service, which was held at his

home in London, were a dozen bishops, who had come to pay their respects to their old colleague.

After the address, Mrs. Clara Hearing, the famous clairaudient, gave clairaudience, remarking before she began that this was done to show how closely related we really were to the other world, and that what she would tell the mourners would be a practical demonstration of the truth of the words spoken by Mr. Trueman in his address which breathed the idea not of *Good-bye*, but of *Au revoir*.

She then pointed to the Bishop of Dogmaham, who was sitting next to the Bishop of Latitudeham, and mentioned one fact after another which she said was being conveyed to her by his mother in Etheria. The bishop acknowledged that it was all true, every word, but when Mrs. Hearing had concluded he protested to Latitudeham about the sacrilege of disturbing the dead and that all these messages came from the Devil.

" Rather contradictory, my friend," said Latitudeham.   " You can't have it both ways.   Just keep calm, and listen to what she tells the others."

Mrs. Hearing then pointed to the Bishop of Creedalbury and reminded him of an incident in his school life.

" You were at Harrow."

" Are you referring to the school?" enquired the bishop.

" Yes, I mean you were educated at Harrow School."

" That is correct," acknowledged the bishop.

" Do you remember your great friend there called Mesyrot?"

" Yes," came the reply.

" Well, he is here standing beside me," re-marked Mrs. Hearing. He tells me. I have not pro-nounced his name correctly. It spells M.E.S.Y.R.O.T. That is letter by letter as I get it, but he tells me that it is pronounced Mesero. Is that correct? "

" Yes, that is correct," came the reply.

" He asks me to say this. He was known to you as JAM because his full name is James Andrew Mesyrot. He got that nickname on the first day he arrived at school, because on all his boxes were the initials J.A.M. He remained your friend at school and at college, and when you got married he gave you a solid silver tea-tray. He was of French-Canadian descent and joined up with the Canadians as an officer during the Great War. He was killed at Vimy at Easter in 1917 during the push for Vimy Ridge. He left a wife and two sons. You were responsible for getting his younger son into a good business in London where he has done well. His other son is in Canada and his wife has married again."

" Yes, that is all true," replied the bishop.

Mrs. Hearing then gave a correct description of the " dead " officer and then continued :

" All this may sound very trivial but remember you cannot see him and this is the only way he can make you realise that he is here. He wishes to send you his thanks for your kindness to his boy, but he wants to do more than this. He wants to open your eyes to the reality of the world in which he now lives, and what better occasion could be used for this than during a funeral service, when people's minds naturally turn to the question of what has happened to the one for whom they mourn? Is he dead? Has his consciousness become extinguished, or does he still live, retaining his old memories? Your friend Mesyrot has proved to you that he retains his old memories and that he is a conscious living being. What has happened to him has likewise happened to the one whose physical body is being buried to-day. If your friend gave you a philosophic discourse it would not prove his continued existence because it is possible for me to do so. When, however, your friend gives you details about events which took place in your early life, which he and you only know about, then you will be led to the conclusion that your friend still lives. If he lives then all the dead live, and the more recent arrivals there still remember events which took place during their earth life.

Remember, sir," Mrs. Hearing concluded, " I could go on giving you information to convince you that the dead live, but I must give some consideration to the other people present. Your mother and father are here and several of your friends and relations including your Aunt Laura, who was very fond of you. I am being bombarded with messages to give to you but I must switch off and give my attention elsewhere."

Mrs. Hearing then went round about a dozen of the people assembled giving them in turn similar information to prove that their friends were present. She gave particular attention to Mrs. Leader, who was told that her husband was present, having been brought back for the occasion, that he was very interested in all that he had seen and heard at his funeral, and that after he had rested somewhat and become accustomed to his new surroundings, he would come back the first time she sat with a medium.

Thus ended a simple service. What the bishops thought of it all they only told each other, as by now they had ceased issuing Diocesan letters denouncing Spiritualism, the people not appreciating what was so obviously untrue.

Only Mr. Trueman and Mrs. Leader accompanied the coffin to the grave, where it was interred without any ceremonial.

"Funerals, in the years to come, will be such as this," Trueman remarked to her on the way to the grave. "All absurdities spoken by priests at the grave will cease, and laymen will take the service, because in the days to come there will be no priests. It will all come gradually, but, believe me, come it will. The days of priests and parsons are numbered, to the lasting benefit of mankind."

"Yes, I quite agree. Their influence gets less and less every year. A hundred years ago a priest or parson had to be present at the death-bed. Now this is considered unnecessary. In time he will not be needed either at a marriage or a funeral. Spiritualism is slowly winning through, but we cannot hurry the mental development of the people. It will, however, all come in time.

Thanks, my friend, for your kind, sympathetic remarks, which were a great comfort, as was the clairaudience of Mrs. Hearing. Some day the clairaudient will give comfort and consolation at every funeral."

After the interment they parted on the understanding that she would come to Sureway Court in a fortnight's time, to have her first talk with her husband from his new abode.

TWENTY YEARS ON.

The years passed on, the middle-aged had entered old age, and the young had become middle-aged.

John Matterson had given over his materialistic beliefs, as had many of his fellow scientists. Facts had conquered. The materialistic view of life and the mechanistic view of the Universe were now less firmly held by scientific men, who were more and more coming to realise that it consisted of much more than appealed to us as physical matter.

Faith Church had married a parson. As she never read anything except novels her religious views had changed but little. As Frank, on more than one occasion, remarked to Angela, " You will always find that the orthodox never read deeply. I have never all my life met an orthodox person who has read anything but light literature. That is why they are orthodox, I suppose."

Frank and Angela now lived in Harley Street and Frank had attained his ambition of being one of our leading consultants. He was more and more being helped in his cures by having many of his patients treated by psychic healers. He and Dr. Cureall worked together, so far as psychic healing was concerned, as the latter conducted a very successful psychic healing clinic in London.

Angela's mediumship had developed in a remarkable way during the past twenty years. Her clair-audience was most convincing, but it was when she was in trance that the personality of the communicator made itself most evident. She, however, only gave occasional sittings, and these only to her friends, who always considered it a privilege and an unforgettable experience.

Ralph and Hope still lived most of the year in London. Ralph had now reached Cabinet rank and everything pointed to him being a future Prime Minister. Through his efforts the disabilities Spiritualists had suffered from for a hundred years from the out-of-date Witchcraft Act of 1735 and the Vagrancy Act of 1824 had been removed.

During all these years Spiritualists had been liable to prosecution, and were frequently prosecuted and convicted, because mediumship was punishable by law.

Spiritualists had thus been the only body who could not conduct their religious services in freedom, as could all other religious denominations in the country. It had by now also become legal for Spiritualist Churches and Societies to receive legacies for training mediums.

Anthony Goodenough and Diana Hunter had some years previously decided to marry. Their friends had often wondered why two so alike in their outlook on sports did not become man and wife, as they were so often seen together in the hunting field.

Public opinion was noticeably hardening against all blood sports and the opinion was even being expressed by hunting people themselves that this cruel form of obtaining pleasure could end in only one way, by being made illegal.   Fewer and fewer people were being attracted by this form of pleasure as the mental level of the entire community was rising by the spread of education.   Drag-hunting was now much more general than it had been and it was expected that it would eventually replace hunting the fox.

The law against cruelty to animals in every form was being tightened in every direction, and other forms of sport were taking the place of killing for fun.

George Trueman had retired from business, and had by now contributed a great book to the literature of Spiritualism and Psychical Research.   His age was now compelling him to reduce the number of public meetings he addressed.   His wife's mediumship, owing to advancing age, was not at its previous high level, though she still continued her work with Miss Noteall to the great and lasting comfort of many who sought their help.

Fortunately, records had been kept of all the séances held during the period of her mediumship, extending to over forty years.   Trueman, for his book, had picked out many of the most interesting and evidential cases he could find in his large collection, and had produced and published a text book of six hundred pages.   He had still sufficient material to fill several more volumes, which he hoped some day to publish.

Some years earlier he had financed a New Knowledge series by the publication of leading books on Spiritualism, sold for one shilling a copy.   The number of readers of books on Spiritualism had thus increased ten times.

As he remarked once to his wife, " The Rationalist Press Association, by their excellent shilling publications of the best books on Science, Philosophy and Religion, were the first to put the truth about Christianity before the people. My ' New Knowledge Series ' has given the people a religion and philosophy in harmony with present-day knowledge, and not based on myths and legends two thousand years old."

The public press had by now been won over to the new philosophy, and the jeers and sneers which had been accorded to Spiritualism in the first quarter of the century were now things of the past.

History had just repeated itself. First the new idea with faltering steps makes its appearance to be denounced by nearly all. Then it gathers round it a few adherents impressed by the reasonableness of its claims. These slowly grow in numbers, denounced by those whose minds can never lead and must always be led. And so the band of pioneers increases in number, gathering strength from the followers behind, till the time comes when all have joined the vanguard which, because of its numbers and strength, becomes the orthodox. Again and again the same process goes through its circle, just as it has always done since humanity began to reason, and always will do so long as thought exists.

THIRTY YEARS ON.

Professor Horace Storey came down to breakfast one morning and opened mechanically what had always been looked on as Britain's most conservative newspaper, the unfailing supporter of orthodox science and religion. Its silence on any subject, not accepted by official science or the Church, had always been considered an indication of its disapproval. That was thirty years ago, but thirty years had brought its changes here as they had done elsewhere.

" Good gracious ! " the Professor exclaimed to his daughter, who had been his constant help and companion since the death of his wife many years previously. " George Trueman is dead. My greatest and oldest friend gone. What a loss to humanity. Listen dear—

' GEORGE TRUEMAN.
FAMOUS SPIRITUALIST PASSES ON.
A Pioneer, a Scholar, and Leading Chartered Accountant.

We much regret to announce the death, which occurred suddenly last night, of George Trueman of Sureway Court in the County of Sussex, a leading man in the City of London, one of its foremost accountants, a scholar, a scientist, and one of Spiritualism's great pioneers. His loss will be felt far and wide as, though he retired from business and his various directorships about ten years ago, he has devoted his greater leisure to the furtherance of the cause he had so much at heart. His great book on Spiritualism has become not only a national asset of great value, but international as well, it having been published in nearly every civilised country.

George Trueman was eighty years of age and is survived by his wife, through whose wonderful mediumship he acquired the facts which to all thoughtful people prove without doubt our survival after death. Two sons and a daughter, Mrs. Ralph Leader, the wife of our Foreign Secretary, also survive him. . . . .' "

" Oh, I am sorry," replied Miss Storey. " You were always such great friends. I am sure you will miss him more than anyone. He will be as great a loss to humanity as was Dr. Leader. Yes, Tate, do you want me? "

" It is the telephone, Miss. Will the Professor please speak? I have connected it through to the study."

In reply to his daughter's enquiry on his return the Professor remarked, " A request from Trueman's son that I conduct the funeral service at Sureway Court. I have agreed to do so as I am sure it is what George wishes."

And so it came about that the earthly remains of George Trueman were quietly interred in the presence only of his sons, after a service of rejoicing at the liberation of his great mind into a realm of larger, fuller life. The service, attended by a large company, was conducted by Professor Storey at Sureway Court, who adopted throughout his remarks only the phraseology of Spiritualism, omitting all orthodox expressions, pious hopes and the claim that only through the belief of Christian doctrines could Heaven be reached.

The newspapers throughout the length and breadth of the land emphasised the great help George Trueman had given, by his life and work, to the liberation of the people's minds from superstition. They drew attention to the fact that it was he, as much

as any of the pioneers of Spiritualism, who had helped
to give humanity a knowledge of its destiny and a
more rational idea of its true place in the Universe.

Thus ended the earthly career of a great man
which was suitably commemorated by a monument to
his memory, erected in Sureway village, on which
were inscribed the following words :—

TO THE MEMORY
of
GEORGE TRUEMAN
who devoted many years of his life in
spreading the knowledge that Mind,
which is the individual, and not the
physical body, continues after death to
control the etheric body, in a world of
finer substance, surrounding and inter-
penetrating this earth.   A really great
man, the friend of all mankind, and one
who held high the torch of knowledge,
which   alone   enlightens   and   raises
humanity.

FORTY YEARS ON.

The years passed on.   Changes in the intellectual, social and political life of Great Britain,
Europe and the rest of the world were slowly taking
place.   The League of Nations, helped by the rising
intelligence of the people of all countries, had now a
grip of world politics which had ceased to be so
national in character and had become more international.   The support accorded the principle of this
international method of settling international disputes
had now made war practically impossible between
League members, and armies had everywhere been
reduced to small dimensions.   They had now become

not much more than supplementary to the regular police forces which latter had become more an organisation for regularising the life of the community than for suppressing crime and violence, which had almost ceased.

Education had made such progress everywhere that peace both within and without the nations was now the accepted order of society.

The rational limitation of births had brought about the reversal of the old insane policy, adopted by some Continental countries, of encouraging the increase of the population so as to make each nation strong to resist aggression and equally strong to grab some territory from its neighbours in order to accommodate its increasing population.

Now that the policy of grab had been abandoned, each nation felt safe within itself. Accordingly it had ceased to bring life into the world, at a rate beyond that which the country could support, just for the purpose of having it killed off in the attempt to protect or extend its frontiers. As a result of this change of outlook a falling birthrate was not looked on as a national disaster, but the reverse, because it meant that there was more of the world's wealth to go round to the benefit of the smaller population.

Cruelty to animals had come to an end, and all blood sports had been abolished, much to the annoyance of Tony and Diana and those who thought like them. The Kilforfuns had both passed on, hunting almost to the last. The hope was expressed that the animals they had hunted, maimed and wounded on earth would not haunt them in their new abode by means of mental regrets.

A very different reception, it was agreed, was accorded Mrs. Trueman on her entrance into the fuller life, as her time on earth had been spent in doing good, giving comfort and raising the fallen.   She had passed on five years after her husband and the public sorrow at her death was hardly less pronounced than that shown in respect of her husband.   A suitable inscription to her memory, briefly recalling all she had done for humanity, was added to the memorial erected to the memory of her husband.

Mrs. Leader had also passed on at an advanced age, and as Ralph was her husband's heir, after her death, he inherited his uncle's fortune, which was a great help to him, as being Prime Minister, his expenses were heavy.   Hope, now the foremost political hostess in the country, kept up her husband's great position by entertaining extensively, and in every way was a worthy helpmate to a great man.

John Matterson, who had been for many years Professor of Biology at Cambridge, remained a bachelor, being engrossed in his studies.   As he remarked to Angela on one occasion, " You and Frank have added three strapping boys and one girl to the world's population.   My life is too much occupied in trying to find out the meaning of life, of birth and death.   I have not the time to marry and follow your example."

So John remained wedded to his Biology.

CHAPTER XV.
AU REVOIR!
FIFTY YEARS ON.

Ralph and Hope Leader, Frank and Angela Wiseman and John Matterson were now the only people, who have figured in this story, who remained on earth fifty years from the commencement of this record. As they had then been young people, whose ages had ranged between twenty and twenty-two, it could not be considered that they were now old, in fact they all looked forward to ten or fifteen more years of earth-life.

Christmas had again come round, as it has year by year since this old earth first started spinning on its own. Christmas was again being celebrated, as it has been for thousands of years under different names, because Christmas, though a Christian religious festival, first originated when our ancestors worshipped the Sun.

Christmas in the year we have now reached had ceased in England to be a religious festival, and was looked on only as a time of family reunion and an occasion for the exchange of gifts. The old religious beliefs associated with the day were fading from the people's minds much as Thursday had ceased to be celebrated as the day on which the God Thor was worshipped.

Frank and Angela had invited on this occasion their old life-long friends John Matterson and Ralph and Hope Leader to dinner. The children of the Leaders and the Wisemans had by now all married,

having homes of their own, so that the reunion which
had been proposed by Angela was welcomed by all.

After dinner the conversation turned to past
years by Hope recalling the happy time they all had
had at Turnberry, over fifty years ago.

"What changes have come since then," said
John. "Looking back on those days the people
were just emerging from a long, dark night of superstition, just beginning to find their feet. They were
beginning to rely on themselves and not look back
nineteen hundred years to find a saviour for their
sins. They were beginning to outgrow the idea of
a whipping boy to take their punishment, one of the
crudest ideas that ever entered the mind of man,
though fifty years ago it was still considered wrong
and a sin, as they called it, to doubt the fact that
Jesus was God, or part of God, having come down
from heaven for our salvation."

"Yes," replied Frank. "The Bible was just
beginning to be doubted in earnest, and some historians were beginning to wonder if Jesus had ever
lived. Now the Bible has found its right place in the
library with the Koran, the Buddhist Suttas and
other so-called Holy Books. It is now looked on,
as it always should have been, as an interesting
record of Jewish and Pagan religious thought, but
we don't give it to our children to read and their
morals are better in consequence."

"The controversy still continues as to whether
Jesus ever lived or not," remarked Ralph. "The
historians, when we were young, could find no
evidence of the fact that he had, and they have found
none since."

"Well, does it matter so very much after all whether he lived or did not live?" said John. "Apollonius of Tyana, who was supposed to have lived shortly after the time attributed to Jesus, and who was worshipped for four hundred years with divine honours, may have lived or he may not; but who cares? Fortunately, religion has now ceased to be concerned with the past. The past is only of interest to us as history, and this is as it should be. Our religious and philosophical ideas are now moulded by those who have passed on, and come back to us, as they know more than we do, and that is also as it should be.

If the past were entirely blotted out religion would still remain because the desire to plumb the depths of the Infinite is in everyone. Science tries to explain the various expressions of nature. Religion relates to that which is behind these expressions. Science is only recording what nature reveals. Religion considers the cause behind. Religion needs no label. Consequently sects of all kinds are dying out. Spiritualism was never a sect, only a state of mind and outlook on life, and as this has now come to most thinking people the name Spiritualism is quite unnecessary.

Religion has nothing whatever to do with the past. It is not history. Religion has nothing to do with theology, which is just the opinions of the ancients about the mystery of life and death, which we are much more competent to form an opinion about than they were. Don't you agree, Mr. Prime Minister?"

"I do, my dear Professor, which explains

why parsons are decreasing in number. The people have come to realise that and consequently the clergymen who remain preach the old theology to empty pews. Not one per cent of the population believes their doctrines. Those parsons who have thrown over the old have nothing to put in its place. To preach Spiritualism is to teach the people that the Church is not needed. Church-going is a thing of the past, as the people now attend lectures and instruction classes on all matters relating to this world and the next, and don't reserve a certain day to listen to theological doctrines being taught. Every day is sacred, if well spent, and has been profaned if we have lived only for ourselves. The Roman Catholic Church has still a grip on their people but in another fifty years that too will have gone. Then at last Europe will be free of priestcraft. When I was on the Continent last year I noticed that there remained only a few of those crude shrines with a man hanging on a cross."

"Europe is slowly emerging from a night of darkness," remarked Hope. "I often think of the words of that great pioneer Gerald Massey—

> ' No matter though it towers to the sky
> And darkens earth, you cannot make the lie
> Immortal; though stupendously enshrined
> By art in every perfect mould of mind :
> Angelo, Rafæl, Milton, Handel, all
> Its pillars, cannot stay it from the fall.
> The Pyramid of Imposture reared by Rome,
> All of cement, for an eternal home,
> Must crumble back to earth, and every gust
> Shall revel in the desert of its dust;
> And when the prison of the Immortal, Mind,
> Hath fallen, to set free the bound and blind,

No more shall life be one long dread of death;
Humanity shall breathe with ampler breath,
Expand in spirit, and in stature rise,
To match its birthplace of the earth and skies.' "

" Very much to the point," said Ralph. " The new knowledge has now taken the place of the old beliefs, to the great comfort and happiness of all. Speaking as a politician, or perhaps I may be allowed to say as a statesman, I feel that my task is infinitely easier than that of my predecessors, who had to govern a semi-ignorant people, those who believed that war settled disputes and who were just savages in their treatment of wild animals. What a change the higher range of intelligence, due to greater knowledge, has brought about in the happiness of the race.

Think back and compare anything of the past with anything of the present and you will appreciate the advance which has been made in the comfort and happiness of the race by mental development. Compare the mud hut to the modern house, the camel, horse or runner on foot to modern methods of sending messages, by telephone, wireless or telegram, or of travel by aeroplane, motor car or electric train. Think of the track hewn through a forest and our modern roads, the old rush light and the present-day electric lighting systems, which have turned night into day.

The Atlantic can now be crossed in a day, and our present-day facilities for travel make it possible for most people to travel about the world, which was possible only for the rich fifty years ago. The nations of the world are getting to know each other and this knowledge has brought about real friendship, which is making all the people one great family. This has been one of the contributing factors which has stopped war. To-day only a police force is necessary, and the hundreds of millions spent on keeping men armed, and on instruments of destruction, are saved for productive uses and for making our lives happier and more comfortable. Invention has reduced working hours to four a day and the people are living in greater comfort, in greater happiness, and in better health. They have learned to use their leisure by spending their time in keeping their bodies healthy by outdoor games and by developing their minds by reading and joining dramatic and literary societies.''

'' You all remember how, fifty years ago, we had to pour petrol into the tank of our car,'' Frank remarked. '' Now a small packet of powdered coal, by being turned into gas, takes us for a hundred miles. Our aeroplanes can now carry enough fuel to take them round the world.

By mass production, what in the days when we were young was available only for the minority is now at the service of the majority. If we have come to our present position after only a hundred years of education what will things be like in another hundred years? ''

'' Last century people were so ignorant that the great majority could not read nor write,'' said Hope. ''The working-man to-day is well educated and a gentleman, and his wife is a lady.''

'' Few people realise,'' said John, '' how ignorant were our immediate ancestors. Think, for instance, of our grandfathers and grandmothers believing the story of Noah and the Ark. Anyone has only to read it to see that it was quite impossible.

Jehovah having decided to drown the world told Noah to make an ark. Its length was five hundred and fifty feet, ninety-one feet eight inches wide, and fifty-five feet high, divided into three stories, with one window only twenty-two inches square in the roof.''

"Jehovah couldn't have made much of a study of ventilation," Angela remarked.

"Neither of ventilation nor of anything else because it had only one door, which shut from the outside. Through this door Noah had to get specimens of every living creature within only seven days. Fourteen of each species of birds, and, as there are known to be twelve thousand five hundred species of birds it means that one hundred and seventy-five thousand birds went through the door within the seven days.

Besides that there are at least one thousand six hundred and fifty eight kinds of beasts on the earth and, according to the story, the number which entered the ark came to three thousand two hundred and sixty-six. Then there were one thousand three hundred reptiles, as we know of six hundred and fifty species and are told that a couple of each was taken. Lastly, we know of at least one million different kinds of insects and as they went in in pairs they came to the round figure of two million, a total animal cargo of two million, one hundred and seventy-nine thousand, five hundred and sixty-six, to be fed, watered and kept clean by only eight people.

This goodly company was afloat for a year. Think of the amount of feeding stuff the ark would have to carry and the amount of manure to be lifted each day.   Think of the stench and the only ventilation coming from one window on the roof, twenty-two inches square.''

" And yet,'' remarked Frank, '' our grandmothers and grandfathers fervently believed in the truth of this yarn and that all unbelievers in it would go to Hell.   What a mad world they must have lived in !   What a mentality !   All this was the result of ignorace due to the lack of education in their day, when they were spoon-fed by the Church, accepting all it told them and not thinking for themselves.''

" What a change has come about since the beginning of the twentieth century,'' said Hope.   " I remember my father telling me that when he was a young man of twenty his mother found him reading a book in which the stories about Adam and Eve and Noah were called legends.   His mother took the book and burned it.   He then bought Darwin's *Origin of Species.*   This, too, was seized and burned, and so on it went for some years with every book which threw any doubt on the Bible being word for word true from the first verse of Genesis to the last of Revelation.   He was made to go to church twice every Sunday and was never allowed to go for a walk or read a book other than one dealing with the Bible. He was cuffed even if he whistled or laughed.''

" Surely not when he was twenty,'' enquired Frank.

" No, that was when he was younger, but as a young man he was only allowed to read sacred literature, and had to go to church regularly every Sunday and listen to long, drawn-out prayers and long, dreary sermons, twice every Sunday. I remember him telling me once that in church some children were not sitting still. The parson broke off his sermon and pointing to them he said, in solemn tones, ' You children if you don't sit quiet you will go to Hell and burn and burn and burn.' ''

" Good gracious ! Not, surely, in your father's day. A generation earlier, perhaps, but not so late as his time," exclaimed Frank.

'' Yes, Frank, he actually heard the parson say that. I could hardly believe it when he told me, but he assured me that it was true, and gave me the name of the parson and the church. How would you like to have the House of Commons composed of people with such a mentality, Ralph? ''

'' It would be too terrible for words to express, Hope. No wonder cruelty to man and beast was general when the people believed in such a savage religion. Think of the contrast between then and now. Think of the contrast between pig-sticking, bull-baiting, fox hunting, otter hunting, and stag hunting, and the pursuits of to-day. Think of the constant wars and suffering and the conditions now. Contrast the mentality of our grandparents who worshipped a savage God like Jehovah, the god of war and everything that was cruel, with our idea to-day of God as the Universal Mind, of which we each are part, which is in all and the cause of all we experience.

It is almost as great a contrast as that between the pagan gladiatorial contests, when the people thirsted for more and more human blood, and our humane societies of to-day which have been respon-

sible for the relief of suffering to both man and animal.
Contrast the prisons of a hundred years ago with the
way we deal with offenders to-day, educating and
training them to be good citizens.

It was a red-letter day for this country when it
obtained secular education.   As this has increased so
has the influence of the Church declined.   Likewise
has crime declined, as there is nothing plainer in
history than the fact that in a country with the most
priests there is the most crime.   The fewer the priests
the fewer the criminals.   Why! crime and prisons
are now nearly things of the past.   What a dreadful
time the pioneers had in trying to make our Christian
ancestors humane.''

'' Most diseases have now been conquered,''
said Frank, '' pain and suffering have almost ceased
to exist.   That is what comes from man relying on
himself and not on the gods.   Poverty and misery
have gone.   Slums are no more.   All have decent
houses to live in.   As the people came to believe less
and less in the superstition of the past they became
more civilised because their minds were responding
to a higher level of thought.   The last hundred years
has witnessed the human mind advancing, as the result
of education, to a greater degree than it had done
over the previous two thousand years.''

'' And the communication which has now been
opened up so freely with Etheria,'' remarked Ralph,
'' has enlarged our vision, made us certain of our
destiny, and helped to regulate our conduct one to
another in a way which was impossible in the old days
of ignorance, when everyone thought more or less that
it was every one for himself and that to accumulate

the greatest amount of material gain was the height of wisdom."

"How materialistic would still be our conception of the Universe if the burning of mediums had never been stopped. What an outcry there was over the mere suggestion that it should be stopped," said Hope.

"Mediumship, like everything else not sanctioned by the Church, was sinful," said John. "People now have come to realise that there is only one sin and that is selfishness, because it leads to the unhappiness of ourselves and others. We are constantly sending out boomerangs and they all come back to us just as we sent them. The happiness of each individual and the human race is the only goal for which it is worth striving. Whatever tends to bring about unhappiness is wrong, whatever brings about happiness is right. That is why the old theologies were pernicious. They laid emphasis only on belief in their doctrines being right and unbelief as being sinful, whereas the only sin is selfishness, and the only way to atone for sin is to become unselfish and think of others as much as ourselves. Now we know that mental wealth is what really brings about happiness and that the mental wealth we acquire on earth is all that we can take with us when we die."

"You did not think like that, John," remarked Frank, "when we were talking things over after our game of golf at Turnberry fifty years ago. Now you are Professor of Psychical Research at Cambridge and the people accept all you say as if you were an oracle yourself instead of being one whose business in

life is to study those who were called oracles by the
ancients."

"True, but I have lived and I have learned just
as you have, Frank. You only wondered in those
days whether I was right or wrong. I thought I
knew, but neither of us did. You have Mr. and Mrs.
Trueman to thank for your advance in knowledge.
This would have come in time, just as it has come to
others, but you were fortunate in having the evidence
of the new knowledge put before you so clearly just
at a time when your mental development was
sufficiently receptive to accept it."

"That is quite true, John. When the mind
reaches the receptive stage new ideas are adopted
naturally. No good can be done by argument with
one who is not ready for something new and something better. The old appeals to them, and that
satisfies them till they are ready for a change of
thought."

Angela, who had been sitting passive during the
conversation, then remarked : "Your father is here,
Hope. He says he wants to speak to you all through
me. Just keep quiet. Put on some soft music, and
wait."

Angela then seemed to slip into a peaceful sleep.
She remained upright in her chair and in a few minutes
she spoke in a strong masculine voice :

"Just a few words of greeting. I am George
Trueman. Many of your friends are here with me.
You cannot see us but we can see you. We join
with you in all your good wishes at this your festive

season. We send you all our affectionate remembrances and are sure you return yours to us."

This was received by all quite naturally, as if he were still present on earth.

"Of course we do," all replied. "Please accept our best wishes for a happy New Year."

"Well," he went on, "we do not count the seasons here in quite the same way as you do on earth, but it is your continued love and affection that we appreciate.

Never forget that death is but an incident. You were talking just now about your time at Turnberry, over fifty years ago. I heard all you said and doubtless you were thinking of the broken family circles and how death had severed friendships made on earth. Nothing is further from the truth. Though you cannot see us we are still here and our affections are unimpaired. Our memories are just as they were on earth.

The only difference is that here we are enjoying a fuller, freer life, untrammelled by the limitations of the physical body. Otherwise we are still the same in mind and body, in a world similar to earth but tuned up to a higher degree in beauty and everything else. You will have no difficulty in recognising us when your time comes to make the change, except that we shall all look youthful. And so it goes on, earth filling Etheria, and those here returning to earth, as we are now doing, interested in our friends, until the time comes when they too are here and then we go on together forgetting our earth-life, reaching on to something greater and grander than anyone on earth can possibly imagine.

Now I must go as Edward Leader wishes to say a few words.''

" I am Edward Leader,'' came the new voice. '' I am proud of you, Ralph. You are a worthy successor of my father, your grandfather, who is here with the rest of us. My wife is with me here in this room, also Angela's and Frank's mother and father. Ralph's father and mother are likewise here and your parents also, John Matterson. So we are quite a family party. Some day, as your etheric senses develop, we shall be seen and heard without the need of this human instrument which I require to use to make my presence known.

Now, this is my message. During the ages you have had your dictators and teachers, the former keeping the people in subjection, the latter trying to raise them mentally. The teachers have tried to make them self reliant, the dictators to make them obedient. Both types were needed in the past but as education spreads, as mind develops, the dictator gives place to the teacher.

The people have always worshipped the dictators. Being children they appreciate having someone to think for them. They have seldom appreciated their teachers. The teachers, to be teachers, had to be in advance of their times and in consequence were often persecuted, imprisoned or murdered. That was their fate. In their time they received little or no recognition, whereas the dictators of Church and State received the homage of the mob. These tyrants gloried in mob worship, in parades and processions. Crowns, mitres and crucifixes attracted the crowds whereas books and learning appealed to the few.

The dictators, kings, emperors, popes and bishops built prisons and dungeons and chained both the body and the mind, the thinkers and teachers built schools to free and unshackle the mind. The dictators preached war, the teachers peace. One carried the sword and made force his god. The other advocated study, investigation and invention. They put what was right before might. The dictators made many ignoble people nobles. No one but yourself can make you noble.

Thus as intelligence advances peace takes the place of war. The people learn to eliminate the cause of war. They learn how to increase their happiness and to advance their comfort but the majority forget that the progress of humanity is due to the teachers and not to the dictators, who, at the most, maintain the *status quo*.

Be, therefore, teachers. Advocate everywhere freedom of thought and expression. Encourage learning and knowledge. Put wisdom always first and foremost. You will receive no public recognition. No fanfare of trumpets will herald your approach. The crowds will not kneel for your blessing. No armies will do your bidding, but yours is the greater service. The teachers and thinkers are the real benefactors of humanity but so long as ignorance remains they will be denounced by all who stand for superstition, tyranny, injustice and cruelty.

Carry high the torch of knowledge. Think logically and honestly. Don't allow your emotions to capture your reason. All earth troubles come from wrong thinking. If you think right you will not fear.

Fear comes from ignorance and not thinking aright. Here in Etheria we realise how much the people on earth suffer from this cause and how greatly their happiness will increase when their minds develop. Only within the last few hundred years have you begun to think rationally and your country, which during the past hundred years has permitted the freedom of thought necessary for rational thinking, is just beginning to reap the harvest.   The soil has been prepared for the growth of the tree of knowledge. Cultivate that soil well and your example will save and raise the people elsewhere, because they will profit by your experience and follow where you lead. *Au revoir* to you all and a happy New Year.   Your mother is here, Hope, and she will be the last to speak.''

     " Just my love to all of you, my dear friends. Keep on as you are doing.   Live straight, think of others, help the helpless, raise the fallen, and make your lives shine with love and kindness so that all may realise that they are illumined by the light of the Torch of Knowledge, fed by the oil of wisdom, which will give light and direction to all who are guided by it.   Till we meet again, either as we are doing now, or face to face in this land of freedom from all earth's troubles, where we are freed from all physical limitations.   Here our mind is more the master of our surroundings than with you.   You wish for many things to which you cannot attain.   Here, to think is to experience, so learn to control your thoughts aright as this is the first and the last principle in the attainment of happiness with you on earth and even more so in this world, where mind conditions our place and happiness in a way you will only realise when your time comes to join us.

All our love till we meet again. *Au revoir.*"

" And we here send you all our love in return," replied Hope. " For you it is *Au revoir*, but for us who cannot see you it is—Till we hear from you again. Thanks so much for coming. We shall give you another opportunity before long."

When Angela returned to normal and heard what had been said she also echoed the feelings of the others by saying : " In truth there is no death, it is just the portal leading to a life of greater and greater freedom and happiness for all who know how to live aright. Death is only a change of environment, a bend in the road of life. Our life-story never ends. This we have come to know by our being guided and having followed, without fear or wavering, the Torch of Knowledge."

"True, very true," replied Ralph Leader.

" OUR LIFE-STORY NEVER ENDS."